THE COEN BROTHERS

THE COEN BROTHERS

RONALD BERGAN

Thunder's Mouth Press

Published by
Thunder's Mouth Press
A Division of the Avalon Publishing Group
841 Broadway, Fourth Floor
New York, NY 10003

First published in 2000 by
Orion Media
An imprint of The Orion Publishing Group Ltd.
Orion House
5 Upper St. Martin Lane
London WC2H 9EA

Library of Congress Cataloging-in-Publication Data

Bergen, Ronald.
        The Coen brothers / Ronald Bergan.
            p. cm.
        ISBN 1-56025-254-5
        1. Coen, Joel. 2. Coen, Ethan. 3. Motionpicture producers
and directors—United States—Biography. I. Title.

PN1998.3.C6635 B47 2000
791.43'0233'092273—dc21
[B]

                                                            00-044296

Distributed by Publishers Group West
Designed by Pauline Neuwirth, Neuwirth & Associates, Inc.
Manufactured in the United States of America

Pictures supplied by
The Kobal Collection, Ronald Grant Archive and
Pictorial Press Limited.

SOURCES

N.B. I have taken quotations from various sources and my own notes
when I was present at interviews, and sometimes amalgamated them
into single quotes. All the quotes at the beginning of each chapter
are from the Coen brothers.

CONTENTS

ACKNOWLEDGEMENTS

I would like to thank the following:

Trevor Dolby, my publisher, for encouraging me through thick and thin; Robyn Karney, whose skills I could have done with earlier; my agent Tony Peake; Rena Coen, with apologies, and, in alphabetical order: Gilbert Adair, Professor Paul Benaceraff, Danae Boussevain, Gianna Chatchere, Mark Cousins, Adams Douglas, Margrit Edwards, Anna Faiola, Sir Anthony Forte-Bowell, Catherine Grégoire, Dr. Raymond Geuss, Clive Hirschhorn, Kate Holland, Professor Dennis Jacobson, Roderick Jaynes, Professor Dick Jeffrey, Stacey Mann, Domingo Monet, Lolly O'Brien, Ben Primer, Professor Edward Schulbyte, Alan Schoolcraft, Peter Strickland, John S. Weeren.

For Rik Boulton, Richard Statman and Vito Rocco,
friend, colleague, and idol, respectively.

Turning and turning in the widening gyre

The Falcon cannot hear the falconer;

Things fall apart; the center cannot hold;

Mere anarchy is loosed upon the world,

The blood-dimmed tide is loosed, and everywhere

The ceremony of innocence is drowned;

The best lack all conviction, while the worst

Are full of passionate intensity.

The Second Coming (W. B. Yeats).

O, Brother!

"The way we work is incredibly

fluid. I think we're both just

about equally responsible

foreverything in the movie.'

1 *The Mark of Coen*

"FILM DIRECTOR JOEL COEN
SLAYS YOUNGER BROTHER ETHAN!"

DURING ONE of their writing sessions, Joel Coen (46) suddenly pulled out a gun on Ethan (43), his brother and co-creator of all their movies, and threatened to kill him. Ethan begged him not to do it. "Look into your heart," the younger man pleaded, echoing the words that John Turturro speaks when he is about to be killed in *Miller's Crossing*. But Joel blasted the .44 Magnum into Ethan's chest two or three times in the manner of some of the many violent scenes in their films. He then took Ethan's body into the country around Minneapolis, Minnesota, their home town, and was feeding it into a mechanical wood-chipper when the police caught up with him. Joel then turned the gun on himself. The motive for the killing is still unclear. Some say that Joel could not tolerate the duality of their existence. Scrawled on a piece of paper on his desk was a quote from Edgar Allan Poe's *William Wilson*, a story in which a mean-spirited gambling Austrian officer murders his *doppelgänger*, confesses and kills himself.

> You have conquered and I yield. Yet, henceforth art thou also dead—dead to the World, to Heaven, and to Hope! In me didst thou exist—and, in my death, see by this image, which is thine own, how utterly thou hast murdered thyself.

When the quotation above was submitted to the police grapholo-gist, it was found to have been written by Roderick Jaynes, the mys-terious editor on most of their films, and the writer of the introduc-tions to the published scripts of *Barton Fink* and *Miller's Crossing*.

Naturally, like most people, I was shocked by the totally unex-pected fratricide. But, to be honest, as the brothers' biographer, I was secretly delighted. What a coup! Joel couldn't have timed it better. The tragic event happened just as I was completing my biography and wondering how to end it. There is never much problem in the cases where the subjects are dead, but with the living it is far more difficult because the story has not ended. This gruesome killing gave my bi-biography, or "bigraphy," just the sensationalist element it needed, a *sine qua non* for biographies these days. Up to that point, I had failed to dig up anything even vaguely scandalous about the brothers, though I hoped to suggest that they were abnormally close, a relationship on which new light was cast by the Coencide.

Yet, nobody would ever have imagined that such a thing could ever have happened. There was a clue in something Joel once said when asked how the brothers determined which of them would pro-duce and which direct. "I'm about three years older and thirty pounds heavier, and I have about three inches on Ethan in terms of reach. But then he fights real dirty. I can beat him up so I get to direct." Ethan concurred: "It's those critical three inches in reach that make the difference."

I was reading the screaming banner headlines, when a gust of wind caught the newspaper and carried it away from me. I tried to chase it along the road, but it kept evading my grasp. And then I woke up . . . I was unsure whether I was relieved or disappointed.

There's a guy in No. 7 that murdered his broth-

er, and says he didn't really do it, his subcon-

scious did it. I asked him what that meant, and

he says you got two selves, one that you know

about and the other that you don't know about,

because it's subconscious. It shook me up. Did

I really do it and not know it?

—The Postman Always Rings Twice (James M. Cain)

2   *Being the Coen Brothers*

MY THOUGHTS went back to the day, over a year before, when I was first commissioned to do a biography of the Coen brothers and approached them to ask if they would cooperate. It was a situation that reminded me of a cartoon I once saw of a man opening the door of his apartment to a stranger. "Excuse me," says the visitor. "You don't know me but I'm your biographer." Joel asked me, "Why would you want to write a biography of us? Listen, you've written books on Jean Renoir and Sergei Eisenstein. We can't compare to them in any way. We're boring." I assured him that I, and my potential readers, were more interested in their public lives than their private ones. After all, I wasn't writing a book on some bimbo movie star, male or female. But they were skeptical. "Actually, to tell the truth, we don't want a book written about us." "Come on," I thought, "we're not talking J.D. Salinger here!" However, there was one condition on which they would agree to cooperate, which I will come to later in this chapter.

The Coen brothers, however reluctantly, have submitted themselves to endless interviews and photo sessions, though they are seldom seen smiling in the photos. "We're not usually in a smiling mood when we get our pictures taken," Joel explained. "It's not one of our favorite things. The best interview we ever did was with a guy from *Details* magazine. We did it and then he went away and must have decided we were too boring, so he just made up the entire piece himself." "I have to say," interjected Ethan, "it was a big improvement. But if we keep being interviewed, we'll never get any work done. You can print whatever you want. You don't have to confirm anything."

Ideally, what biographers want is to enter the minds of their subjects, not literally, as in the Spike Jonze film *Being John Malkovich*, but in a figurative sense. "I want you to enter my mind," says cartoonist George Sanders to his "ghost" Bob Hope in *That Certain Feeling*. "Can I bring a toothbrush?" Hope asks. I had my toothbrush ready for the journey. I was willing to act like an ace reporter, responding to the demands of the city editor, like the one in *The Hudsucker Proxy*, which I quote with one name substitution.

"I wanna know what makes the Coens tick! Where are they from? Where are they going? I wanna know everything about these guys! Have they got girls? Have they got parents? . . . What're their hopes and dreams, their desires and aspirations? . . . What do they eat for breakfast? Do they put jam on their toast or don't put jam on their toast, and if not, why not, and since when?"

ALTHOUGH I had met the Coen brothers and seen them a few times previously, I often wondered whether they were for real. Were they, as some headlines have suggested, "Brothers from Another Planet'? Or are we to believe George Clooney, who told an interviewer on the set of *O Brother, Where Art Thou?* that "They are not brothers at all, and Ethan is really a woman. Don't let the whiskers fool you'?

When I first spoke to Joel, he was just about to embark on the screenplay of *O Brother, Where Art Thou?* with Ethan. He told me he would speak to Ethan about the biography and that I could contact them through Alan J. Schoolcraft. Having already been forewarned of the prankster nature of the brothers, I skeptically questioned the existence of Mr. Schoolcraft, but Joel insisted there was such a person. The name struck me as invented. Knowing of Alan Jay Lerner, the lyricist of *My Fair Lady*, I put two and two together: Lerner, Learner, Learning, School Craft. QED.

I admit that I subsequently spoke regularly to Schoolcraft on the phone, although his voice sounded suspiciously like Joel's. He seemed to act as the Coen brothers' factotum. A sort of Figaro, which is an anagram of *Fargo* without the I. Then I read a diary by one Alex Belth who worked as an assistant on *The Big Lebowski*. He writes: "I was introduced to Alan J. Schoolcraft, a recruit sent over from Working Title . . . I took one look at the Schoolcraft and thought there just wouldn't be enough for two. He was a hulking slab of a lad with a fuzzy blond head and devilishly raised eyebrows over his shiny Irish eyes. The guy was pushing thirty and had been out in La-La land for a few years." This piece of purple prose convinced me that Schoolcraft was a figment of the Coens' imagination and that Belth was playing along.

I was further frustrated when I tried to contact their editor Roderick Jaynes, who lives in Haywards Heath, not far from London where I live, but I kept being told that he was either abroad or unavailable. I even stupidly began to question his existence, though I knew he had been nominated for an Oscar for his work on *Fargo*. As with Schoolcraft, I analyzed Roderick Jaynes' name. From where did the name derive? I remembered that Roderick Usher was incestuously attracted to his sister in Poe's *The Fall of the House of Usher* and Jaynes echoes Janus, the two-faced Roman god. And that is how the Coens were mostly seen — as a two-headed, film-making mutant.

3   *The Ministry of Silly Names*

BOTH JOEL and Ethan are Biblical names. Joel is Hebrew for "Yah is God," meaning "Jehovah is the only true god." In the Bible, Joel was a minor prophet, though he had a book named after him. According to nameologists, Joels are considered ambitious, intelligent, caring and creative. Ethan means firm and strong. In the Bible, Ethan the Ezrahit is an obscure figure, only mentioned as being surpassed in wisdom by Solomon. The only other Ethan as famous (yes, there is the actor Ethan Hawke) is a fictional one, Edith Wharton's *Ethan Frome*. There are not too many celebrated Joels either, although two appear in these pages—Joel Silver, the Hollywood producer of *The Hudsucker Proxy*, and Joel McCrea, the star of Preston Sturges' *Sullivan's Travels*, from which the Coens took the title *O Brother, Where Art Thou?*

Joel and Ethan might be considered silly names by some, but they are not nearly as silly as the ones they have invented for their characters. Like one of their emulatees, Preston Sturges, they take a Dickensian delight in the comical cognomen. Gertrude Kockenlocker (Betty Hutton) is the heroine of *The Miracle of Morgan's Creek* (1944), who gives birth to sextuplets (one better than the mother in *Raising Arizona*), but can't remember the father's name. She only remembers that his name was something like Ratsky-Watsky.

In Sturges' *The Palm Beach Story* (1942), Rudy Vallee plays millionaire Hackensacker III, not too distant a name from millionaire Hudsucker. (From a different world comes J.J. Hunsecker, the vicious newspaper columnist played by Burt Lancaster in Alexander Mackendrick's *Sweet Smell of Success*.) The ruthless businessman Sidney J. Mussburger (Paul Newman) starts toying with changing the name of Hudsucker Industries to Mussucker Industries, Hudburger Industries, Sidsucker Industries . . .

The slogan of wealthy furniture dealer Nathan Arizona, the father of the quins in *Raising Arizona*, is "If you can find lower prices anywhere my name ain't Nathan Arizona," when actually his name is the even sillier Nathan Huffhines. "Would you buy furniture at a store called Unpainted Huffhines?" he says. In the same movie, there are the Snopes brothers, Gale and Evelle, and the terrifying "Lone Biker of the Apocalypse" with the incongruous name of Leonard Smalls. The leading characters are H.I., or Hi (as in drugs) and Ed (as in Edwina).

The Big Lebowski, a funny name in itself, features a video porn producer called Jackie Treehorn and a Chicano bowling fanatic called Jesus Quintano; the Soggy Bottom Boys, Wash Hogwallop (obviously a hick) and Vernon T. Waldrip (an uppity drip) appear in

O Brother, Where Art Thou?. *Fargo* has Gaear Grimsrud and Carl Showalter. The "funny looking" Steve Buscemi, who plays Showalter, also plays Mink, a little rodent, in *Miller's Crossing*. However, the most emblematic of their characters' names, in the tradition of Restoration comedy, is Barton Fink (John Turturro), "fink" meaning a sneak or unpleasant person.

4 *First Sighting*

FRIDAY 24 May 1991—the Duke of York's Cinema in Brighton, Sussex, England. We have just watched *Miller's Crossing* as part of the Brighton Festival. Joel and Ethan are being interviewed on stage after a screening. Although I knew already from having met a number of film directors, and interviewed some of them, that they are no longer whip-wielding, eye-patch and jodhpur-wearing megalomaniacs, I still have a romantic notion of these "helmsmen" of the cinema. Now they are just like you and me, and sometimes much younger. Little did I know, that evening almost a decade ago, that I would attempt to play their Boswell, although Dr. Johnson was over twenty years older than his biographer. The reverse would have seemed quite risible. Of course, a biographer can be older than a deceased subject.

After coming out of my reverie of how young the brothers looked, I became aware of a nasty aroma from Ethan's trainers. It was the price I paid for being too much of a fan and sitting in the front row. Some of the audience challenged them on the film-maker's "responsibility" with regards to representing violence. Joel and Ethan brushed off any sense of responsibility, which didn't go down too well with some of the more prissy questioners, but the Coens didn't seem at all bothered.

5 *Double Whoopee*

"WE RECEIVED your fax regarding a biography, but due to our exceedingly busy schedule we will be unable to participate in the book for some time. However, in going over your résumé we noticed a prior bio on Laurel and Hardy. If you wished to reissue that particular book and substituted 'Joel and Ethan' for 'Laurel and Hardy' you would have our blessing."

I decided to try it. Below is an extract from the original first chapter of this biography.

> Although it took a few more films to develop the fixed personalities that Joel and Ethan Coen would be loved and acclaimed for, it was clear that *Blood Simple* was the beginning of a perfect comic partnership—Joel displaying his pomposity and outraged dignity, and Ethan innocently unaware of the havoc his idiocy causes. In their T-shirts, jeans and trainers, they were vagrants from bourgeois pretensions. However, despite their deference to authority, their unfailing courtesy, and their reverence for property, they inevitably left a trail of destruction in their wake. Yet if they had been merely idiots they would never have attracted the love and laughter of generation after generation. Much of their appeal lay in a child-like innocence—children suddenly finding themselves having to behave as adults in a harsh adult world. When Ethan cried, he cried not out of anger or hurt, but because he was confused. Even as married men, they behaved like naughty boys trying to escape from their nannies.

Unfortunately, it was too difficult to continue in this vein, because I started getting into a fine mess when certain real discrepancies between the lives of The Thin One And The Fat One and those of The Thin One and The Thin One kept creeping in. Yet, the Coens have often been referred to as a double act, and they do identify with the comic duo to a certain extent, though which is which is hard to tell. Oliver Hardy might not have been the explicit model for the many fat men (mostly John Goodman) in the Coens' movies, but his influence on them is evident. However, Ollie was the master of the slow burn—when Stan landed him in a fine mess, he would just glare at the camera and twiddle his tie—while the Coens find "howling fat men" funny.

In *Raising Arizona*, the two cons, Gale (John Goodman, the Hardy one) and Evelle (William Forsythe, the Laurel one), escape from jail and come out in the mud, a scene reminiscent of one in *Pardon Us* (1931), Laurel and Hardy's first feature. Stan and Ollie are sent to prison for bootlegging. When they make their escape, they find themselves in cotton fields, where they black up and join the cotton pickers undetected. The three escaped convicts in *O Brother, Where Art Thou?* pretend to be black when they record a "Negro song" as the Soggy Bottom Boys for a blind record producer, and later black up to effect an escape from a chain gang. Of the two cons in *Raising Arizona*, the Coens remarked: "We first imagined Gale and Evelle to be sort of the Laurel and Hardy of the Southern penal society. Gale being the bigger older one and Evelle more the Stan Laurel type. They looked like grown-up babies."

As in *Their First Mistake* (1932), in which Laurel and Hardy have to look after an adopted baby, Gale and Evelle have Nathan Arizona Jr, the infant they have abducted, on their hands. When Evelle holds up a store to get diapers and balloons for the baby, he asks the shopkeeper if the balloons are a funny shape. "Not unless you find around funny," says the shopkeeper. The Coens obviously found "round funny" like the hula hoop—"you know, for kids"—in *The Hudsucker Proxy*, and big, around men like business tycoon Waring Hudsucker (Charles Durning), the detective (M. Emmett Walsh) in *Blood Simple*, gangster Johnny Casper (Jon Polito) in *Miller's Crossing*, and John Goodman.

In *Liberty* (1929), Stan and Ollie are back in prison but quickly make a break for it and somehow find themselves on the top of a partly-built skyscraper, not the best place for Olly to discover that a crab has sidled into his pants. Panic reigns as much as when Paul Newman falls out of a skyscraper window in *The Hudsucker Proxy* with only the Laurel-like innocent, Tim Robbins, to hold him up by his feet.

In *The Big Lebowski*, John Goodman attacks a Corvette with a crowbar, smashing the windshield and the driver's window, thinking it's the car of someone on whom he wishes to inflict revenge. Unfortunately, it's the wrong car, and the Mexican owner takes the crowbar away from him and starts to smash what he believes is Goodman's car. This derives almost directly from *Big Business* (1929), in which a splenetic James Finlayson and Laurel and Hardy wreck each others' Tin Lizzies with abandon.

Stan and Ollie are known in France by the singular sobriquet of "Laurelardee." As the brothers speak with one voice, it seemed an unnecessary chore to divide their enunciations into "said Joel," "added Ethan," "Joel interrupted," "Ethan interjected," "explained Joel," "ejaculated Ethan" throughout the book. I, therefore, considered calling the Coens, in order to vary the prose Jethan, Ethoel, Joethan, Jethco, or even Ethel. How much better to quote them as one? e.g. "When we're writing the script, we're already starting to interpret the script directorially," remarked Jethco. However, more often than not I have synthesized their individual utterances into one quote, so that when one reads "said the Coens," it does not mean that they literally spoke in unison.

ED: You mean you busted out of jail?

GALE: Waaal . . .

EVELLE: We released ourselves on our own recognizance . . .

GALE: What Evelle means to say is, we felt the institution no longer had anything to offer.

—Raising Arizona

6 Coencidences

According to Ephraim Katz, "the brothers work in perfect harmony as a synchronized unit, planning and writing their films together and taking turns at directing scenes." The brothers referred to here are not the Coens but the Italians Paolo and Vittorio Taviani. Co-directed films and sibling film-makers are not as "singular" or uncommon as has been made out. After all, in the beginning were the Lumière Brothers, August and Louis, whose surname has a poetic congruity. Let There Be Light!, and there was Cinema! Twin brothers John and Roy Boulting interchanged as producer and director, and Albert and David Maysles made their Direct Cinema documentaries together. At another extreme are twin brothers Mike and George Kutcha, camp, low-budget, underground New York directors. Like the Coens, they were first let loose with 8mm cameras in their childhood, but unlike the Coens, the Kutcha brothers never graduated to 35mm. "I'm afraid of working on a big picture," explained George. "I really wouldn't want anyone to sink their money into a project of mine and then lose the money." More recently, there has been Peter and Bobby Farrelly (*There's Something About Mary*), Larry and Andy Wachowski (*Matrix*), and the Belgian prize-winning brothers Luc and Jean-Pierre Dardenne (*La Promesse, Rosetta*).

NOMINALLY, JOEL directs and Ethan produces, but they are jointly involved in every aspect of production, and share the credit as screenwriters. So why does Joel take credit for directing while Ethan takes credit for producing? "We really co-direct the movies," Joel explained. "We take separate credits but actually do pretty much everything together. There really isn't a good reason. We got in the habit with *Blood Simple*, just to stake out these two areas, to say, 'Look, he produces. Don't give us a producer.' We could just as easily take the credits— 'Produced, written, and directed by' the two of us. We've considered changing it, but we'd just get asked why we changed it at this point, so we might as well let it be. The credits on the movie don't reflect the extent of the collaboration. I do a lot of things on the production side, and Ethan does a lot of directing stuff. The line isn't clearly drawn."

ETHAN: "We tend to see the movie on the same terms. There are no fundamental disagreements of what we are dealing with since we created it together."

JOEL: "We share the same fundamental point of view toward the material. We may disagree about detailed stuff, but it's just a case of one person convincing the other that their point of view is truer to the final objective. It gets talked out and decided through discussion. Also, by that point we are also collaborating with a lot of other people."

ROGER DEAKINS, the Director of Photography on all their films since *Barton Fink*, was initially concerned about the logistics of working essentially with two directors. "I soon realized, though, that I could ask either of them if I had a question. It didn't matter who I turned to. It was whoever was free and nearest or most convenient. They were so totally in sync."

William Preston Robertson, a friend of the Coens, described their way of speaking as "a word jazz of monosyllables and demi-sentences, halting advances into non sequitur and abrupt retreats into coma." When Robertson interviewed them separately, "the isolated Coen being queried would utter half a sentence, then look around curiously (Joel) or in panic (Ethan) when no one interrupted him to complete his thought."

Barry Sonnenfeld, the cinematographer on their first three pictures, commented that a typical discussion on the set after a take would consist of nothing more than Ethan saying, "Joel," and Joel responding, "Yeah, Ethan, I know. I'll tell them." Another trademark is to punctuate their sentences with "heh-heh" or "yeah-yeah," nervous verbal tics that seem to indicate amazement that anything they say should be taken seriously. John Turturro calls them the "yeah-yeahs."

"At times it was like being directed in stereo," said Jon Polito, who played Johnny Caspar in *Miller's Crossing*. "It's the yin and yang of one being," remarked close friend and erstwhile collaborator Sam Raimi. "They're like identical twins. Alike, but very different," according to Sonnenfeld.

BUT THEY are not identical twins, or even unidentical twins. For many years, they looked like a pair of perennial post-graduates—

Coen clones can still be seen on every campus in America. Today, Joel, with his unkempt, long hair, resembles a nutty professor, while Ethan, his hair and beard more neatly trimmed, could be a lecturer in business affairs. They both wore granny glasses, though Joel's were sometimes dark tinted, while Ethan's were wire rimmed, and frequently T-shirts, jeans and trainers. One or the other or both have beards and mustaches from time to time. Joel's beard is often an attempt at a Van Dyke, and he likes to tie his straight black hair back in a pony tail, whereas Ethan seems to be able to do nothing with his gingery curly mass. Joel is taller and darker. Ethan is ginger and slight of build. One commentator separated them by saying that "Joel has the sort of good looks and elegantly casual clothes you'd expect from a semi-retired west coast musician. Ethan, with his frizzy hair and more animated expression, seems closer to the kind of movie geek that you might expect."

According to William Preston Robertson: "Joel is lanky, dark-haired and pony-tailed. In his more pensive moments, he will sit slouched in a chair with an expression that resembles an afghan catching the faint scent of game in the wind. Ethan is somewhat shorter, but has a larger fuzzier head, and, in his more pensive moments, exhibits a propensity for tireless, outside-the-delivery room-style pacing."

The brothers, then still in their twenties, first emerged blinking into the spotlight after *Blood Simple*, yet to find a distributor, had excited audiences at film festivals around the USA. For one reporter "they made a comical appearance" at the New York Film Festival. "Petite, self-effacing and soft-spoken, they gave an air of pleasant tranquillity . . . looking like a couple of nuclearfreezeniks from a Quaker college."

Gabriel Byrne, who played the lead in *Miller's Crossing*, commented on working with the Coens. "I had no idea what the brothers looked like and here they were, this double act who could be in movies themselves. They looked like somebody Diane Arbus could have shot, the one with long black hair who looks a bit like Peter Sellers in *The Wrong Box* [Joel] and the other curly-headed guy [Ethan] who chews biros all the time. And they paced up and down the floor, as they tend to do, nodding furiously one to the other."

Joel once tried to explain away their duet for two voices in a mundane manner. "A lot of journalists write about how we finish each other's sentences. What they don't realize is that, frequently, it's in an interview session where you've often been asked the question before." "Two heads are better than none," Ethan put in.

However, there are some divergences in their characters. Although they both smoke Camel Lights, Ethan likes good coffee from Starbucks, while Joel will drink "any-store-will-do" coffee that is handed to him and, when they write, Ethan does most of the typing. Joel is more talkative and sociable. Ethan takes books to parties. (When Barry Sonnenfeld told director Penny Marshall, "They're so easy to work with. It's like working with one person," she replied, "Sure, one of them's mute.") They live at opposite ends of Manhattan and, of course, they are married to different women, Joel to the actress Frances McDormand, and Ethan to the film editor Tricia Cooke.

Their tastes in films differ in one aspect. "I really like dog movies," claimed Joel. "I'm not sure Ethan is into those." "*Old Yeller* and that kind of thing," replied Ethan dismissively. "It doesn't irritate me, it's just not an enthusiasm I share." But Joel remarked that "Ethan is unbelievably sentimental and sloppy. He's always trying to sneak it into our movies." "Joel refuses to go to sentimental movies with me because my weeping embarrasses him. But don't tell anyone in the press."

It obviously amuses the brothers to express some disunity, but it is the sort of badinage they resort to in order to deflect any deep probing. However, if we were to take Joel's remark at face value, then the slightly sentimental endings of *Raising Arizona* and *Fargo*, rare examples of sentimentality in their work, could be blamed on Ethan.

Sam Raimi remarked: "Ethan has the literary mind and has more of a say on scriptorial matters, leaving Joel more time to worry about visual issues." Frances McDormand commented: "It's not like you can say exactly that one scene or one line is Joel's idea and another is Ethan's. It's a smooth, rolling process. Ethan is literary. He's published short stories outside of their work together. Because of Joel's earlier work as an editor, he's much more visual."

NEVERTHELESS, THE more one tries to separate the sibling Coens, like operating on Siamese twins, the more they knit together.

Like Alexander Dumas' *The Corsican Brothers*, The Minnesotan Brothers seem to have a "physical telepathy." The fact that they come from the twin cities of Minneapolis and St. Paul adds a further relish to the binary aspects of their lives.

There is a passage in a short story called *Greenleaf* by one of the brothers' favorite authors, Flannery O'Connor, that sums it up. " 'Which is boss, Mr. O.T. or Mrs. E.T.?' She had always suspected they fought between themselves secretly. 'They never quarls,' the boy said. 'They like one man in two skins.' 'Hmp. I expect you just never heard them quarrel.' 'Nor nobody else heard them neither.' "

Tweedledum and Tweedledee

Agreed to have a battle;

For Tweedledum said Tweedledee

Had spoiled his nice new rattle.

Just then flew down a monstrous crow,

As black as a tar-barrel;

Which frightened both the heroes so,

They quite forgot their quarrel.

–Through the Looking Glass (Lewis Carroll)

KINGS OF THE INDIES

"You sort of do it by feel

and not with reasons.'

7 *Independents' Day*

IN 1996, around the time of the release of *Fargo*, an interviewer suggested that the Coens "were at the beginning of the independent film-maker movement, doing it your way and all that." "Yes, we were at the beginning of that bullshit," replied Ethan facetiously. "We are grandfathers of the independent." It was also intimated that they had become "the elder statesmen of indie cinema." Joel's reaction was, "When it comes to elder statesmen, I think Robert Altman still holds that position. Personally, I don't want to be an elder statesman of anything. I don't even want to be a statesman."

But Independents' Day was declared as long ago as 1919, when four of the biggest names in motion pictures, Mary Pickford, Douglas Fairbanks, Charles Chaplin and D.W. Griffith, formed United Artists and published their aims. "A new combination of motion picture stars and producers was formed yesterday, and we, the undersigned, in furtherance of the artistic welfare of the moving picture industry, believing we can better serve the great and growing industry of picture productions, have decided to unite our work into one association . . . We believe this is necessary to protect the exhibitor and the industry itself, thus enabling the exhibitor to book only pictures that he wishes to play and not force upon him other program films which he does not desire, believing that as servants of the people we can thus serve the people. We also think that this step is positively and absolutely necessary to protect the great motion picture public from threatening combinations and trusts that would force upon them mediocre productions and machine-made entertainment."

It was claimed at the time that "the lunatics have taken over the asylum." But as Jack Lipnick, head of Capitol Studios in *Barton Fink* says, "The lunatics are not going to run *this* particular asylum. So let's put a stop to that rumor right now." Unfortunately, the lunatics (and that includes the Coens) have never really run the asylum (i.e. Hollywood) but have often managed to influence those over-sane, reactionary people who run the place to change the regime slightly, and allow their charges a little more freedom from time to time.

The first idealistic attempt at true independence failed. By the end of the 1920s, Griffith was ruined, Pickford and Fairbanks were heading for retirement, Chaplin's divorce cases and politics were beginning to tarnish his reputation, and United Artists, "the company built by the stars," passed out of their hands and into those of producer-businessmen. United Moguls might have been a more appropriate name.

In the 1930s and 1940s, the major studios consolidated their grip on the movie industry, despite the increased artistic freedom accorded to producer-directors such as Alfred Hitchcock and William Wyler, and writer-directors like John Huston and Joseph L. Mankiewicz. In the 1950s, a growing number of independent producers gradually broke the stranglehold of the majors. In fact, by 1958, 65% of Hollywood movies were being made by independents, discounting the avant garde and underground movements that had always been there. Units such as Hecht-Hill-Lancaster, the Mirisch Corporation and Otto Preminger Productions were able to tackle more daring subjects, delving into those areas from which Hollywood had previously shied.

At the other end of the financial scale, Roger Corman, as "King of the Z movies," and John Cassavetes, whose *Shadows* (1959) was made for a mere $40,000, provided hope and inspiration for a new generation of directors. Martin Scorsese, who was seventeen at the time of the release of *Shadows*, declared: "It had a sense of truth and honesty between its characters that was shocking. And since it was made with a 16mm camera, there were no more excuses for directors who were afraid of high costs and cumbersome equipment." (Joel was then five years old and Ethan was two.)

At the same time, the French New Wave directors were turning their backs on conventional filming methods. They took to shooting in the streets with handheld cameras and a very small team, using jump cuts, improvization, deconstructed narratives, and quotes from literature and other films. In particular, Jean-Luc Godard with *Breathless* (1960), dedicated to Monogram Pictures (the all-B movie studio), attempted to recapture (and comment on) the directness and economy of the American gangster movie. Then, with *Une Femme est Une Femme* (1961), Godard paid homage to the MGM musical, and, in *Alphaville* (1965), he used the trappings of American pulp fiction and *film noir* to tell a futuristic story. The methods and subject-matter of Godard, François Truffaut and Claude Chabrol were taken up and adapted by young directors in other countries. The French New Wave was the most seismic event in the history of the cinema since the coming of sound.

In the 1960s, Hollywood found itself with an audience now increasingly drawn from the 16 to 24 age bracket. This younger generation expressed a growing aversion to traditional values and political and social processes, an attitude which culminated in the anti-Vietnam War movement in 1968. Furthermore, with the demise of the old Production Code, the limits of language, topics and behavior were considerably widened, almost enough to satisfy the tastes of the young. They were pandered to mainly by the low-budget youth-oriented movies of Roger Corman such as *Wild Angels* and *The Trip*, both starring Peter Fonda who produced and featured in *Easy Rider* (1969), the film whose combination of drugs, rock music, violence, and motorcycles caught the imagination of youth.

This movement was ignored by fifteen-year-old Joel and twelve-year-old Ethan, beginning their first experiments with Super 8 and influenced by more mainstream movies. While smaller-scale independently produced pictures were attracting the young, the major studios continued to target family audiences with the sort of movies that had attracted Doris Day fans such as little Joel and Ethan. As the producer Samuel Goldwyn Jr said, "Movie audiences have become like political groups. They are much more splintered than they used to be."

In the 1970s, the majority of those people who regularly went to the cinema were in their teens and early twenties. In order to cater to their tastes, the studios turned more and more to a quartet of talented young film-school graduates who would dominate the cinema of the decade, and whose films would be among the biggest grossers in the history of motion pictures. Francis Coppola, George Lucas,

Martin Scorsese and Steven Spielberg were known as the "movie brats." They were exposed to classic American films at just the historical moment when these films were becoming intellectually respectable, convincing them that the Hollywood tradition was an honorable one. But this group also realized that the tradition was ready to be reformed and revitalized from within. The New Hollywood, according to critics David Bordwell and Janet Staiger, "has absorbed narrational strategies of the art cinema while controlling them within a coherent genre framework."

Joel and Ethan were still students when *The Godfather*, *Star Wars*, *Taxi Driver* and *Jaws* came out, and when Woody Allen's sophisticated and hilariously angst-ridden cycle of New York movies took off with *Annie Hall*, introducing the most persuasive and pervasive strand of Jewish neurosis yet into screen comedy. When the Coens made their debut with *Blood Simple* in 1984, their elders David Lynch (*Eraserhead*), John Waters (*Pink Flamingos*), John Carpenter (*Dark Star*) and David Cronenberg (*Scanners*) had already entered the kingdom of indiedom. But in 1984, the year John Cassavetes released his final film, *Big Trouble*, Lynch was making a $40 million movie, *Dune*; Waters had begun dipping into the mainstream with *Polyester*; Carpenter was swimming in it after *Escape from New York*, and Cronenberg had just made his first Hollywood movie, *Dead Zone*.

The unrepentant maverick Robert Altman, out of step with the more bland Hollywood of the Eighties, had moved to New York, formed his own company, and was concentrating almost exclusively on transforming modern American plays into films. The field was now open for a new generation of "independent" directors, as distinct from "underground" film-makers such as Andy Warhol, with a different perspective. It was Sam Raimi, Jim Jarmusch, Spike Lee and the Coens who led the way, lucky to have emerged at the time when indies were ready to bloom. But it was the Coen brothers' genre-bending style, alternating between spoofery and seriousness, that had the greatest influence on most of the American independent movies that followed.

In one way, however, the lessons of the Fluxus artists, which the Coens satirized in *The Big Lebowski*, could be related to the independent film movement. As Yoko Ono said: "Fluxus is a very important movement in that sense. They let people know that they don't I think have an excuse. They can't say, 'Well, I can't buy any materials, and I don't have enough money, therefore I can't make art,' or, 'I didn't go to school, so therefore I can't make art.' Anybody can do it if they put their minds to it. Each of us has a song of our own, and you can express that, either visually or in music . . . and in writing, too."

The indies were supposed to be geographically situated at the antipodes of the hypercapitalist mentality of studio film-making. Though the borders have often since become blurred, the indies represent the hip side of cinema. The self-effacing, geekish Coens accepted the hip mantle with amusement, pleasure and some irony. To paraphrase a couple of their lines from *Barton Fink*, "We all have that Coen feeling. But since you're the Coens, you should have it in spades."

Asked how they felt about the new phase when directors get treated like rock stars, Ethan replied, "Well, that's good. Joel's pretty happy about that. People have always mistaken Joel for Joey Ramone. I've always been treated like a rock star. Nobody mistakes me for the other Ramone." In Ethan's short story *Have You Ever Been to Electric Ladyland?* the obnoxious record producer says, "It is hipness that will kill this great industry. I am as hip as the next person. But I am from fucking Cleveland . . ." Substitute Minneapolis, and you get the picture.

JACK LIPNICK: I respect your artistry and your methods, and if you can't fill us in yet, we should be kissing your feet, for your fine efforts . . . (*He gets down on his knees in front of Barton.*) You know in the old country we were taught, as very young children, that there's no shame in supplicatin" yourself when you respect someone ... On behalf of

Capitol Pictures, the administration and all

the stockholders, please accept this as a

symbol of our apology and respect.

–Barton Fink

8   *Our Way*

SINATRA-ISTICALLY, the Coens have always done it their way, despite having big studios bankrolling them. More aptly, they have stuck to their guns both figuratively and literally. (There is a shooting in all their films, excepting the aberrant *The Hudsucker Proxy*.) In fact, they turned down a Warner Bros. offer of millions to direct *Batman* because the project didn't originate from them, a *grande geste* that stood out from the pervasive venality of Hollywood. There were also plans to turn *Fargo* into a TV series, and Kathy Bates was already working on a pilot episode when the Coens decided to drop the project.

According to Carter Burwell, the composer on all their films, "The Coens are different from any other film-making enterprise I've ever worked on, because we're entertaining ourselves a lot of the time. I've never heard Joel and Ethan discuss an audience at this point—the audience will get this, or get that, or we'll sell tickets. It's certainly never been brought up in my presence. In other films, the process does seem more geared toward the audience—they test them, to see what they do and don't understand. The concept of an audience is very different from how Joel and Ethan make a film. They have their own quality; they're not bent out of shape to fit whatever the market demands. Those films are made inexpensively, so they're able to make more of them. When you make a movie for $6 million, you can hardly lose money, and it keeps their careers going for as long as they do."

This was said at the time of their second film, *Raising Arizona*. Those were the days! *The Hudsucker Proxy* would cost $25 million, and the Coens started the new century with *To the White Sea*, budgeted at $60 million. After *The Hudsucker Proxy* was given the cold shoulder by the critics, the brothers commented defensively: "It's like the lower budget makes them [the critics] feel safer. Maybe you don't seem like such underdogs when you're doing the big budgeted stuff. Maybe that's it. That's probably a large part of it. Critics are usually kinder to cheaper movies than to those they perceive to be big Hollywood releases. In some of the bad reviews of *Hudsucker*, it was reported that the movie cost $40 million. In fact, it cost $25 million. It's true that a lot of money seems like a stick they want to beat you with. They cut you a lot more slack if you spend less money, which makes no sense."

It never entered their minds that *The Hudsucker Proxy* was their least commercially successful movie, not because of bad reviews, but because it was their most referential film and thus excluded much of the audience. It was also mooted that American audiences found the title off-putting as "proxy" was not a word in most of their vocabularies. But all the Coen titles are enigmatic. How many people understand what *Blood Simple* or *Raising Arizona* mean? In France, for example, they were given the more elucidatory titles, *Sang Pour Sang* (*Blood for Blood*) and *Arizona Junior*, while *The Hudsucker Proxy* was called *La Grand Saut* (*The Big Jump*). *Miller's Crossing* is a rather tangential title (only two scenes, albeit crucial, take place there) and only one short scene transpires in the town of Fargo. *The Big Lebowski* is really about The Small Lebowski (Jeff Bridges) and Barton Fink is the protagonist's real name, not a nickname. As for *O Brother, Where Art Thou?*, only independent film-makers like the Coens could get away with such a title. Big studios would have, at least, asked for it to be called *O Brother*. The titles are symptomatic of the Coens' independent spirit.

However, huge budgets, such as the one for *To the White Sea*, begin to separate the Coens from the younger wannabee directors and move them, whether they like it or not, into the Establishment, despite cinematographer Roger Deakins' conviction that, "You'll never see them selling out and going to Hollywood and shooting someone else's script."

Pauline Kael put the question on the release of *Blood Simple* as long ago as 1984: "What's the glory of making films outside the industry if they're Hollywood films at heart, or, worse than that—Hollywood by-product?" At the same time, Joel commented, "Ethan has a nightmare of one day finding me on the set of something like *The Incredible Hulk* wearing a gold chain and saying 'I've got to eat, don't I?' "

> NORVILLE: You know, for kids! It has economy,
> simplicity, low production cost and the poten-
> tial for mass appeal, and all that spells out
> great profitability . . .
>
> *—The Hudsucker Proxy*

9   Auteur Biography

THE COENS claim to take responsibility for everything in their movies as true auteurs do. How does one tell an auteur from a hack? One indication is when a new film is referred to by the name of the director(s) rather than the title, e.g. the new Altman, Almodóvar, Von Trier, Oliviera, Kaurismaki, Coen Brothers. Whereas few people would ever refer to the new Howard, the new Reiner or the new Cameron. In keeping with their genuine reticence, the brothers discreetly append their names to the end of the picture, the only directors ever to do so exclusively (they broke the rule with *The Big Lebowski*). Of course, no artists with distinctive, instantly recognizable voices, in whatever art form, need to put their names on their creations. Does one have to squint down to the bottom of a painting by Picasso to read his name, or be told that a symphony one has just listened to is by Mahler?

One critic saw *Blood Simple* as a "grab-bag of movie styles and references, an eclectic mixture of Hitchcock and Bertolucci, of splatter flicks and Fritz Lang and Orson Welles." Another wrote, "It looks like a movie made by guys who spent most of their lives watching movies, indiscriminately, both in theaters and on TV and for whom, mostly by osmosis, the vocabulary and grammar of film has become a kind of instinctive second language."

The fashionable label (1980s — 1990s style) of "postmodernism" is often conveniently attached to the Coen brothers. If the world is meaningless, then why should art be meaningful? One should relish the non-sensical. According to Jean Baudrillard, in postmodern society there are no originals, only copies, or "simulacra."

But what some critics have failed to see is that the Coens, from their very first film, were interested in working inside the rules of a genre, and then breaking them from within. They distil the essence of the genre so that each film contains every element that we expect from a *film noir*, gangster movie, detective thriller, or cons-on-the-run picture, the boundaries being pushed as far as they can go, deconstructing conventional narratives. Their films evoke the atmosphere of classic genre movies, sometimes quoting from specific ones obliquely, without nudging the audience's awareness of them. They have found a visual language (and a verbal one) that translates the past into the present. The ironic inverted commas that inevitably cling like crabs around most postmodernist movies are restricting (especially to audiences not as steeped in American movie history), while the Coens find them liberating.

All their movies are comedies, and all of them, excepting *The Hudsucker Proxy*, are fundamentally *films noirs*, disguised as horror movie (*Blood Simple*), farce (*Raising Arizona*), gangster movie (*Miller's Crossing*), psychological drama (*Barton Fink*), police thriller (*Fargo*), comedy (*The Big Lebowski*), social drama (*O Brother, Where Art Thou?*). Yet, however different they are on the surface, each of the films contains elements of the other, horror edging into comic-strip farce, violence into slapstick and vice versa. One thing is clear: the Coens have little interest in what passes for "realism" in Hollywood mainstream movies. As W.P. Mayhew, the William Faulkner figure in *Barton Fink* says, "The truth is a tart that does not bear scrutiny." Like Hitchcock, the Coens enjoy progressing from the prosaic to the baroque. They could also concur with Hitchcock, who observed: "Most films are 'slices of life', mine are slices of cake." *Pieces* of cake, they aren't!

MOST OF the movies are influenced, in one way or another, as much by other films as by the holy trinity of American crime writers: Raymond Chandler, Dashiell Hammett and James M. Cain. *Blood Simple* was a variation on Cain's *The Postman Always Rings Twice* and *Double Indemnity*. (The 1944 Billy Wilder film of the latter was co-written by Chandler.) The models for *Miller's Crossing* were Hammett's *Red Harvest* and *The Glass Key*, and much of Chandler's written prose was metamorphosed into cinematographic prose in *Barton Fink* and *The Big Lebowski*. Ethan had no qualms about spoofing Raymond Chandler, one of the most pastiched of American authors, in his short story *Hector Berlioz, Private Investigator*. Written completely in dialogue as a radio play, it still manages to convey Chandler through the younger Coen's quirky, deadpan humor. "Berlioz: I'd seen it all, or thought I had. Then one day—September 14, 1947—*she* walked in. Since then, I *have* seen it all."

Crime is the core of the screenplays, because "we feel that criminals are the least able people to cope in society." The Coens are fascinated by losers, who appear as the "heroes' of all their films. Kidnapping, which allows for comic or dramatic tension, occurs in five of the pictures, and they are littered with brutal murders. But they are intrinsically fables of good vs evil. The Coens seem to have heeded Sam Raimi's recipe for films: "The innocent must suffer, the guilty must be punished, you must drink blood to be a man."

There are unmitigated symbols of evil who challenge the good at the climax as in any traditional kiddie matinée adventure. The sleazeball detective against the "innocent" wife (*Blood Simple*); the showdown between the Lone Biker of the Apocalypse and Hi, the naïve hero (*Raising Arizona*); Eddie Dane, the vicious gangster's henchman, and the ambivalent gambler hero Tom Reagan (*Miller's Crossing*); the good/bad salesman Charlie Meadows/serial killer Karl Mundt wrestling with himself (*Barton Fink*); Aloysius, the malevolent sign-painter, struggles with Moses, the black clock-keeper, as the guileless Norville plunges forty-four floors ("forty-five counting the mezzanine") toward the ground (*The Hudsucker Proxy*); the sinisterly taciturn Gaear Grimsrud confronts the cop, Marge Gunderson, hurling a log at her as she holds him at gunpoint (*Fargo*); the bowling pals Dude, Walter and Donny stand up to the three German nihilists in black leather who are demanding money from them (*The Big Lebowski*), and Cooley, the persistent sheriff with the mirrored sunglasses, pursuing the escaped convict hero Everett, who is saved by the flooding of the valley (*O Brother, Where Art Thou?*). The German critic Georg Seessien proffered:

> Evil exists in Coen films in three very different forms. Firstly, in the very real form of power, power that is generally in the hands of fat, older men [Nathan Arizona Sr, Leo O'Bannion, Jack Lipnick, The Big Lebowski], power which is deeply rooted within society and whose continuation is guaranteed by capitalist exploitation and family order. Secondly, in the travails of young protagonists [Hi, Tom Reagan, Barton Fink, Norville Barnes, Jerry Lundegaard, the Dude, Ulysses Everett McGill] whose desire for something or other brings them into confrontation with the fat, older man. And thirdly, evil exists in the form of a very unreal, murderous projection, in wandering killers and monsters [Gale and Evelle, Johnny Caspar and Eddie Dane, Carl Showalter and Gaear, Treehorn's Thugs and the German nihilists], which come into being at the point where the power of the old man meets the desires of the young hero.
>
> The Coens paint pictures of a disenchanted America. Their heroes are imprisoned in the ideology of consumerism, little men (Capraesque at one remove) often being pitted against big business and entrepreneurs. (They make a jokey reference to this in *O Brother, Where Art Thou?*, in which a candidate for governor uses a midget for his campaign slogan "Homer Stokes, Friend of the Little Man." "Pappy O'Daniel, *slave* a the Innarests; Homer Stokes, *servant* a the little man!"). Mammon dominates *Raising Arizona, Miller's Crossing, The Hudsucker Proxy* and *Fargo*, in the latter of which, near the end, Marge delivers a rather unconvincing homily to the crook she has just captured. "There's more to life than a little money, you know. Don't you know that? . . . And here ya are, and it's a beautiful day."

The Coens approach each film as a new stylistic challenge according to the nature of the setting, the period and the plot, yet there are always certain stylistic devices that crop up in a Coen movie such as wide-angle lenses, complicated tracking shots, creative sound, color, and art direction. Each film can be represented by one potent image: a hat, a typewriter, a skyscraper, snow, a bowling alley, leg irons.

Joel: "I don't think there's a thread, at least a conscious thread, anyway, between the different stories we're telling. Sometimes when people point out to us things that are common to the different movies, it's almost like, 'Oh, yeah, I guess that's the case' as opposed to 'Right, that's how it was designed.' "

Ethan: "It's what you call style in retrospect only. At the point of actually making the movie, it's just about making individual choices. You make specific choices that you think are appropriate or compelling or interesting for that particular scene. Then, at the end of the day, you put it all together and somebody looks at it, and, if there's some consistency to it, they say, 'Well, that's their style.' "

JACK LIPNICK: We're only interested in one thing: Can you tell a story, Bart? Can you make us laugh, can you make us cry, can you make us wanna break out in joyous song? Is that more than one thing? Okay, the point is, I run this dump and I don't know the technical mumbo jumbo. Why do I run it? I've got horse sense, goddamit. Showmanship.

–Barton Fink

10   Credit Sequence

LIKE WOODY ALLEN'S movies, the unity of the Coens' pictures is created by the use of a repertory company in the tradition of non-American films such as those of Ingmar Bergman, Yasujiro Ozu or Federico Fellini.

Producer: Ethan Coen. *Director:* Joel Coen. *Screenplay:* Ethan Coen, Joel Coen (or Joel Coen, Ethan Coen). *Cinematographer:* Barry Sonnenfeld (*Blood Simple, Raising Arizona, Miller's Crossing*), Roger Deakins (*Barton Fink, The Hudsucker Proxy, Fargo, The Big Lebowski, O Brother, Where Art Thou?*); *Production Designer:* Jane Musky (*Blood Simple, Raising Arizona*), Dennis Gassner (*Miller's Crossing, Barton Fink, The Hudsucker Proxy, O Brother, Where Art Thou?*). *Music:* Carter Burwell. *Editor:* Roderick Jaynes. *Costume Design:* Richard Hornung (*Raising Arizona, Miller's Crossing, Barton Fink, The Hudsucker Proxy*), Mary Zophres (*Fargo, The Big Lebowski, O Brother, Where Art Thou?*). *Storyboards:* J. Todd Anderson. *Actors:* Frances McDormand, John Goodman, John Turturro, Jon Polito, Steve Buscemi and Holly Hunter.

11   Critics' Choice

Suddenly, there is the sound of two Coens laughing in their characteristic hiccuping manner. It is in response to attempts to submit their films to any kind of aesthetic, textual or thematic analysis. They consider that to take intellectual stock of their work, to delve beneath the surface, is a vain exercise. In this they are in the tradition of macho directors like John Ford, Howard Hawks and Raoul Walsh, who believed they were merely good old-fashioned story tellers, and gobbled up over-intellectual interviewers for breakfast. The Coens are less cannibalistic. When questioned about the content of their films rather than the technicalities behind the making of them, they become reticent, evasive, facetious or make like philistines.

> I suppose when you're landed with a question you don't really know how to deal with you clam up. People interviewing us often look at the movies in different ways from ours, and when they present them on their own terms and ask the meaning of this or that, it's sometimes hard to know what to make of the questions. People read things into our work we didn't know existed. In certain films we've done, where there is an ambiguity designed into the movie, it's frequently the case that the reviewer won't let it rest as being simply ambiguity. And the audience then feel that they're missing something, not understanding something, and have to analyze something into a concrete answer when in fact the movie itself is designed so that you should just be able to watch it and enjoy it. Those journalists have a hard job. They could say, "This is a kind of funny movie and I laughed at it," and leave it at that, but they have to write a certain number of words, so they indulge in all sorts of things that will justify that number.

There is, therefore, some sincerity behind the jokey sarcasm of their comments on critics. "Young writers just starting out and eager to make good should know that the world teems with critics—ugly, bitter people, fat and acned for the most part, often afflicted with gout, dropsy, and diseases of the inner ear. Always they know better; always they recognize exactly what is missing; always, always they can point the way to the finer choice. That is why, on occasion, we search them out. Though the critic can tell you how to improve, he will never tell you what is equally important, when to stop improving. The critic is a lonely man, and a crafty one."

Their attitude to criticism makes the role of the critic and/or biographer redundant, or reduces them to ciphers. But, as François Truffaut wrote: "No artist ever accepts the critic's role on a profound level. In his early period he avoids thinking about it, probably because criticism is more useful to and also more tolerant of beginners. With time, artist and critic settle into their respective roles; maybe they grow to know each other, and soon they consider each other, if not exactly adversaries, in some simplistic image—cat and dog. Once an artist is recognized as such, he stubbornly refuses to admit that criticism has a role to play . . . The artist in a sense, creates himself . . . and then places himself on display. It is a fabulous privilege, but only provided he accepts the opposite side of the coin: the risk involved in being studied, analyzed, notated, judged, criticized, disagreed with."

The Coens have never been able to come to terms with this. Right from the start, the critical reaction to their work has puzzled them. "We thought when we were making *Blood Simple*, it was just a murder story. So imagine our surprise when we started reading reviews and discovered it was the bust of Homer. Or something in that league."

Critics (more often than audiences) hunger for explanations of intentions, sometimes getting their knickers in a twist trying to seek them. When it was suggested by an interviewer that the scene where a woman is reading Russian literature while the creatives in *Hudsucker Proxy* are trying to come up with a name for the "extruded plastic dingus," might be a critique of capitalist society, Joel laughed off the idea. "We weren't really thinking of a critique of capitalism. That didn't mean much to us." It is, in fact, a pretty obvious joke about the passing of time, as she is reading *War and Peace* (always shorthand in American comedies for a long and difficult book) and is on *Anna Karenina* by the time they decide to call it the hula hoop.

Asked to explain the end of *Barton Fink*, where Barton is on a beach, with a box (which might contain a woman's head), seeing the girl in the picture in his hotel room materialize, Joel agonized. "Boy that's a tough one. That's a really funny question!" Ethan helped out. "There's a guy on a beach with a head in a box. What do you say beyond that? We got some very interesting interpretations of *Barton Fink*. What was that by that French critic? 'God checks into a hotel'? He had it all worked out. In a way it was much more clever [sic] than anything we could have come up with."

Naturally, it had to be a French critic, always the object of the moviegoing Joe Public's scorn. There is a tradition of anti-intellectualism in American (and British) films. Hollywood has long been synonymous with mindless, crass, and meretricious mass entertainment. When Hollywood does treat important subjects, it manages, on the whole, to drain them of any depth, presenting the most simplistic and basic reactions to the so-called serious pursuits of existence: politics, philosophy, religion and the arts. Movies have been a kind of antidote to solemnity and "high art," which is why any sociological, philosophical or psychological approach to them is generally greeted with deep suspicion.

Film psychiatrists are often pompous gurus or of the crazy Viennese variety as consciously stereotypified by Dr. Hugo Bronfenbrenner in *The Hudsucker Proxy*. "Patient dizplayed liztlessness, apathy, gloomy indifference and vas blue und mopey. Ven asked vut four Rorschach stains reprezented, Patient replied, 'Nussink much,' 'I don't know,' 'chust a blotch,' und 'sure beats me.' Patient shows no ambition, no get-up-und-go, no vim. He is riding ze grand loopen-ze-loop . . ."

An intellectual writer like Barton Fink, according to John Turturro who portrayed him, was "living too much in his head. The film is all about heads and, at the end, his head is cut off metaphorically." When the derisable Barton is turned on by the servicemen while dancing with a girl at the USO hall, he reacts by pointing to his head and tapping his skull. "This is *my* uniform! This is how I serve the common man! This is where . . ." Finally, the common man (John Goodman) turns, shrieking, "Look upon me! I'll show you the life of the mind!" In contrast, Jackie Treehorn (Ben Gazzara), the Hugh Hefner-type Sixties swinger in *The Big Lebowski*, taps his forehead with one finger, and says, "People forget that the brain is the biggest erogenous zone." "On you, maybe," replies the Dude.

Wisdom comes not from intellectuals, but from Moses, the black clock-keeper (*The Hudsucker Proxy*), the cowboy (*The Big Lebowski*) and the black blind seer (*O Brother, Where Art Thou?*)—the kind of folksy characters who have all the answers, to whom classic Hollywood movies have always given credence, and who are acknowledged by the Coens, with postmodern irony.

VLADIMIR: Moron!

ESTRAGON: Vermin!

VLADIMIR: Abortion!

ESTRAGON: Morpion!

VLADIMIR: Sewer Rat!

ESTRAGON: Curate!

VLADIMIR: Cretin!

ESTRAGON (with finality): Crritic!

VLADIMIR: Oh!

He wilts vanquished, and turns away.

–Waiting for Godot (Samuel Beckett)

12 Cheech and Chong Coen

IN *THE* Making *of* The Big Lebowski William Preston Robertson, trying to elucidate the cowboy voice-over and the tumbleweeds at the beginning of the film, expostulated: "It is an arch statement on America's Great Western Expansion, with Los Angeles being the far-thest geographic point in that expansion . . . and the chauvinism of

Western Expansion, and, indeed, the absurdity of the pioneering masculine mystique itself. But more than that, it is about the past, and the irony of a land professing a doctrine of newness and expansion that is in reality a vestige of its cowboy past."

Ethan's reaction to this was: "Yeah, I mean, probably. It's not that there's some connection between the West and LA. It's that it's kind of wrong in a way. I mean, even the things that don't go together should seem to clash in an interesting way—like, you know, a Cheech and Chong movie, but with bowling. You sort of do it by feel and not with reasons."

Frances McDormand once chipped in during an interview with an earnest reporter: "You see that's the problem talking to these guys. You can't get them on the grand themes." Asked if they were postmodernist, Ethan replied: "I'm not real sure. The honest answer is I'm not real clear on what postmodernism is." Actually, the brothers may act like Dumb and Dumber, but they are really Smart and Smarter, or intellectual Beavis and Buttheads.

WHEN ASKED what the image represents that accompanies the main title of *Miller's Crossing* and the parallel dream sequence in which a black hat is being blown through a forest, Ethan replied, "It doesn't represent anything. It's just a hat being blown in the wind." Joel added: "That hat in the dream is not a symbol, it doesn't mean anything in particular. It's an image that pleased us. You mustn't look for any deep meaning."

Gabriel Byrne, whose character of Tom Reagan dreams of the hat, asked Joel on the set one day, "What's the significance of the hat? I need to know." Joel said, "Ethan, come here, Gabe wants to know what the significance of the hat is." Ethan said, "Hmm. Yeah, it was significant," and then walked away leaving Byrne none the wiser.

In fact, this deflection from the search for significance is built into the screenplay. When Tom Reagan wakes up he tells his girlfriend Verna (Marcia Gay Harden), in bed with him, about the dream. "Yeh, and you chased the hat and it turned into something else." "No, it stayed a hat. And I didn't chase it." He further comments, "There's nothing more foolish than a man chasing his hat." Perhaps, there's nothing more foolish than a critic chasing a symbol that evades him.

To quote Ludwig Wittgenstein: "In order to recognize a symbol by its sign, we must observe how it is used with a sense" . . . or to quote the Coens' patron saint Raymond Chandler: "Scarcely anything in literature is worth a damn except what is written between the lines."

On *The Hudsucker Proxy*, an interviewer proposed that the characters represent Capitalism versus Labour. "Maybe the characters do embody those grand themes you mentioned, but that question is independent of whether or not we're interested in them—and we're not."

This is in contrast to the movie director John L. Sullivan (Joel McCrea) in Preston Sturges' *Sullivan's Travels* (1941) who sees a fight in a Western on the roof of a train as "Capital and Labour destroying each other." Sullivan wants to make *O Brother, Where Art Thou?* "I want this picture to be a commentary on modern conditions. The problems that confront the average man . . ."

The Coens echoed this by making the pretentious playwright Barton Fink say: "We have an opportunity to forge something real out of everyday experience, create a theater for the masses that's based on a few simple truths . . . The hopes and dreams of the common man." Naturally, the Coens were sympathetic to the satiric intent of Sturges' film, and agree with the final sentiments expressed. "I don't want to make *O Brother, Where Art Thou?* There's a lot to be said for making people laugh. That's all they've got in this cockeyed caravan."

James Agee's comments on Preston Sturges' films might serve equally for the Coens' work. "They seem to be wonderfully, uncontrollably, almost proudly corrupt, vengeful, fearful of intactness and self-commitment . . . their mastering object, seems to be to sail as steep into the wind as possible without for an instant incurring the disaster of becoming seriously, wholly acceptable as art."

THE BROTHERS GEEK

It was an odd choice, Minneapolis. To be sure, it

was virgin turf; its Swedes, Poles, and German

Lutherans had never organized on the model of

eastern towns. But there seemed little to organ-

ize. The city had not much serious crime. It was

dotted with scenic lakes. The people were polite.

Many owned boats. In the summer they engaged

in water sports; in the winter they skied. The

stolid northern stock seemed immune to the

great miseries and grand passions upon which

crime traditionally feeds.

−Cosa Minapolidan (Gates of Eden by Ethan Coen)

13 *Minnesota Nice*

MINNEAPOLIS, MINNESOTA, was an odd choice for Jewish families to make. Anyway, the Diaspora scattered many of them across the United States, some landing in the oddest places. The Coens found themselves in St. Louis Park, a middle-class suburb of Minneapolis, a rather staid and boring Midwest city. Maybe its very dullness pushed young Joel and Ethan toward a more imaginative life and an escape into a more exciting world, most of it gained from books and the movies. "It was to compensate for the fact that our lives were terribly mundane," the brothers explained. "It was the suburbs, you know. I cannot think of a single, seminal childhood event," Ethan remarked. "Bob Dylan got out of there at an early age and you can see why," said Joel. "When I had the chance, I wanted to get as far away as possible as fast as possible."

Yet, Minneapolis, for all its lack of excitement and particular visual resonance, is used as background to some of Ethan's short stories, full of insights into a Jewish childhood filtered through fiction, and makes an appearance in *Fargo*, the film that some say put Minnesota on the map. (Other film-makers followed, particularly Sam Raimi with A *Simple Plan*, who took on the Coens on their own ground, both literally and figuratively.)

Ethan refers to his native city in a story called *I Killed Phil Shapiro*, in which the young narrator commits patricide in his imagination/in actuality. "He moved us to Minneapolis. I lived in that strange frozen city where people's breath hovers about them, where fingertips tingle and go dead, where spit snaps and freezes before it hits the ground."

Minneapolis is among the coldest cities in the USA. During an average winter, the temperatures reach –29C to –34C.

"WHAT THEY really remind me of is two guys who grew up in bunk beds," says a long-time friend. Joel and Ethan did share a room and were closer to each other than to their older sister Deborah Ruth (now a psychiatrist).

"I saw almost nothing of my sister from the outset of her puberty until she left for college six years later," writes Ethan in the short story *The Old Country*. "She spent those years in the bathroom washing her hair. Very occasionally she emerged for food or to use the telephone, her head wrapped in a towel." This came partly from life and partly from those Sandra Dee movies of the 1960s, on which the boys doted.

The brothers skied a little and were bored at school. Bright but unexceptional, they went to the local public school attended mostly by Jews, but there were also Protestant kids of Scandinavian origin with names like Gustafson and Lundegaard. The Minnesota phone book is full of Olsons, Johnsons, Svensons and Ericsons, descended from nineteenth-century immigrants who farmed the land when it wasn't covered with three feet of snow. The Coens were brought up on Sven and Ole jokes, rather than Paddy or Polack jokes as in other parts of the country. Perhaps the Coens missed a beat by not naming a couple of characters Olsen and Johnson in *Fargo* as a homage to the madcap stars of *Hellzapoppin'*, although there is an Officer Olson in it.

It has been mentioned that there is something Japanese about the way the natives of Minnesota refuse to express emotion. In *Fargo*, in order to stress the point or subvert it, a Japanese Minnesotan named Steve Park (Mike Yanagita) breaks into tears in a bar, lies about his wife dying of leukemia, and tries to make a play for his heavily pregnant former schoolfriend Marge Gunderson (Frances McDormand). She plays it like an Oriental woman, looking around embarrassed, eyes lowered over her Diet Coke, while he is talkative and tactless.

The scene was filmed in a replica of the Radisson café in downtown Minneapolis that the Coens knew well. Another scene, where Jerry Lundegaard discusses the ransom with his father-in-law and

Stan Grossman, a business associate, was shot in Embers Family Restaurant in St. Louis Park where, in his teens, Ethan once worked as a dishwasher.

Statistically, Minnesotans, considered backwoodsmen by the rest of America, are less likely to take part in television talk and game shows than citizens of other states. "Minnesota Nice" is given to the slow manner of speech of many of the state's inhabitants of Scandinavian origin. It is said that they have to be cheerful and co-operative because they are holed up together through long winters. "The Coens exhibit that region's economy of speech and resistance to overt displays of emotion. They share a common Minnesotan reserve," explained a friend. In fact, in the Coens, natural Jewish volubility seems restrained by the "Minnesotan reserve," or conversely, the "Minnesotan reserve" is liberated by their Jewish volubility.

HOOKER ONE: They said they were going to the

Twin Cities.

MARGE: Oh, yah?

HOOKER TWO: Yah.

HOOKER ONE: Yah. Is that useful to yah?

MARGE: Oh, you bet, yah.

—Fargo

14   The Old Country

JOEL (BORN 29 November 1954) and Ethan (21 September 1957) and their sister Deborah Ruth, a few years the brothers' senior, grew up in an intellectual family in St. Louis Park. Their parents, Edward, an economics professor at the University of Minnesota, and Rena, a professor of art history at St. Cloud State University, both retired, were nominally orthodox (*frum*) Jews. "We were brought up relatively traditionally," Ethan explained. "Our mother made sure of that, but it wasn't very important to our father. They were moderately strict, however."

Quite a lot of Jewish families had congregated in St. Louis Park and its environs. It grew into a substantial Jewish community, and boasts the oldest and largest co-ed Jewish day school, though the Coen parents opted not to send their boys to it. In the 1990s, the synagogues and other local Jewish groups helped Russian-Jewish families settle there.

Joel and Ethan's paternal great-grandfather was a Polish Jew who emigrated to London. He changed his long Polish name to Coen thinking he would be taken for Irish and be better treated than as a Polish Jew. Their grandfather worked for a diamond importer in London, blew the whistle on some irregularity in the business and as a reward was given a diamond which he used to put himself through law school. He ended up as a barrister in London, wig and all.

Their paternal grandmother emigrated from Tsaritsin in Russia to New York as an adolescent after the Revolution. (She died in Hove, on the south coast of England, in 1991.) Towards the end of her long life, she began to lose her memory, her speech lost its sense and then she stopped speaking altogether. But, a year before she died, she began to speak again . . . in Russian. Strangely, she had used her native tongue only rarely over 80 years. For some reason, she encouraged her grandchildren to memorize the phrase "Yayik do Kieva Dovedet," meaning "By your tongue you will get to Kiev," not a terribly useful phrase for three children living in Minneapolis. But its sense is "If you don't know just ask," a good maxim for biographers, and even film directors.

Their paternal grandparents were staying in New York when their father Ed was born. "Though technically he's American, he was brought up in London and went to the London School of Economics. Being English, he has a distinctive sense of humor, but different from ours."

The boys' parents were religious, but not to excess. In contrast, their maternal grandfather and grandmother were orthodox Jews. Their grandmother, who came from Riga in Latvia, would not drive on the Sabbath. "When they paid us a visit on the Sabbath, my mother used subterfuge to make them believe we obeyed all the laws and that we didn't do anything forbidden. That's where we learnt about acting."

But the Judaism that the Coens were brought up in didn't really stick, though they still keep the religious holidays. Perhaps, like the British stage director and sometime comedian Jonathan Miller, they were Jew-ish, they "didn't go the whole hog." Nevertheless, they realized that to stop being Jewish is not as simple as "turning in your library card," to quote the converted Jew Walter Sobchak (John Goodman) in *The Big Lebowski*. As Ethan wrote in his university thesis: "A distinguishing mark of religious attitudes is that one is forbidden to abandon them . . . the converted (to and from a faith) are a small minority (not counting as a 'conversion' someone's outgrowing his kiddie-faith.) That they are exceptional shows that there is some rule at work."

The boys attended Hebrew school as preparation for their bar-mitzvahs. Ethan evokes the sort of school it was (with poetic license) in his semi-autobiographical story *The Old Country*. It is set in 1967, is written in the first person, and is about a ten-year-old boy, the age Ethan was at the time.

"There was one, and only one, all-school assembly during my years in Talmud Torah [Torah Study]. It was at the outbreak of the 1967 Six-Day War . . . and for want of an auditorium, it was held in the snack bar. We were called together so that the faculty could tell us about Israel's performance and prospects in the fighting just started. The main speaker was Ken Jacobson, an earnest teacher unlike most of the rabbis inasmuch as he was less than seventy years old, and who stockily strode the halls of the Talmud Torah in a cardigan sweater and knit yarmulke. (The old rabbis favored skullcaps of a slick black synthetic gathered into a hard button center.)"

In the same story, Ethan describes, with obvious envy and admiration, an anarchic student, whose rebellion goes too far one day and is taken out of school for a week, only to return a docile shell of his previous self. "For the next several months Michael was a model student, if somewhat robotic, until his family moved to California, where (it was common knowledge) all meshuggenehs end up."

> What mysteries have been preserved, what
>
> lost, and what transformed in our migrations
>
> from Canaan to Eastern Europe to New York
>
> City and finally this far-flung garden suburb?
>
> **–I Shot Phil Shapiro** (Gates Of Eden)

15 *Jew Reckoning*

THERE ARE few overtly Jewish characters in the Coen brothers' films, most of which are populated by goys and rednecks. Those Jews, including Walter Sobchak, the adopted Jew, are pretty unsympathetic. In *Miller's Crossing*, Bernie Bernbaum (John Turturro) or "the Schmatte," as he is referred to, is a cowardly, double-dealing, crooked weasel of a man. *Schmatte* is Yiddish for cheap goods. Police chief O'Doole says of him, "It ain't right all this fuss over one sheeny. Let Caspar have Bernie—Jesus, what's one Hebrew more or less?" However, the Italian-American Turturro gives the character more than his due. "Bernie is a guy who's trying to be a survivor. He's constantly on the move. Which is kind of Jewish history." But Joel put it into perspective. "People objected to the fact that the character was Jewish and about the way Gabriel Byrne takes him out in the woods to shoot him. It's such a stretch to take this old Chicago school gangster behavior and turn it into a train ride to Auschwitz."

Nevertheless, it is not forcing the issue to suggest that the Holocaust hovers over *Barton Fink*, which is deliberately set in 1941, on the eve of the bombing of Pearl Harbor. Even the Coens reluctantly admitted that "the whole movie was supposed to feel like impending doom or catastrophe. And we definitely wanted it to end with an apocalyptic feeling." Most horrifying of all, whether intended or not, is the knowledge that the affable insurance salesman Charlie Meadows (John Goodman), "the average working stiff. The common man," who Barton wants to write about, turns out to be "Madman" Karl Mundt, "who likes to ventilate people with a shotgun and then cut their heads off." At the moment when he shoots a cop, he shouts, "Heil Hitler!"

It is also no coincidence that the two cops sent to question Barton about the murder in the crummy Hotel Earle, turn out to have Italian and German surnames, Mastrionotti and Deutsch. "Fink. That's a Jewish name, isn't it?" says Mastrionotti. "Yeah." "Yeah, I didn't think this dump was restricted."

Barton is Jewish as is the vulgarian head of the studio, Jack Lipnick (Michael Lerner), an amalgam of Louis B. Mayer, whom he physically resembles, and the hated Harry Cohn. "I'm bigger and meaner and louder than any other kike in this town," says Lipnick, who originally comes from Minsk, where Mayer was born.

"What's interesting, is that you have these guys who were Jews from the old country, and they used to build synagogues for their parents on the backlots and make them as much like the synagogues in the old shtetls as possible," Joel mused. "On the other hand, they wouldn't admit anything about their own Jewishness and went around calling people kikes."

"We were thinking about these characters as Jews, but we weren't thinking about Jewishness," Ethan added. "It just made sense to us that Barton would be Jewish, given where a lot of these people came from."

IT HAS taken a long time for Jews in the cinema to be treated as well or as badly as any other minority group. Jews as Jews were more or less invisible in Hollywood. Stars such as Tony Curtis (Bernard Schwartz), Kirk Douglas (Issur Danielovitch), Lauren Bacall (Betty Perske) and Jerry Lewis (Joseph Levitch) hid their origins behind Aryan names. In the rare cases when Jewish characters appeared in the movies, it was usually as victims of anti-Semitism as in *Gentleman's Agreement* and *Crossfire* (both 1947). Because most of the Hollywood moguls were Jewish, Jews, when they appeared, were always handled with kid gloves while blacks, Orientals, Native Americans and Mexicans were humiliated for years.

It was Woody Allen who first made the breakthrough with *Annie Hall* (1977), much as Spike Lee—initially greeted as "a young, black Woody Allen"—did with blacks in *Do the Right Thing* (1989). "He [Allen] has vacillated in his attitude toward Jews and Gentiles," wrote Peter Biskind. "One moment sentimentalizing Jews as life-saving agents of passion and vigor, capable of revitalizing desiccated WASPs as he does in *Interiors*, the next denigrating them for their vulgarity, as he does in *Stardust Memories*, or romanticizing WASPs as vessels of truth and beauty put on earth to redeem eternally ambivalent Jews, as he does in *Manhattan*." Allen himself repudiated this. "I use my Jewish background when it's expedient for me in my work, but it's not really an obsession of mine, and I never had that obsession with Gentile women."

The Coens are more relaxed than either Allen and Lee on the racial issue, and have never cared for the sensitivities of minority groups, treating Jews as they do other characters. After all, Martin Scorsese and Francis Coppola never had any qualms about presenting Italian-Americans in the worst light.

In a way, it has only been permissible for Jews to be anti-Semitic, or rather, to create unpleasant Jewish characters. Put Jackie Mason's jokes into a non-Jewish comic's mouth and they would sound offensive. One of the most obnoxious creations in Ethan Coen's stories, which contain many Jews, is the Jewish record entrepreneur in *Have You Ever Been to Electric Ladyland?* In a dazzling monologue, steeped in "fucks' and "cunts," he gives the police an endless list of enemies who could have poisoned his dog. "His first wife was Jewish, looked like a goddam horse, I used to call her Mrs. Ed—last year I sent the daughter an enema bag. 'On the occasion of your bar mitzvah, so you'll know the way to a man's heart.' "

If Jews in the Coens' movies get a rough ride, they are no more done down than other religious, ethnic or social groups. In fact, as much as the Coens enjoy bending genres in their image, they are happy to play with stereotypes. In *Fargo*, Shep Proudfoot, a Red Indian mechanic on parole for dealing in narcotics and other criminal activities, is a sullen, unsympathetic and violent man. (The Coens knew that the Dakota Indians gave their name to Minnesota, meaning "sky-tinted water.") When Shep beats up the petty criminal Carl Showalter (Steve Buscemi), Carl yells, "Stay away from me, man! Hey! Smoke a fuckin" peace pipe, man!"

Miller's Crossing is peppered with characters who express racist remarks; Hi's obnoxious boss in *Raising Arizona* has a fund of Polack jokes, which he can't even get right, and Visser, the sleazy private eye in *Blood Simple*, when presenting the bar owner with evidence of his wife's unfaithfulness, says, "It ain't such bad news. I mean you thought he was a colored . . . You're always assumin" the worst."

However, the blacks seem to be treated in a slightly gentler manner than most other groups. Meurice, the black barman in *Blood Simple*, is the only character who has a certain amount of control over his life. Other noteworthy blacks like Tommy Johnson, who believes he sold his soul to the devil to be "taught to play the guitar real good," and the blind seer in *O Brother, Where Art Thou?* and the clock-keeper in *The Hudsucker Proxy*, are repositories of wisdom.

In *The Big Lebowski*, Turturro's Chicano bowler Jesus Quintana is broadly caricatured. Accompanied by O'Brien, "a short fat Irishman with tufted red hair," he warns Walter and the Dude, "I see you rolled your way into the semis. *Dios mio*, man. Seamus and me we're gonna fuck you up . . . Nobody fucks with the Jesus." When the Dude refers to the guy who peed on his rug as a Chinaman, Walter points out that "Chinaman is not the preferred nomenclature. Asian-American, please."

In their introduction to the script of *The Big Lebowski*, the Coens announced that they had won the 1998 Bar Kochba award, "honouring achievement in the arts that defy racial and religious stereotyping and promote appreciation for the multiplicity of man." The award was given by Rabbi Emmanuel Lev-Tov, author of the memoir *You With the Schnozz*.

WALTER: It's shabbas, the Sabbath, which I'm allowed to break only if it's a matter of life and death—

DUDE: Walter, come off it. You're not even fucking Jewish, you're—

WALTER: What the fuck are you talking about?

DUDE: You're fucking Polish Catholic—

WALTER: What the fuck are you talking about? I converted when I married Cynthia! Come on, Dude!

DUDE: Yeah, and you were—

WALTER: You know this!

DUDE: And you were divorced five fucking years ago.

WALTER: Yeah? What do you think happens when you get divorced? You turn in your library card? Get a new driver's license? Stop being Jewish?

—The Big Lebowski

16   Private Eye and Public Ear

WHAT SPECIFIC qualities the brothers inherited from their parents are hard to pin down. One could assume that their knowledge of the economics of film came from Ed Coen. Rena thinks that Joel's "wonderful eye" might have come from her. Ethan, of course, has a "wonderful ear" as anyone reading his collection of short stories, *Gates of Eden*, will testify. Dialogue dominates these stories, some of them written entirely in direct speech, and dialogue is one of the main strengths of their films. Certain phrases like "scare me up a gargle" meaning "get me a drink," from *Miller's Crossing*, were thought up by Ethan.

"He'll end up with a phrase flying around in his head and it will reappear throughout the movie," according to Sam Raimi. In fact, both brothers are masters of the word, especially colloquial language. It is fair to say that they didn't pick it up by frequenting the Minneapolis underworld. A Coen linguistic tic, and a humorously effective one, is to put bombastic language into the mouths of their characters, often in stark contrast to the circumstances or the personalities involved. For example, the terminology used by Carl Showalter (Steve Buscemi), the kidnapper in *Fargo*: "I'm not gonna debate you, Jerry." "You're tasking us to perform this mission." "Circumstances, Jerry. Beyond the, uh . . . acts of God, force majeure . . ." To a state trooper: "That's my license and registration. I wanna be in compliance." To a car park attendant: "I guess you think, you know, you're an authority figure . . . You know there are limits to your life, man. Ruler of your little fuckin" gate here."

In *O Brother, Where Art Thou?* Everett (George Clooney), a con on the lam with his two dim-witted companions, Pete and Delmar, is insulted by Pete as they walk along a dusty road. "Pete, the personal rancor reflected in that remark I don't intend to dignify with a comment, but I would like to address your general attitude of hopeless negativism. Consider the lilies a the goddam field, or—hell!—take a look at Delmar here as your paradigm a hope."

The Coens explained: "We often get going on a script by thinking about the rhythms and the way that people speak. Finding a voice for a character kind of helps you make them real and figure out what to do with them. It's a way of making them specific instead of just saying 'this is the good guy or whatever.' "

Much of it is a heightened form of colloquial speech derived from pulp fiction, as well as the Coens' innate ability and sense of humor, but also from being steeped in the crime literature of Raymond Chandler and Dashiell Hammett, and more modern writers like Elmore Leonard.

Ethan remarked: "It's funny that people who write about our films always refer to other films whenever they want to make comparisons. It's often down to contemporary narrow-mindedness that these literary references are overlooked."

"An interesting bit," he said negligently. "I picked it up just the other day. Asta Dial's *Spirit of Dawn*." "I thought it was Klopstein's *Two Warts on a Behind*," I said . . . "You have a somewhat peculiar sense of humor," he said. "Not peculiar," I said. "Just uninhibited."

–**Farewell My Lovely** (Raymond Chandler)

17   Movie Brats

WHILE STILL in their teens, both brothers were enrolled at the quaintly named Simon's Rock College of Bard, a fee-paying college situated in the small community of Great Barrington in Massachusetts, west of Boston and two and a half hours north of New York City. Located among 275 acres of wood, hills and ponds, it was a world away from their suburban home in Minneapolis. The rebellion of the Sixties hardly penetrated its walls and squeaky-clean students.

The college was founded in 1964, with the idea of admitting students from sixteen years old, too young to go to university. Joel Coen entered Simon's Rock in 1971 and stayed for two years. Ethan arrived in 1974 and spent one year there. As the school claims in its brochure: "Simon's Rock is the only college of the liberal arts and sciences in the United States specifically designed to provide bright, highly-motivated students with the opportunity to begin college after the tenth or eleventh grade . . . It is designed for students who seek a serious alternative to the last year or two of high school because they and their parents find that their ambitions and interests are no longer being met—for students who are searching for something more." It seems as though Simon's Rock met the requirements of the sharply intelligent Coen brothers.

Adams Douglas, a contemporary of the brothers, said they were not involved in the small film-making program they had there. "I recall them as unremarkable. I have no strong memories of the topics of intellectual discussions in the Dining Hall (a favorite Simon's Rock pastime), nor do I recall them being in any serious trouble for anything (another way one might become memorable). I do know they seem to have aged little. Unlike many of us, they look essentially the same as they did in the '70s, including their hairstyles." In fact, they sound like a couple of real dorks.

BEFORE GOING to graduate school and then onto university, the Coens were drawn to popular culture, especially the movies. "All that cold weather drives you inside to watch movies," they explained. Pete Peterson, an English and Media Studies teacher, remembers the

Coens as budding *cinéastes* who attended his Eight and a Half Cinema Club at the High School during the early Seventies. "The kids had very sophisticated tastes in film, so we catered to that by showing 'underground' films. It was at the club that the Coens first saw François Truffaut's *The 400 Blows*. I remember, they thanked me for it."

But their tastes were generally on a lower level. Ethan has cited *All Hands on Deck* as being the first movie he ever remembers liking. Certainly he can be forgiven for enjoying this unhilarious 1961 CinemaScope navy musical, starring the anemic Pat Boone and the cretinous Buddy Hackett, that only a four-year-old could like. Joel's primal choice demonstrated rather better taste, though he was six years old when he saw *The Magnificent Seven*, "the first film that made an impression on me."

Unlike Steven Spielberg, whose ambition was to make the sort of movies he enjoyed as a child, and who became a raider of the lost RKO, there is very little discernible influence of the films the Coens saw as children on their own pictures. Among the films the brothers saw (and liked) were naff Walt Disney kiddie movies with animals in the title starring boring, cleancut Dean Jones: *That Darn Cat*, *The Ugly Dachshund*, *Monkeys Go Home!*, *The Horse in the Gray Flannel Suit* and *The Love Bug*. The fact that Joel was just into his teens and Ethan was a pre-teen almost mitigates these tastes.

Francis Ford Coppola determined to become a film director after seeing Sergei Eisenstein's *October*. Martin Scorsese was turned on by the movies by another famous screen tandem, Michael Powell and Emeric Pressburger, and delved into Ingmar Bergman's universe. The Coens enthused about glossy Doris Day vehicles: *Pillow Talk*, *That Touch Of Mink*, *The Thrill of It All*, and *Move Over, Darling*. Actually there is something of Doris Day's spunky wholesomeness in Marge Gunderson, the pregnant policewoman in a parka in *Fargo*. Little Joel and Ethan also giggled through the very worst of Bob Hope movies like *Bachelor in Paradise*, *A Global Affair*, *I'll Take Sweden*, and *Boy, Did I Get a Wrong Number!*, and looked with favor into the pits of Jerry Lewis' career, *The Family Jewels*, *Three On a Couch* and *Boeing-Boeing*. They were particularly taken by the latter and remembered the opening credits in which, to calm top-billing egos, the names of Jerry Lewis and Tony Curtis revolved on an axis. Many years later, as a joke, Ethan suggested that he and Joel do the same with the credits of their own pictures. "If I could keep only one film on video for all time it would have to be *Boeing-Boeing*, a terrible 1965 sex comedy," Joel later claimed.

Tony Curtis was a favorite in *Sex and the Single Girl, Not With My Wife, You Don't!* and *Drop Dead, Darling*, as was lanky Jim Hutton in comedies such as *The Horizontal Lieutenant, The Honeymoon Machine* and *Walk Don't Run*. According to Ethan, "It's a very weird, wooden aesthetic that nobody's interested in anymore."

Sometimes nostalgia overrides quality so that the films we see as children have a special place in our hearts, and even seeing them again as an adult, and being able to assess them for the crap they really are, they still retain a glow completely incomprehensible to those of another generation.

On television, Andy Devine, the raspy-voiced buffoon character actor, who rather resembled John Goodman, had a show on television called *Andy's Gang* in which Devine introduced *Ramar*, a serial set in India, starring Jon Hall stripped to the waist. The Coens' predilection for exotic trash extended to those late *Tarzan* movies of the 1960s with Jock Mahoney in *Tarzan Goes to India*, and Mike Henry in *Tarzan and the Valley of Gold* and *Tarzan and the Jungle Boy*. The boys had seen the earlier and better *Tarzans* on television with Johnny Weissmuller, their favorite being *Tarzan's New York Adventure*, probably because of the strange Coenesque incongruity of the Ape Man in a suit, comparable to placing an old-time cowboy in modern downtown Los Angeles in *The Big Lebowski*.

Steve Reeves was another muscle man that the unmuscled Coens revelled in. Reeves was the star of badly dubbed peplum pictures made in Italy, such as *The Giant of Marathon* and *The Trojan Horse*. They developed a shared sense for kitsch as they sat through hours of wooden epics on *Mel Jass' Matinee Movie*. They were also entranced by an eccentric late-night movie show on Minneapolis TV. "All the films would be Italian productions, but very different. It might be a Fellini film one night, then *Sons of Hercules*. A highbrow Italian movie followed by Steve Reeves." (It's typical that Joel mentions the Reeves title, which doesn't actually exist, but not the "highbrow" Fellini.) This blurring of categories has rubbed off on their work. They often undercut their most dramatic films with dark humor, and switch between styles and genres. "We always liked subject matter that wasn't just flat-out comedy. But it's hard for us to write without amusing ourselves at a certain level, which means making ourselves laugh. We never did anything we didn't try to leaven with humor."

It was only later that the Coens discovered that there were Hollywood films from an earlier era that had a true quality, like those of Billy Wilder, Frank Capra and Preston Sturges, on whom they drew more directly. And yet, among their best-loved pictures was *The Fortune* (1975), which is "our favorite Mike Nichols movie, with all its heavy style and humor." The film revolves around a Laurel and Hardyish pair of bumbling, small-time conmen (Warren Beatty and Jack Nicholson), who pretend to kidnap an heiress to get her father's money. Sound familiar? John Goodman and William Forsythe in *Raising Arizona*; and Steve Buscemi and Peter Stormare in *Fargo* are also bumbling, small-time conmen who attempt kidnappings. Another of their favorite films was Sam Peckinpah's *Bring Me the Head of Alfredo Garcia* (1974), although they claimed, cheekily, never to have seen it. It contains a menacing biker (see *Raising Arizona*), indiscriminate violence (see *Blood Simple*, *Miller's Crossing*), and a head in a box (see *Barton Fink*).

18 First Fumblings

MINNEAPOLIS MAY not be the most exciting city in the USA, but its 'burbs were even less so, and St. Louis Park, despite its population of 44,000 residents, 60 neighborhood parks, its library on Library Lane, with a large section of Russian-language books, the Jewish Community Centre on South Cedar Lake Road, the one movie theater at Shelard Park and the exclusive Minneapolis Golf Club not far from the Coen family's house in Flag Avenue, there was not much for active and intelligent teenagers to do.

Three such teenagers were Joel and Ethan Coen, and Ron Neter. One day, as the three of them were lounging on the sofa of the basement den where the brothers and their friends hung out, Joel thought of a way of relieving the boredom. Why don't they make movies? Super 8 movies! This was the late 1960s, only a few years after Super 8 had replaced the standard 8mm film. Both optical and magnetic sound tracks could be used, and the larger picture area produced images of greater definition and higher color quality than the standard 8mm film. Until it was replaced by the much easier and cheaper videotape, Super 8 was very popular with home-movie enthusiasts, enabling more and more people to make movies. But they were beyond the means of your average teenage boy.

Ron Neter, now a commercial producer in Los Angeles, suggested the boys mow neighborhood lawns in order to earn enough money to buy a movie camera and film stock. Eventually they were able to purchase a lightweight Vivitar camera and some film, and started making their own films in Super 8, "incredibly cheesy even by Super 8 standards," remarked Ethan. The tyro film-makers didn't realize that in New York, underground film directors searching for a more personal, anti-commercial form of expression were turning to Super 8. The home movie was suddenly cool, and there were manifestos on the revolutionary purity of 8mm over 16mm.

ON THE day the boys bought their camera, they returned to the basement den to discuss what to film. So they looked up the TV Guide and waited for a movie that interested them, pointed the camera at the television set and filmed *Tarzan and the She-Devil*, starring Lex Barker as Tarzan and Raymond Burr as the heavy. It was a pre-postmodernist act. They had made a film of a film, something they have done, less literally, ever since. It was an equivalent of the short story by Jorge Luis Borges, *Pierre Menard, Author of Don Quixote*.

"He did not want to compose another *Don Quixote*—which is easy—but *Don Quixote* itself. Needless to say, he never contemplated a mechanical transcription of the original; he did not propose to copy it. His admirable intention was to produce a few pages which would coincide word for word and line for line—with those of Miguel de Cervantes."

Borges goes onto write that Pierre Menard's *Don Quixote* was "more subtle" than the original although identical. The Coen brothers' first film *Ethan and Joel Coen, auteurs of Tarzan and the She-Devil* was more subtle than the original although identical, and far more subtle than Gus Van Sant's near shot-by-shot version of Hitchcock's *Psycho* many years later. Actually, it was probably the first and last time they didn't have full control over their material.

The Coens then decided to start filming from life. Out they went to their nearest park where Joel, the nascent movie director, filmed his sneakered feet as he descended a slide. This plotless, debut location film could have been called *Feet First* if Harold Lloyd hadn't got there earlier. Then Joel lay on his back beneath a tree, pointed the camera upwards and filmed children jumping from the tree down around him.

It was now time to move into the realms of narrative film with actors. Luckily, they found their first star in one of the neighborhood kids, Mark Zimmering, nicknamed, for some cryptic reason, Zeimers. He was a lively boy with a shock of dark, unruly hair *à la* John Turturro, orthodontic braces, and a wide grin. "I was the one with most charisma, I guess," recalled Mark Zimmering, now a distinguished endocrinologist.

"We remade a lot of bad Hollywood movies that we'd seen on TV. Movies that never should have been made in the first place," Joel commented. According to the brothers, two of their most successful films were *Lumberjacks of the North*, "because we owned a couple of plaid shirts," and the remake of *The Naked Prey*. The latter was a naïve, message-laden adventure film directed, produced and starring the unsmiling Cornel Wilde. Filmed in Africa, it told of how the hero, a white hunter, is stripped and made defenseless by savages and pursued like a wild animal. The Coens' version was called *Zeimers in Zambia*, in which Zeimers, fully clothed and wearing a fuzzy winter cap with earflaps is pursued by Ethan, in Buddy Holly glasses, and reddish mop of hair, as a savage native waving a spear.

"At that time, we didn't really understand the most basic concepts of film-making," remembered Joel. "We didn't know that you could physically edit film—so we'd run around with the camera, editing it all in the camera. We'd actually have parallel editing for chase scenes. We'd shoot in one place, then run over to the other and shoot that, then run back and shoot at the first spot again. We had very weird special effects in that film. We actually had a parachute drop— a shot of an airplane going overhead, then a miniature, then cut to a close-up of a guy against a white sheet hitting the ground." Ethan explained: "It was hell waiting for the airplane to fly by. We were nowhere near a flight path."

Ed . . . A Dog, naughtily named, like Holly Hunter's ex-cop in *Raising Arizona*, after their father Ed Coen, was a remake of the kids' weepie boy-loves-dog classic *Lassie Comes Home*. (The most vicious gangster in *Miller's Crossing* is Eddie Dane.) Zeimers loves Ed and asks his parents if he can keep him. He is met with rejection from both the father (Ron Neter) and mother, played by Ethan in his sister Debbie's tutu. Zeimers lifts the small and slight Ethan up and hurls him across the room with ease. As a result, the father agrees to let Zeimers keep Ed. The film ends with Zeimers turning toward the camera and grinning from ear to ear. This classic might have been the reason Ethan expressed antipathy toward dog movies in later years because of the abuse he suffered during its making.

Another piece of juvenilia was *The Banana Film*. Originally intended to be viewed while listening to Frank Zappa's *Hot Rats* album, it was about a man (well, actually Zeimers), now without his braces, who has a passion for, and an uncanny ability to smell out, bananas. Ethan, in Debbie's tutu again, is slung out of the front door of his house into the snow, a shovel following close behind. Ethan staggers to his feet, begins shovelling the walk, and soon has a heart attack and dies. Zeimers approaches Ethan's corpse, and smells something. He discovers a banana in Ethan's pocket. Zeimers goes off eating it, then suddenly stops, clutches his stomach, looks despairingly into the camera, and vomits. "They [the brothers] really had an affinity with vomit in their films," said Ron Neter. Perhaps, it would be apt to describe the vomiting in their films by the vivid Australian expression of a "Technicolor yawn," though it is not applicable to the films as a whole.

19   Barf Time

IN *BLOOD Simple*, when the bar-owner Marty (Dan Hedaya) sees the photos of his "dead" wife and lover, he says "I think I'm gonna be sick," and heads for the bathroom. Previously, Marty has a finger broken and is kicked in the groin by his wife Abby (Frances McDormand) during a rape attempt. He sinks to his knees, drops forward on one hand and vomits. In the dream sequence, when Abby confronts the dead Marty, he disgorges bucketfuls of blood.

In *Miller's Crossing*, Tom Reagan (Gabriel Byrne) retches after a post poker-game hangover, and then with fear when he is led into the forest thinking he's going to be shot. The alcoholic Southern novelist W. P. Mayhew (John Mahoney) has a good chunder in the toilet after meeting Barton Fink, and the mysterious Charlie Meadows alias Karl Mundt alias John Goodman pukes after discovering the murdered woman (Judy Davis) in Barton's bed.

Norville (Tim Robbins) spews up (off-screen) after carrying the "swooning" scheming ace reporter Amy Archer (Jennifer Jason Leigh) up the fire stairs of the Hudsucker Industries building to the top floor. Norville: "Excuse me—I—executive washroom . . ." Amy: "Are you all right? . . . Is it your lunch? The chicken à la king?"

In *Fargo*, Marge suddenly doubles over, putting her head between her knees down near the snow. Lou: "Ya see something down there, Chief?" Marge: "Uh—I just, I think I'm gonna barf." Lou: "Geez, you okay, Margie?" Marge: "I'm fine, it's just morning sickness."

> He went in, and I let everything come up. It
> was like hell, the lunch, or the potatoes, or
> the wine. I wanted that woman so bad I
> couldn't even keep anything in my stomach."
>
> **The Postman Always Rings Twice** (James M. Cain)

> Ned Beaumont went down the stairs, loose-
>
> jointed, pallid, and bare-headed. He went
>
> through the downstairs dining room to the
>
> street and out to the curb, where he vomited.
>
> **The Glass Key** (Dashiell Hammett)

20   *My Son the Philosopher*

FROM REGURGITATION to education. Joel went to study film at the Tisch School of Arts at New York University in 1974. Contrarily, when Ethan went to Princeton University three years later, he studied philosophy. All Joel has to say about his time at NYU was that the school gave him a camera and left him alone. "I was a cipher there. I sat at the back of the room with an insane grin on my face." He went because "it had a late application deadline—I missed all the others." After four desultory years there—"I made some movies, then some more"—he graduated and "chased a woman" to the University of Texas graduate film school in Austin. He married the woman, who wishes to remain unnamed, but quit after a semester and the couple returned to New York to an apartment on Riverside Drive. He did, however, remember the barren roads and roadhouses he had seen around Austin when it came to writing *Blood Simple*.

At Princeton, Ethan's senior thesis was a 39-page document entitled *Two Views of Wittgenstein's Later Philosophy* which he submitted "in partial fulfilment of the Degree of Bachelor of Arts' on 7 May 1979. (A "senior thesis' is a longish essay required of AB candidates in their final year and written under the supervision of a faculty member.) Dr. Raymond Geuss, now at Cambridge University, England, supervised Ethan's independent work. "I do very vaguely remember teaching Ethan Coen as an undergraduate in the late 1970s, but you will appreciate that was a very long time ago," said Dr. Geuss. "If I try to think back I recall him as a slightly built under-graduate who was very quiet, seemed self-possessed, and smoked a lot. I can't honestly say that Coen made any strong or distinct impression on me."

"I didn't study philosophy with the idea of making a career out of it. It's just an indication that I had no idea what career I wanted to pursue. My parents, being Jewish intellectuals, thought that because I studied philosophy I was doing something useful."

One could venture to guess as to how, or whether, Ethan's philosophy studies had an influence on his profession of film-making. Dr. Geuss, the author of many philosophical works, and a collection of poems, most of them translations or imitations from the Greek and Latin under the title *Parrots, Poets, Philosophers and Good Advice*, offers a caveat. "If you are looking for connections between Wittgenstein's philosophy and Coen's films you will want to be very careful. Wittgenstein's work is a kind of Rorschach pattern; everyone finds something different in it and people tend to project into it what they think is true on other grounds." One thing we do know is that Wittgenstein loved the movies.

Paradoxically, in an essay on Wittgenstein, Ethan mainly quotes the American philosopher John Wisdom, an "epigone" of the Austrian-born philosopher. He then proceeds to use Wittgenstein to criticize the Wittgensteinian because this "promises to be more informative than using him to criticize some steely-eyes positivist or existentialist rowdy."

Even in a thesis of such seriousness, Ethan's absurdist sense of humor emerges. After quoting from Stanley Cavell's *The Availability of Wittgenstein's Later Philosophy*, in which he compares Wittgenstein and Freud, Ethan writes, "Holy cow! What an Aha! Stanley must have felt! . . . Actually for Stanley it was only a brief lapse, but I'm still groping after the point of John's [Wisdom's] meandering, apparently purposeless philosophico-artistic-scientific-religious synthetic essays. Puzzles don't get solved, as they do in Wittgenstein. All we get is a few lousy Aha!s." Towards the end of his paper, Ethan writes, "I see that we're running out of time so I'll skip the rest of the dull stuff. I don't think it made things more coherent anyway . . ." and ends, "Wittgenstein might say here: If you want something more, you'll have to cook it up yourself."

Ethan was also an admirer of the Wittgensteinian film critic Sir Anthony Forte-Bowell, who wrote a scholarly essay on the linguistic philosophical aspects in the work of The Three Stooges. "I will pause to note . . . the whimsy implicit in the name given Curly either in wry acknowledgment or in absurd refusal to acknowledge what is striking about his physical appearance, *videlicet* his want of hair, *et ergo a fortiori* his want of curly hair. Analysis reveals no comparable whimsy at work in the assignment of names to Larry and Moe, and an historian might here note that Lawrence and Morris were the given names of the actors by whom they were respectively depicted." This extract from the magazine *Cinema/Not Cinema* (April 1998) was used in the introduction to the published screenplay of *The Big Lebowski*.

Before he plunged into Ludwig Wittgenstein's *Tractatus Logico-Philosophicus*, and while Joel was in New York, Ethan conceived of a film called *Froggy Went a Courtin'*. He saw it as a montage of run-over toads with a recording of Odetta singing the title song in the background, but he could not find any squashed toads. (Over twenty years later, Ethan was finally able to satisfy this curious whim: a toad was to make a significant appearance in *O Brother, Where Art Thou?* when John Goodman squeezes one to death in his ample hands.) But Ethan would have to put all these notions behind him when he too left Minnesota for university in 1977, with fame and notoriety another seven years away.

Is it a matter of the believer's operating with a more sophisticated conceptual apparatus, which he might bring us (nonbelievers—hello out there) to share by means of some fancy dialectic? No—this isn't how people become religious. Is the believer smarter than we are? No. I'm not saying that he's stupid. I'm saying that I can't imagine what sorts of distinctions he could draw to make his statement make sense for me. And the Catholic's insistence that it is literally the blood and body of Christ that he eats—he wants to emphasize that he gives those words no special sense, that he didn't "have recourse" to them for want of better—underscores the point that here we haven't to do with some quasi-scientific insight.

—Two Views of Wittgenstein's Later Philosophy (Ethan Coen)

FIRST BLOOD IV

"We wanted to trick people into thinking we'd

made a real movie."

21 Dough–Raimi

IN THE spring of 1980, Sam Raimi drove a station wagon from Detroit to New York, with canisters of the raw footage of *The Evil Dead*, his debut feature, in the back seat. "I'd never driven into New York before and I knew there'd be all sorts of hoodlums and bad characters about. When I pulled up to the building where the cutting room was, this guy came up to the car with long scraggly hair down to his chest, looking undernourished. I thought he was trying to rip us off. That was my first meeting with Joel." Joel had been hired to be the assistant editor to Edna Ruth Paul on *The Evil Dead*.

The Coens and Sam Raimi had much in common. Raimi is a couple of years younger than Ethan, but got his start before the Coens. Like the brothers, Raimi spent his childhood making 8mm movies, experimenting with comedy, horror and adventure.

Sam was the fourth of five children and grew up in Franklin, Michigan. His father ran a furniture and appliance store. (In *Raising Arizona*, the father runs a furniture store and has five children.) Sam's mother owned a store called Lulu's Lingerie. Sam's eldest brother Sander was drowned aged 15, an incident he said colored everything he did for the rest of his life.

Raimi formed a student film-makers' society with his brother Ivan while at Michigan State University, and was also close to a younger brother, Theodore, who appeared as a demon in *Evil Dead 2*. After Sam and Ivan left college, they formed their own independent production company, making a 30-minute version of *The Evil Dead* to screen at parties for well-heeled intellectuals, inveigling investment from dentists, lawyers and other professional men in Detroit. It was financed independently on a subscription basis and made for $380,000, with Raimi acting for much of the time as his own grip and gaffer.

The full feature, shot on 16mm, was completed in 1980 but only released three years later. *The Evil Dead*, "the ultimate experience in grueling horror," concerned five clean-cut All-American kids in a mountain cabin in Tennessee, who find an old book of the dead which helps them summon up dormant demons from a nearby forest. All except one, Bruce Campbell, become possessed and turn into hideous and murderous creatures who start chopping each other up. The ludicrously lurid film, merely a fright machine, has all the clichés of the slasher movie, eerie sound effects and plenty of blood splashing everywhere. Characters are set up to be slaughtered. But it has some spectacular point of view (POV) ground-level tracking shots, overhead shots, and amazing make-up effects (by Tom Sullivan). The unsteady, racing shots were done with the use of a "shakicam" nicknamed Sam-Ram-a-cam. It was a camera which could be carried along at ground level.

Horror was chosen as a genre by many neophyte film directors because of its appeal to the drive-in market which would offer the best chance of recouping the investors' money. "I didn't really like horror films," Raimi explained. "They frightened me. But as I studied them I saw there was an art to them. Back then it was a much more infantile goal. Get a response, get a visceral, audible response. Will they jump and how high? I appreciate the artistry of the horror film, but the movies I see are not those. They are stories of real people, or a mix of real people and adventure, like *The Treasure of the Sierre Madre*, which I love." Raimi's passion for the John Huston picture was reflected in his 1998 movie *A Simple Plan*, the publicity line being "Sometimes Good People Do Evil Things," which could have served for quite a few of the Coen movies. It was about a pair of geeky brothers who come across a crashed airplane that contains millions of dollars. They plot to keep the money—but greed causes distrust between them. It all takes place in a snow-covered Minnesota, and was also plainly influenced by *Fargo*.

However, the influence was stronger the other way. Those hours spent in the editing room helping to cut *The Evil Dead*, which contains a premature burial, knives being stabbed into flesh, some char-acters refusing to die and rising from the grave, must have affected Joel when he came to make *Blood Simple*.

Raimi co-wrote *The Hudsucker Proxy* (in which he appeared in sil-houette), written some time before *Blood Simple*. In *Miller's Crossing*, Raimi had a cameo playing the baby-faced, machine-gun toting plainclothes cop, who shoots a man coming out of the Sons of Erin Social Club, and snickers with satisfaction.

While trying to get *Blood Simple* distributed, Ethan, Joel and Sam wrote the chaotic slapstick comedy *Crimewave* (1985), directed by Raimi, in which the Coens appeared in a cameo as press photogra-phers. In the same year, Joel and Sam had cameos as drive-in securi-ty men in the John Landis spoof *Spies Like Us*. They were among a group of more established directors, such as Michael Apted, Costa-Gavras, Martin Brest and Terry Gilliam, who had walk-ons. Both Raimi and Coen had made only one feature, but being considered in this group was an indication that they were thought of as comers.

MANY ASPECTS of the Coens' style derive from Raimi: the ground-level, high-velocity tracking shots, the odd angles, the relentless Hitchcock-on-speed POV shots. In *Blood Simple*, the camera run-ning up on the front lawn is attributable to Raimi's shakicam method. There is a point in *Evil Dead 2* (1987) when a character looking at someone who has been beaten senseless, says, "Crazy buck's gone blood simple." (Much knowing laughter from a section of the audi-ence.) In the same movie, there are similar spectacular long takes to the ones in *Raising Arizona*, of the same year.

But Raimi's early films are as uninhibited and vulgar as the Coens' are pre-planned and precise. The Coens, self-conscious, literary and thoughtful as they are, often pretend to be like Raimi—intuitive craftsmen, interested in nothing but entertaining their audience. And as *A Simple Plan* proved, inside Raimi are the Coen brothers trying to get out.

AFTER JOEL had worked on *The Evil Dead*, cinematographer Barry Sonnenfeld, who had been a classmate of Joel's at NYU, hired him as a production assistant on an industrial film he was shooting.

"Without a doubt the worst PA I ever worked with," Sonnenfeld recalled. "He got three parking tickets, came late, set fire to the smoke machine. He was better in the cutting room."

In 1981, Joel also worked as assistant editor on *Fear No Evil*, directed by 23-year-old Frank Laloggia, another horror-gore film about a possessed high-school student. Joel then spent a week, before being fired, on *Nightmare*, directed by sex-movie man Romano Scafolini, which contained a catalog of gruesome murders. Make-up effects expert Tom Savini got top billing in the original ads, although Savini claimed never to have worked on the film. When he threatened to sue, Savini's name was covered up with tape on all the posters.

This was the kind of film background from which Joel and Ethan emerged to make their gory debut feature.

POSSESSED CHERYL: Why have you disturbed our sleep? Awakened us from our ancient slumber? You will die! Nightmare is before you. One by one we will take you.

SCOTT: What happened to her?

LINDA: Did you see her eyes? Oh Ash, I'm scared. What's wrong with her. *Possessed Cheryl stabs Linda in the ankle with a pencil.*

SCOTT: Cheryl! Stop it!

POSSESSED CHERYL: Join us!

SCOTT: I think we ought to get out of here.

ASH: Yeah.

SCOTT: We still have a few more hours before morning.

SHELLY: I don't think I can wait that long.

SCOTT: You have to. We all have to! And then in the morning, we'll get in the car, and we'll take the bridge. And—

SHELLY: Why does she keep making those horrible noises?

—The Evil Dead

22   Life is a Pitch

WHILE JOEL was doing his assistant editing on *Evil* movies, Ethan worked for a temporary employment firm as a statistical typist, typing rows and columns of numbers, at Macy's department store, the New York State Power Authority, a law firm and other companies. Ethan particularly remembers spending his days at Macy's typing up numbers for the tags on men's bathrobes and pajamas. So when it came to writing their screenplays, it was Ethan who did most of the typing.

Ethan also earned some cash by doing some writing for the TV cop show *Cagney and Lacey*.

Barry Sonnenfeld, who hung out with the Coen brothers in Central Park around 1980, recalled: "They would play this game where they would have to write a ten-minute movie in ten minutes." Sam Raimi and the Coens began to write *The Hudsucker Proxy* in the Riverside Drive apartment that Ethan now shared with Joel and his wife. "Writing with them was like watching a badminton game," said Raimi. "Joel would mention a line of dialogue, and Ethan would finish the sentence. Then Joel would say the punch line, and Ethan would type it up. When things weren't clicking, they would pace, following each other in designated tracks. I could subtly torture them, by altering the speed of my pace."

But, in early 1981, Joel and Ethan finally felt they had a shootable script, which they had written without Raimi over some months. Then both brothers moved back to Minneapolis for a while to stay with their parents for about the year it took to raise the $1:5 million budget for their debut feature.

HOW DID two young unknowns come to make their first feature? How does anybody get to make a first feature? These are questions that most young would-be directors always ask. For one thing it helps to have chutzpah and self-confidence, both of which the Coens had. Or, rather, they were able to give the impression of confidence.

What did they have going for them? The only experience they had had in making films consisted of their amateurish Super 8 efforts. The sum total of Joel's experience was his work as an assistant editor on a couple of cheap gore pictures, but that was not enough to convince producers to put up money for a feature, no matter how gory the subject or low the budget. So they decided to finance their first movie themselves. It has been suggested that this decision was made because they had seen other directors lose creative control of even low-budget movies. In fact, there was a less idealistic reason. "It came about by accident. We raised money ourselves because we had to. No studio would give us money to make our first feature—we had no production experience."

Inspired by the 21-year-old Sam Raimi's success in getting *The Evil*

Dead made three years earlier after shooting a 30-minute version, the Coen brothers decided, much less ambitiously, to show what they could do by shooting a three-minute trail as if the movie was completed and was about to appear. It would show prospective investors that they could make something that looked like a real film, and it was something to invest in that had a recognizable form, unlike a treatment or script, in which none of the investors had any expertise.

All very well, but if you have no money nor even a camera, even a three-minute trailer could only be made in their dreams. In order to rent a 35mm camera and lights for five days, at the cost of only a one-day rental charge, they waited until President's Weekend—Washington and Lincoln's birthdays. They then shot it from Thursday to Tuesday in Robbinsville early in 1982.

The 30-year-old photographer Barry Sonnenfeld had never looked through a 35mm camera before, and he taught his cousin Kenny, a neuro-pharmologist, how to pull focus. Oh my God, they recruited Kenny! When they watched the footage the next day, Sonnenfeld thought it looked great. But Joel only said, "Okay, bye." "I was crushed," recalled Sonnenfeld. "Later, I found out he was really excited, too. But because they don't need compliments, they don't realize other people do. That's another thing that gets people mad at them. They never notice."

The "trailer" consisted of a gun being loaded, a man being buried alive, gunshots being fired through a wall and light streaming through the bullet holes, all of which ended up in the finished picture. Joel then took this clip to Minneapolis, where he went straight to Hadassah, the Jewish philanthropic organization. They supplied him with a list of the hundred richest Jews in town, and he raised $750,000 from them in nine months. They also scraped up pledges of $550,000 from 68 investors in bits as small as $5000.

Quite a lot of money was raised in their home town, although some of it came from New Jersey and Texas (where they were going to shoot the picture) in the form of a limited partnership. "We would pitch it to them from a financial point of view, explaining to them what the risks were, and what the potential rewards were. We had the most luck with entrepreneurs, people who had started out thirty years before with $200 and were millionaires now. We went to people who were gamblers. We said, you can lose all your money. On the other hand, you can make money. We would sit there and argue with them for a long time, until they either threw us out or gave us a check. . There were over sixty investors in it. All the investors were small. They each put up $10,000 to $20,000. We were able to tell them, you're taking a risk, but we're also risking a couple of years, and we won't make any money until you go into profit." (The final budget was $855,000 plus $187,000 in deferred costs.) As for salaries, the Coens offered everyone in the largely inexperienced cast and crew "a chance to work on a higher level in exchange for less money."

THE COENS certainly had to look across a lot of wide desks to make their pitch, an image that frequently appears in their films—power in the form of "a blustery titan," at the other end of a desk. For example, the table in the conference room in *The Hudsucker Proxy* was so long it had to be delivered in five different pieces and assembled in the studio. Young protagonists wanting something from older, wealthier men: Nathan Arizona, Johnny Caspar (*Miller's Crossing*), Jack Lipnick (*Barton Fink*), Sidney J. Mussburger (*The Hudsucker Proxy*), Wade Gustafson (*Fargo*) and Jeffrey Lebowski.

Wade Gustafson (Harve Presnell), the overbearing business tycoon father-in-law, was based on a number of money-men that our young wannabee directors were courting. "When we were raising money for *Blood Simple*, we did a certain amount of it in the Midwest. I [Joel] remember having meetings with these hardened businessmen who would hang out in the local coffee shop and then put their parkas and galoshes on and slog out into the Siberian landscape, get in their cars, and fishtail off through the snow."

Ed and Rena Coen contributed to the funding of the film. "They were not exactly overjoyed with our decision to become film-makers, but they came around to the idea. Our parents were always supportive and encouraging. Even though film-making fell outside their realm, they were very open-minded."

In Ethan's story called *The Boys*, a father contemplates his two sons' futures. "His anger swelled at a world he was certain would make losers of both of them, the one a suck-ass [Joel?], the other a mute [Ethan?]. Why should disappointment be propagated through another generation, a cruel snap traveling down an endless rope?" Ed was able to see his sons' success.

> NORVILLE: Well, sir, I've got something for you from the mailroom, but first if I could just take a minute or so from your very busy time . . . a little something I've been working on for the last two or three years . . . You know, for kids! Which is perfect for Hudsucker—not that I claim to be any great genius; like they say, inspiration is 99 percent perspiration, and in my case it's at least twice that, but I gotta tell ya, Mr. Mussburger, sir, this sweet baby—
>
> **–The Hudsucker Proxy**

23 *Raising Cain*

BEFORE EMBARKING on the shoot, in order to get the tone they were after, one would think that the Coens would have watched *Double Indemnity* or one or more of the four film versions of *The*

Postman Always Rings Twice, both adaptations of novels by James M. Cain, the prime literary influence on Blood Simple. But that would have been too obvious, and might have led them into pastiche, conscious or otherwise. What they did watch was Bernardo Bertolucci's *The Conformist* (shot in color by Vittorio Storaro) and Carol Reed's *The Third Man* (shot in black-and-white by Robert Krasker), both pictures far removed from the world of *Blood Simple*.

Coincidentally, cinematographer Richard H. Kline and director Lawrence Kasdan watched the same two films while preparing *Body Heat*. Made a few years before *Blood Simple*, *Body Heat* has some similarities in plot—a married woman and her lover want to bump off her husband. Thus, an evocation of pre-war Italy and post-war Vienna would influence the style, but not the subject of *Blood Simple*. "What they wanted was a real non-diffuse image, the kind of image Storaro achieved in *The Conformist*," remarked Sonnenfeld.

Somewhat closer in time and content was Wim Wenders' *The American Friend* (1977), which they watched a number of times. One of the reasons was that the brothers were big fans of Robby Müller, Wenders' and Rainer Werner Fassbinder's favorite cinematographer. The flashily photographed *The American Friend* was based on a Patricia Highsmith thriller about a dying man forced to take a job as a hit man in order to have money to leave to his widow. But it is much more poker-faced than the Coens would ever allow, and the distracting myth-making works against the plot through which the director's real-life heroes Sam Fuller, Nicholas Ray and Dennis Hopper wend their way.

Blood Simple was the prime spark which helped ignite the independent film movement from the mid-1980s, but its form and content were made possible by a number of steamy and violent films that had just preceded it: Stanley Kubrick's *The Shining*, Martin Scorsese's *Raging Bull*, David Lynch's *Eraserhead*, David Cronenberg's *Scanners*, Brian De Palma's *Scarface* and *Body Double*. Closest of all, however, were Bob Rafelson's *The Postman Always Rings Twice* (1981), which was able to be truer to the book in its sexuality than previous screen versions, and Kasdan's *Body Heat*.

Taylor Hackford attempted a remake of *Out of the Past*, Jacques Tourneur's archetypal 1940s *film noir*, as *Against All Odds* (1984). In

France, François Truffaut made *Vivement Dimanche*, based on an American pulp novel (*The Long Saturday Night* by Charles Williams), shooting it in monochrome in an effort to capture the style of 1940s Hollywood *noir*. There was also *Dead Men Don't Wear Plaid* (1982), a one-joke parody in which Steve Martin interacts with *noir* stars of the past. What made the Coens' film more interesting was their quirky postmodernist take on the genre which was neither pastiche, parody nor remake, but had the soul of the genuine article.

The murder of the husband by the detective was influenced by the five-minute sequence in Alfred Hitchcock's *Torn Curtain* (1966), when Paul Newman, with the help of a farmer's wife, batters an East German security guard to death and then disposes of the body. "The idea is that it's very difficult, and takes a very long time to kill some-one. It's not necessarily just bang, and the character keels over dead. Hitchcock took ten minutes [sic] to kill that guy in *Torn Curtain*. We decided to stretch it out to twenty."

In *Blood Simple*, however, the husband is shot once and is pre-sumed dead by the audience and by the detective and the barman Ray, who finds him. Ray, thinking his lover Abby has shot her hus-band, tries to get rid of the "corpse." In a long, wordless sequence, reminiscent of the nine minutes Norman Bates takes to clean up the shower and take Marion Crane's body into the car in *Psycho*, Ray car-ries the "dead" Marty to his car and takes him out on the road, then stops to bury him in a field. After he has stopped the car, he finds that Marty has crawled out and is attempting to escape. He has to bury him alive in a shallow grave, shovelling the sand over him as he groans, beating the top of the grave with a spade. The ghost of Edgar Allan Poe, the author of *The Premature Burial* and *The Tell-Tale Heart*, as much as that of Hitchcock, hovers over this scene.

THE SOMEWHAT cryptic title of the Coens' debut movie came from Dashiell Hammett's *Red Harvest*. The unnamed detective hero in the fictional town of Personville, nicknamed "Poisonville," believes that after a person kills somebody, "he goes soft in the head—blood-simple. You can't help it. Your brains turn to mush," and "If I don't get away soon I'll be going blood-simple like the natives . . . I know it. That's what I've been telling you. I'm going blood-simple."

The film shows the influence of hard-boiled detective fiction writers such as Hammett and Raymond Chandler, whom the Coens read avidly, as well as Southern writers like William Faulkner and Flannery O'Connor, the title of whose novel *Wise Blood* could be the opposite of *Blood Simple*. The term "warthog from hell," applied to the Lone Biker by "Ed" (Holly Hunter) in *Raising Arizona*, was from an O'Connor short story called *Revelation* in which a well-meaning, pig-farming Southern woman is suddenly physically attacked by a fat young girl, who tells her, "Go back to hell where you came from, you old warthog!"

But it was James M. Cain who prompted the screenplay in the first place. The brothers' admiration for Cain knew no bounds. "We've always thought that up at Low Library at Columbia University, where the names are chiselled up there above the columns of stone— Aristotle, Herodotus, Virgil—that the fourth one should be Cain," they declared hyperbolically. "We started reading Cain's novels five years ago [1979]. We especially liked *The Postman Always Rings Twice*, *Double Indemnity*, *Mildred Pierce* and *Career in C Major*. We liked the hard-boiled style, and we wanted to write a James M. Cain story and put it into a modern context."

Although the basic geometry of the film is a James M. Cain triangle, and the character of the Greek bar-owner Marty was lifted from Nick Papadakis in *The Postman Always Rings Twice*, "but a little less cheerful and fun-loving," the plot has the husband wanting to murder the illicit lovers, rather than the other way around. "We wanted to avoid the clichéd story of two lovers plotting to kill the husband or wife. We also wanted a double-cross because we liked the idea of somebody having a killer who faked it and then killed the guy who hired him. We hadn't seen that one before." *Blood Simple* is also more violent and less sexy than Cain, as well as moving into horror movie territory.

There is also a husband who wants "pictures of his wife in the act" in Ethan's story *Destiny*. "Shut the fuck up. I got a personal situation. I got a wife here fuckin" someone else. His dick. Her pussy. Woom-pah, woom-pah, woom-pah. Do I gotta draw yas an illustration?"

We didn't say anything. She knew what to do.

She climbed back and I climbed front. I looked at the wrench under the dash light. It had a few drops of blood on it. I uncorked a bottle of wine, and poured it on there till the blood was gone. I poured so the wine went over him. Then I wiped the wrench on a dry part of his clothes, and passed it back to her. She put it under the seat.

–The Postman Always Rings Twice (James M. Cain)

24 Be Prepared

THE COENS started with the premise of a murder story/thriller set in Texas and worked from there. In the autumn of 1982, eight months after the trailer was shot and shown, the brothers had their money and arrived in Austin, Texas, to make *Blood Simple* on an eight-week shooting schedule. There was a tendency for the Coens, coming from the icy Midwest, to choose warm climes for their shoots: Texas, Arizona, Louisiana (*Miller's Crossing*), Los Angeles (*Barton Fink, The Big Lebowski*), and Mississippi (*O Brother, Where Art Thou?*)—the frozen exception being *Fargo*, which was consciously at the opposite extreme.

"But what I know about is Texas," says the voice-over of the detective at the opening of *Blood Simple*. However, the Coens didn't know Texas, nor Arizona, nor Louisiana, nor Mississippi. Texas was chosen for *Blood Simple* because, "the weather's good. It seemed like the right setting for a passion murder story. And people have strong feelings about Texas, which we thought we could play off of. And again your classic *film noir* has a real urban feel, and we wanted something different."

The less familiar rural Texas landscape is used very effectively and, paradoxically, although the film is set in the wide open spaces, a claustrophobic atmosphere is created. Like *Raising Arizona* and *Fargo*, it concentrates on a small community, with only a few houses and a bar. There does not seem to be a world outside.

For the Neon Boot bar, where a great deal of the action takes place, the Coens benefited from being granted free use of a mainly disused bar. "The only thing was, they opened it up at weekends for swinging singles nights, so we had to keep moving our stuff out." On the first day of shooting, which happened to be in the bar, Joel was so green that the assistant director had to tell him to yell "Action!" instead of "OK" when he was ready to shoot.

ONE OF the challenges of shooting a $1.5 million movie was to make it look ten times that amount. For the Coens the only effective way to bring the low-budget film in on budget was to pre-plan everything, so every scene was meticulously storyboarded, a process that was to be an essential element in their film-making henceforth. "We storyboard our films like Hitchcock. There's very little improvisation, because we're chicken basically. Pre-production is cheap compared to standing around the set with a crew, scratching your head and saying things like, 'What would it look like if we put the camera over here?' "

The other reason, besides economics, that *Blood Simple* was storyboarded was the intricate nature of the plot. Certain visual elements repeat themselves in ironic visual ways. Devices such as match cuts, sound overlaps and dissolves are all cheap and easy to do if they are thought about ahead of time.

To help them draw the storyboards, they got three local people from Austin. "It was weird. One guy would do storyboards. Another guy would do floor plans. And a woman was there who seemed a sort of secretarial help. We'd sit there with three people. It was odd. It was very quiet. They were perfectly nice. But you'd sit there and describe the shot and they would stare at you, pencils poised. They treated us like royals. And the storyboards were square and stiff."

Ethan, Joel, and Barry Sonnenfeld storyboarded the whole film together. At the beginning of every day, the three of them and the first assistant director, Deborah Reinisch, would have breakfast at Denny's in Austin—the Grand Slam special—and go through the day's shots and talk about the lighting. (A Denny's is where the anarchists confer in *The Big Lebowski*.) It was in Austin that they saw a sinister hotel across the street from where they were staying which became known to them as The Hotel Across the Street. They discovered that its stationery was blazoned with the logo: "The Hotel for a Day or a Lifetime," a slogan they used for the Hotel Earle, the rundown Los Angeles hotel in *Barton Fink*.

On the set, according to Joel, "We'd put it all together and look through the viewfinder. Barry might have an idea, or Ethan would come up with something different, and we'd try it. We had the freedom to do that, because we had done so much advance work." Sonnenfeld added: "Also we'd try to torture each other. For example, I didn't allow smoking, which meant that only one of them would be on the set at any given time, because the other one was off having a cigarette."

25 *Black and White in Colour*

"WHEN PEOPLE call *Blood Simple* a *film noir* they're correct to the extent that we like the same kind of stories that the people who made those movies liked," Ethan commented. "We tried to emulate the source that those movies came from rather than the movies themselves." Joel added: "It utilizes movie conventions to tell the story. In that sense it's about other movies—but no more so than any other film that uses the medium in a way that's aware that there's a history of movies behind it. For us it was amusing to frame the whole movie with this redneck detective's views on life. We thought it was funny but it also relates directly to the story. It was not our intention to make an art film but an entertaining B-movie."

The greatest *films noirs*, those of the 1940s, were shot in black-and-white. When black-and-white films were almost entirely phased out in the 1960s, much of the atmosphere of the genre was lost. There were some directors, frustrated at being forced to use color, who tried to suggest monochrome by the way color and shadows were used. The Coens, like other directors of the time, had no choice.

"There was a big practical consideration. Since we were doing the movie independently, and without a distributor, we were a little leery of making a black-and-white movie," commented Joel. "But we never really considered that a sacrifice. We wanted to keep the movie dark and we didn't want it to be colorful in the *Touch of Mink* sort of way."

According to Sonnenfeld: "What we talked about early on was having the elements of color in frame by sources of light, at least as much as possible, like with the neon and the Bud lights, so that the rest of the frame would be dark. That way it would be colorful but not garish. Joel, Ethan and I felt strongly that we wanted our blacks to be rich, with no milk quality. I think we were afraid that to shoot the film in black-and-white would make it look too 'independent,' too low budget." Actually, with the yellow light, and the khaki-colored Texas landscapes, *Blood Simple* is more of a *film jaune* than a *film noir*.

"We also used the lighting as a psychological tool," explained Sonnenfeld. "For the film to be effective, the film had to be dark and contrasty. The lighting itself became a character. The evil detective, in a bright bathroom, starts shooting bullets through a wall into a dark adjoining apartment where our heroine was hiding. As each bullet slams through the common wall light streaks through the darkened apartment at all kinds of crazy angles. By the time the detective runs out of bullets, the darkened room is sliced up into 30 tubes of light bleeding out of the six bullet holes."

THE BROTHERS decided early on that they wanted to move the

camera around a lot, and "when the camera wasn't moving, we sometimes would dolly or raise or lower lights during the shot, so there was
always some kind of apparent movement," Sonnenfeld explained.
When they filmed the tracking shot along the bar and the camera
hops over a passed-out drunk, Joel said, "No. It's too self-conscious."
Ethan replied: "The whole movie is self-conscious."

There is an odd low, subjective tracking shot which sweeps across
the lawn toward Marty trying to rape Abby. It seems to be from the
German shepherd dog's POV. (There is a similar dog's eye view in
Raising Arizona.) It was achieved by having two grips racing the camera along the ground at full speed, approaching Abby and Marty.
Owing to the extreme wide-angle lens, in a matter of a couple of seconds, the camera moves from an extreme wide shot into a super
close-up of Abby as she bends back and breaks Marty's fingers. "In
effect, all the shaking is smoothed out by the time the shakes reach
the middle of the 12-foot shakicam, and the camera seems to float,"
explained Sonnenfeld. "I would run behind the camera, not looking
through the viewfinder, but still getting a sense of level and angle."

26 Enter Frances

FOR THE role of the wife, the Coens wanted to cast a Southern
actress, and approached 25-year-old Holly Hunter, who was born in
Georgia. They met when she was performing on Broadway in the
Beth Henley comedy-drama *Crimes of the Heart*, the story of three
Mississippi sisters, and asked her to be in *Blood Simple*. But she had
another commitment and suggested Frances McDormand, the same
age, who had been her room-mate when they were both aspiring
actresses. However, Holly warned Frances that it was a low-budget
film being made by two brothers who had never made a feature
before. Nevertheless, Frances went to an audition.

"Holly and another friend told me they'd met these two really weird guys and auditioned for a movie they were making. I thought they were much too young to make a movie, and geeky, two geeks sitting there," McDormand recalled. "They were my own age for one thing, which was odd. They were chain-smoking at the time and had this huge ashtray on the table, full of cigarette butts. They asked me if I wanted to smoke, which was amazing in an audition."

The brothers asked her to come back at four o'clock that afternoon, to read with John Getz, who was cast as the lover. To their amazement, she said she couldn't because she had to watch her then boyfriend in his first acting job, a small role in a TV soap opera which was being broadcast at the same time. "Joel later told me that they thought I was crazy to watch a soap opera instead of coming to an audition. Anyhow, they changed the time to five o'clock. When finally I did come, they cast me. I was in total cultural and professional shock. That's why I look the way I do in the movie. When you look at the movie now, where other people think I made the choice of looking dumb—that was me. I stood paralyzed until they told me what to do. When we were shooting, I remember saying to Joel, 'Don't try to articulate intellectually what the scene's about. Just tell me whether to breathe harder, breathe softer, talk louder, talk softer.'"

FRANCES MCDORMAND was born in 1958 in Illinois and grew up with her older brother and sister in Pennsylvania. Her father, a preacher with the Disciples of Christ, moved the family around from one small town to another. "There's a popular perception of preachers being fanatical, but my father's denomination was really mild. It wasn't like I grew up in a strict religious background—definitely not as strict as an Irish Catholic background. My mother was always in the choir and still is, and she's the secretary of the church now. They still worry when I don't have a job. 'You doin' okay? Lemme give you five bucks.'"

Frances realized that she wanted to become an actress when she was playing Lady Macbeth in a high school production. (Little did she know that she would be involved in an even more bloody affair with her first film.) After graduating as the only theater major in her class at Bethany College in West Virginia, she went onto study in the graduate program at Yale Drama School. "I had no choice," she says.

"I literally couldn't do anything else. I went to Yale when I was 21, which was good because I would have died if I'd gone to New York first. I'd always lived in small rural towns, so going to New Haven, Connecticut was a really big transition for me."

From Yale she began her career in some heavyweight productions around the country—George Bernard Shaw's *Mrs. Warren's Profession*, Anton Chekhov's *The Three Sisters* and Arthur Miller's *All My Sons*, to name a few. She then took the plunge in New York, very quickly learning how difficult it is to support oneself in classical theater, and she made extra money as a waitress and sought out work in commercials and episodic television until *Blood Simple* helped her on the way to fame.

Despite her initial opinion of the Coens, and their very different backgrounds, Frances and the brothers soon clicked, especially she and Joel. They were soon living together in his uptown New York apartment. (Joel was about to get a divorce. "There was no ugliness and no money," he insisted.) A couple of years later, after the release of *Blood Simple* in 1984, Joel and Frances were married—a "mixed" marriage, as she was from a strong Christian background and he from an orthodox Jewish one.

27 Private Dick

WHEN IT came to casting their first movie, the Coens hardly put a foot wrong. The part of Loren Visser, the sleazy private eye, was written for M. Emmett Walsh. The brothers had seen Walsh in *Straight Time*, and the 1978 movie, directed by Ulu Grosbard, was at the back of their minds when they wrote the script. In *Straight Time*, Walsh plays a cruel and slimy parole officer who seems to have a personal vendetta against ex-con Dustin Hoffman. The last we see or hear of him is when Hoffman blows his top, attacks him while he is driving, and leaves him handcuffed to a fence on the freeway, with his trousers around his ankles, and cars buzzing around him refusing to stop. Not quite as terrible a fate as the Coens had in mind for Walsh in *Blood Simple*.

"When I read the script, I said, 'This character is so much fun. I'll flesh him out and use him in an important movie six or seven years down the road.' Because no one was going to hear about this movie. At best, it would be the third bill at an Alabama drive-in," Walsh commented.

Walsh met the Coens for the first time in Austin just before shooting, and he thought, "These two scrawny kids must have rich parents who're putting up the money. They showed me this two-minute film. I thought, 'What the hell is this?' Then I saw the storyboards and the shooting schedule, and I realized they knew exactly what they were doing."

During the shooting, however, Walsh would sometimes say to Joel, "Let's cut this sophomoric stuff. It's not NYU anymore." They would have arguments and disagreements, but, according to Joel, they would generally be fruitful. "One time I asked him to do something to humor me and he said, 'Joel, the whole damn movie is just to humor you.'"

"IF I need you again I'll know what rock to turn over," says Julian Marty, the husband who hires Visser to take photos of his wife and her lover together. This venomous gumshoe has a cigarette lighter—pointedly seen in close-up as he leaves it at the scene of his crime—marked "Loren Visser—Elks Man of the Year," a comment on his so-called social respectability.

It is the detective's voice we hear at the start of the film. "The world is full of complainers. But the fact is, nothing comes with a guarantee. I don't care if you're the Pope of Rome, President of the United States, or even Man of the Year—something can always go wrong. And go ahead, complain, tell your problems to your neighbor, ask for help—watch him fly. Now in Russia, they got it mapped out so that everyone pulls for everyone else—that's the theory, anyway. But what I know is Texas, and down here, you're on your own."

Although the detective seems to be the narrator, he is not omniscient like the clock-keeper in *The Hudsucker Proxy* or the cowboy in *The Big Lebowski*, and a few seconds into the film the narrative device is abandoned in favor of a wider perspective. However, in the opinion of the German critic George Seessien, by putting Reaganite philosophy into the mouth of the "most immoral and unappetising figure in the film," *Blood Simple* is "a radically anti-American film." If there was any political intent in this, or in their other films, despite a number of teasers along the way, the Coens want it kept a secret.

The obese and oily detective, in his canary yellow suit and stetson, has the air of a Western heavy, and represents unadulterated evil, but his driving a beat-up Volkswagen bug adds an absurdist element to his character. (The fat private snoop in *The Big Lebowski* drives a similar car: the Coens find big men in small spaces amusing.)

Visser himself seems to appreciate the absurdity of the situation in which he finds himself. At the end of the film, as he lies dying under a sink, watching the rotting pipes, he utters a high-pitched Coenian laugh.

VISSER: I'm supposed to do a murder—two murders—and just trust you not to go simple on me and do something stupid. I mean real stupid. Now why should I trust you?

MARTY: For the money.

VISSER: The money. Yeah. That's a right smart of money. In Russia they make on fifty cent a day.

–Blood Simple

28   The Postmodernist Always Rings Twice

THE ABOVE title of a collection of essays by the British writer Gilbert Adair could apply equally to *Blood Simple*. Whether or not Ethan understands the term, the film is postmodernist in the way it alludes to 1940s *film noir* through a number of inverted commas. The *film noir* was a product of the psychology of post-war America, which expressed the nihilism and depression brought about by the Second World War and intensified by the Cold War—resulting in a general distrust of human nature and institutions. But *Blood Simple* does not come directly out of the social or political malaise. Most of the *noir* elements are there: oblique lighting, odd camera angles, compositional tension, chiaroscuro, the depiction of a dark world of crime and corruption, betrayal, cynicism and a fatalistic mood, which the Coens used as a basis on which to build an amoral structure.

But this is no mere smart-ass film buffery. The film captures the soullessness of much of American pulp fiction. The main characters, though classic archetypes of the genre—The Husband, The Wife, The Lover—are caught in a Greek tragedy of errors. (The Greek husband tells the detective, who brings him the incriminating photos, "You know in Greece they cut off the head of the messenger who brought bad news.") Everyone is in the dark (*noir*). None of them knows what is going on as they only see part of the whole. The audience knows everything and can only watch helplessly as the characters on screen stumble around without all the facts.

The restless, roaming camera reflects the mood of the characters, the atmospheric photography exactly fits the murky story. It is also littered with enough quirky images to please any Coenhead. A cigarette is stuck in the mouth of a stuffed bear, fish lie on an office desk, a surreal still life that one can almost smell. The husband holds a gun, his finger in a splint, the lover tries to mop up a pool of blood with a nylon jacket that will not absorb it. The climactic *tour de force* sequence when the private eye tries to free his pinned hand by shooting holes in the wall, is one of the most bizarre and memorable in all their films.

IN ASSESSING *Blood Simple*, some critics, not entirely flatteringly, evoked Hitchcock and Welles. Besides the *Torn Curtain* episode, Hitchcock's ability to create menace out of commonplace situations is apparent throughout, especially in the moment, during a tense scene, when a newspaper is thrown at the front door, sounding like a gunshot. And with many of the shadowy, high-angle shots, the film is as close to Welles' *Touch of Evil* as it is to *The Evil Dead*. It is only the latter's influence that is detrimental to *Blood Simple* in the more unsubtle horror movie elements.

The residue of slash picture mentality is most evident in the premature burial scene, and in the completely dispensable dream sequence. Abby wakes up coughing, goes to the bathroom and washes her face. A wide-angle shot reveals the door behind her. There is a creepy rhythmic thumping sound coming from the next room. Abby goes into the living room. The camera tracks around the room. The dead Marty is there. He tells Abby he loves her before he vomits copious blood. She then wakes up. Because the whole sequence is shot realistically, and there is no hint that it is a dream, the Coens have tried to hoodwink the audience into believing that Marty has actually come back from the grave. It is a rather cheap trick that is risible rather than blackly comic. But, on the whole, the film rises above the crude idiocies of *The Evil Dead* and its kind.

29   *Post-Production Trauma*

AFTER THE main shoot of *Blood Simple*, the Coens ran out of money. Therefore, during re-shoots, the brothers were forced to stand in for actors. "After the body was covered with dirt that was me squirming under there," Ethan revealed. "I'm proud of that." As for the editing of the movie, they had the idea of approaching the Englishman Roderick Jaynes, who was credited with the editing on

Beyond Mombasa, a ropy 1956 jungle film, starring Cornel Wilde and Donna Reed, which they admired for some perverse reason. What the Coens didn't know was that Jaynes had been taken off the picture after less than a week, because the director George Marshall found his cutting "too damned Prussian," and he was replaced by Jack Tuttle. Owing to union rules, Jaynes' name remained on the film. As Tuttle had since died, the Coens decided to ask Jaynes, who had not worked on a film for almost thirty years, to edit their first movie.

"I decided to accept . . . under two conditions: that I be left alone in the cutting room, that I not be asked to read the script before starting in cutting," Jaynes recalled. "Given a free hand on *Blood Simple*, I was rather proud of my first cut, but when I screened it for the lads they responded to the action scenes with silence and to the dramatic scenes with alarming asthmatic laughter. They took the picture away and, along with a friend of theirs named Don Wiegmann, made rather a mess of things, I'm afraid, but due to union rules my name remains on the picture."

WHILE TRYING to sell *Blood Simple* in Los Angeles, Ethan, Joel and Joel's new wife, Frances McDormand, were so broke that they moved into Sam Raimi's apartment. "They crashed on the floor," recalled Raimi. "For some reason, Joel and Fran got the bedroom and Ethan and I ended up crashing on the floor. After the Coens moved out, Fran's friend Holly Hunter moved in. After she left, we took on a new tenant, named Kathy Bates."

Having failed to find a distributor in Los Angeles, they returned to New York where they killed time concocting "thought experiments"—high concept movies they would have liked to see but couldn't bother making. One such was called *Adolph "Terry" Hitler*, which had young Adolph growing up and becoming a big Hollywood agent nicknamed Terry, running the Adolph Hitler Agency (AHA). He wears baggy suits, takes lunches at Mortons, waves to everybody and reads *People* magazine. Where it went from there is anybody's guess.

However, their main preoccupation was trying to get *Blood Simple* distributed. All the major distributors passed on it, and a lot of the smaller ones as well. The word was that it was too gory to be an art film, too arty to be an exploitation film. "It wasn't easily pigeon-holed generically," Joel explained. "That was very frustrating for us, because at the same time we were being turned down, we were watching it at festivals with large audiences and knew that it worked, that audiences liked it. It's much easier for those guys to say no than it is to say yes."

They got their first big break when a talkative friend on a plane happened to be sitting next to the member of a panel that chooses films for the USA Film Festival in Dallas. But the watershed was when *Blood Simple* was shown at the Toronto Film Festival, where there were about four distributors who saw the film with an enthusiastic audience. "When you screen a movie for most distributors, they look at it all alone in a room while they're taking telephone calls. But seeing it with an audience is a very different thing. After that we started to get offers."

Finally, they found a distributor in Circle Films, a Washington DC-based independent distribution company, with whom they signed a four-picture deal. Ben Barenholtz, the executive producer, said, "I've seen a lot of first films and there was something about this first film that was so good and natural. The only first film that impressed me as much was *Eraserhead*."

ON THE whole, *Blood Simple* gained good reviews, although one critic described it as having "the heart of a Bloomingdale's window and the soul of a résumé." The influential Pauline Kael of the *New Yorker* wrote: "It comes on as self-mocking, but it has no self to mock. Nobody in the movie-making team is committed to anything, nothing is being risked except the million and a half." But it appealed to a wide spectrum. *New York's* film critic David Denby called it "one of the most brazenly self-assured directorial debuts in American film history." *Fangoria*, a fanzine dedicated to gore movies, called it "an art film, a comic tragedy, a splatter film, a murder story that honors Hitchcock without insulting his memory."

To their surprise, the brothers began to be lionized. Steven Spielberg asked them to visit him, and Hugh Hefner invited them to his mansion. But they had no desire to make a picture for Spielberg and refused to hobnob with other Hollywood directors, nor did they go to many parties. They thought Hefner and his mansion a joke. Many years later, in *The Big Lebowski*, they created the character of Jackie Treehorn (Ben Gazzara), a mordant portrayal of a Hefner-like producer of "interactive erotic software."

The success of their first film did not change the Coens much. They took a dingy office on the sixth floor of a West 23rd Street industrial building, occupied by graphics and printing shops, that might have served for Philip Marlowe or Sam Spade, remaining aloof from both the big studios and the arty independent-film scene.

The independent movies that we see are not really avant-garde [Joel explained at the time]. John Sayles is an independent film-maker that I like. I like what Alan Rudolph does. Also I like low-budget horror movies that are made independently. They're mass audience pictures. I've worked with a lot of people who have done that stuff like Sam Raimi. Those are the kind we feel closer to rather than, say, more avant-garde artists. I liked *Stranger Than Paradise* [Jim Jarmusch], though, which is closer. Our movies are a no-bones-about-it entertainment. If you want something other than that then you probably have a legitimate complaint. What's the Raymond Chandler line? "All good art is entertainment and anyone who says differently is a stuffed shirt and juvenile at the art of living." The distinction between art and entertainment is one we've never understood. If somebody goes out to make a movie that isn't designed primarily to entertain people, then I don't know what the fuck they're doing.

At the time of the release of *Blood Simple*, the Coens talked big about remaining small.

You can't get anymore independent than *Blood Simple*. We did it entirely outside Hollywood. To take it a step further, we did it outside any established movie company anywhere. It was done by people who have had no experience of feature films, Hollywood or otherwise. We'd like to continue as independently as possible. Not independent necessarily of the Hollywood distribution apparatus, which is really the best if you want your movie to reach a mass market. But as far as production is concerned, there's a real trade-off involved. It's true that certain movies require more money to produce right than *Blood Simple* did. But the difference with us is, while we may need more money for the next one than we did for *Blood Simple*, we're still not talking of the kind of budgets that the studios are used to working with. We did this film for $1 and a half, and for me $3–4 million is an incredible amount of money to make a movie. And that's attainable without going to the studios. If they're giving you the money, they can legitimately say, "Hey, it's our money, we're gonna have our input here." If you can keep it away from Hollywood studios, you can make it a lot cheaper. By virtue of the fact that it's cheaper, and it's away from the bureaucracy of Hollywood, the film-makers can retain more control over the project."

Blood Simple grossed about $1.5 million in its first six months, and it was reckoned that a typical backer who put up $1000 made about 150% return on his investment. How things have changed since 1984! Sixteen years on, the Coens were ready to take on *To The White Sea*, budgeted at $60 million. But now they were ready to raise more than just money.

HI STAKES

"Does it look wacky enough?

F. SCOTT Fitzgerald, in the notes to his Hollywood novel, *The Last Tycoon*, wrote, "There are no second acts in American lives." After the success of *Blood Simple*, audiences and the Hollywood establishment were watching to see, from different viewpoints, what the precocious Coen brothers were going to come up with next. More importantly, they wondered whether Ethan and Joel would be able to stick by their wish to "continue as independently as possible."

Ben Barenholtz, 52-year-old top man at Circle Releasing Corp., was determined that they should. A long-time distributor, and one of Circle's founders, he had previously been unable to answer the Coens' appeal for financing on *Blood Simple*. But he, along with his partners, Ted and Jim Pedas, distributed the film. Barenholtz sat down with Joel and Ethan on either side of a long desk and explained to them that they needed a buffer from the studios.

"They didn't come on in the same way most people do that are trying to pitch movie ideas," Barenholtz explained. "And they certainly didn't look the typical young film-makers. But there was a determination to them, not a cockiness, but they were so self-assured that you sort of felt, 'Yes, they'd do it.' They're sensitive, determined and know what they want. Their objective is to have total artistic freedom. The priority was never the money. They want to work without interference. So I created a context. What director do you know who had final cut and total artistic control on his second picture? Well, that's what Joel had."

Raising Arizona was the much awaited second picture. It was half-financed by Circle, who put up about $4 million, the other half coming from Fox, which distributed the film. And the only strings that were attached were purse strings. Joel remarked: "We became victims of our own choices. We became spoiled. We'd financed *Blood Simple* ourselves, by going through the laborious process of finding individual investors, and we had complete freedom. We part-owned the movie as a limited partnership and we could do whatever we wanted in terms of production. So from then on, we figured that was our prerogative. It seemed perverse to make a second movie and relinquish the control we had on the first one. So we insisted on it. If we had had the chance to sell out on *Blood Simple*, our whole history would have been defined by that experience. It wouldn't have been a good thing. The fact that we didn't have any options and no one was willing to give us the time of day was probably the best thing that could have happened to us."

31 Looney Tunes

THE COENS wanted to make their next movie totally the opposite of *Blood Simple*, which was slow and deliberate. "We were labeled *film noir*, so we wanted to try something faster and lighter." In fact, throughout their career, although their films can be linked thematically and stylistically, they have tried to change the tone of each from the movie that preceded it.

Crimewave (the initial title, *X, Y, Z Murders*, was changed for video release), the film the Coens wrote with and for Sam Raimi the year before, prefigured *Raising Arizona*. Set in Detroit, where Raimi, Robert Tapert, the producer, and the leading actor Bruce Campbell all went to school, *Crimewave* has many elements that anticipated their second feature. "*Raising Arizona* is definitely influenced by Sam, because we were working with Sam at the time," Joel acknowledged. Like *Raising Arizona*, *Crimewave* had a naïve loser hero and two-dimensional comic-book characters, including a pair of murderous pest exterminators, screaming wildly, who drive a van with a giant stuffed rat on top and the slogan "We Kill All Sizes' painted on it. (See Gale and Evelle in *Raising Arizona*.) Called Crush and Coddish, they resemble malign versions of Laurel and Hardy as itinerant mouse-trap salesmen in *Swiss Miss*.

Unfortunately, Crimewave suffered from studio interference, a salutary lesson for the Coens to learn. They were not happy with this "lost" film. "We like it lost. It's no big deal for us, but Sam wasn't thrilled with it. He never had his own cut."

Before *Blood Simple* was released, the Coens and Raimi were writing the script of *The Hudsucker Proxy*, but the shooting was delayed nine years until they were able to obtain the kind of high budget the film needed. As *The Hudsucker Proxy* had been shoved into a drawer, optimistically awaiting the propitious moment when it would be filmed, some of that script found its way into *Crimewave*. Somebody falls from the window of a building and survives (like a cartoon character), and a "miracle" takes place involving a black man. The prison in which the protagonist, Victor Ajax, finds himself awaiting execution is called Hudsucker State Penitentiary. Hi in *Raising Arizona* works for Hudsucker Industries, where M. Emmett Walsh (from *Blood Simple*) has a cameo as a gabby machine-shop worker.

Variety thought *Crimewave* was "more storyboarded than directed." "Storyboarding has always been an important part of our figuring out how to do a movie," admits Joel. Because of this "security blanket" dependency on storyboarding, the Coens were lucky to find J. Todd Anderson, a storyboard artist from Dayton, Ohio. Everybody calls him J. Todd, the single initial lending a whisp of mystery to this pleasant, forthright man. It seems that he and the brothers are so empathetic that Anderson has continued to storyboard every film of theirs since *Raising Arizona*. "I just try to be their extension cord," J. Todd explained. As well as being a storyboard artist, Anderson is a perfect sounding board for their ideas.

"They pretty much have a good idea within twenty or thirty degrees what they want. Though, over time, I've noticed that they see shots from opposite directions. Ethan will see it running from left to right and Joel will see it running from right to left," J. Todd said after some years of working with the Coens.

What is a storyboard but a sort of wall-size comic strip? There is a horror-comic book feel to the scene in *Blood Simple* of the detective punching a hole in the wall with one hand in order to pull the knife out of his other one trapped in the window on the other side. In both *Crimewave* and *Raising Arizona*, there is a *Road Runner* Coyote-like indestructibility to some of the characters. Tom Reagan in *Miller's Crossing* gets brutally beaten up so many times but, like a cartoon character, he keeps bouncing back with hardly a scratch.

THE LOOK the Coens wanted for *Raising Arizona* was "sort of pop, like opening an illustrated children's book. Everything's sharp and bright." In order to reinforce their visual ideal, they screened *The Conformist* and *The Third Man* again. The influence of these two films on *Raising Arizona* seems even less discernible than on *Blood Simple*. In *The Conformist*, according to cinematographer Barry Sonnenfeld, "expressionistic visuals vie with the plot for your attention; Venetian blind shadows prowl across the screen. We wanted to give you the impression there was a real director and DP working on this. Though I regret that some of it's grainy, low contrast, and has a salmon cast."

More pertinently, they also watched *Mad Max*, mainly in order to see how to stage the fight at the end, which is a semi-homage to the George Miller money-spinner, a film that proved that an Aussie film could out-bike, out-stunt, out-Corman, and out-cult any Yankee exploitation movie. *Mad Max* was certainly at the back of the Coens' minds when they invented the incongruously named Leonard Smalls, the Lone Biker of the Apocalypse, played by the intimidating-looking black-bearded ex-boxer Randall "Tex" Cobb. The only thing Hi and Leonard Smalls have in common are similar tattoos which resemble Woody Woodpecker.

Actually, Randy Cobb was lousy on a bike and often missed his mark during the shoot and stalled. In one scene, when he has to drive up to the hole out of which the fugitives made their escape, the bike kept rolling, fell into a hole and threw Cobb face down in the dirt. There was an ominous pause, before Cobb let out a muffled "Cut." Joel grinned and said, "Print that take. I liked it." However, it didn't make it to the finished movie.

In the final cartoon confrontation between Hi and the Biker, the latter hurls a knife at Hi, who swings a plank as a shield at the last moment, and the knife sticks in the plank. The effect was designed by Ethan; the knife was already in the plank, spring-loaded on the non-camera side. Nicolas Cage as Hi released the spring to sync with Cobb's throw, and it jabbed through the plank. He is then blown up by his own hand grenade, and all that is left of him is a smoking boot with his foot in it.

32   Casting Around

AFTER HANDING in the script to Circle, who sound like the last altruistic producers in the universe, the Coens finally got some money, which they used to upgrade their lifestyles somewhat. Ethan moved downtown to a big sublet in Chelsea—"more pacing space"— with his girlfriend Hilary. Frances immediately set about redecorating Joel's Riverside Drive apartment, disposing of Ethan's *Blood Simple* souvenir—a huge bloodied wall used for the hand-stabbing scene. The Coens also rented a share in a Chelsea office. One day in December 1985, just before filming began on *Raising Arizona*, Ethan asked Joel, "Is it okay if I cut out early today?" Joel said, "Sure. What for?" Ethan said, "Hilary and I were thinking of going down to City Hall and getting married. Wanna come?" "Sure," said Joel, who served as best man.

JUST AS Holly Hunter recommended Frances McDormand for *Blood Simple*, a gesture which led to her stardom and marriage, so Frances reciprocated by suggesting her friend Holly to Joel and Ethan for the part of Prison Officer Edwina ("Ed"), and they duly wrote it with her in mind. It was a big-screen break for Hunter, who had previously appeared in a lousy schlock horror movie *The*

Burning, and who had only had small roles in three other films. (In *Raising Arizona*, Frances, with big earrings and blond, has the small part of Dot, the vulgar wife of Hi's boss, with all the unruly children.)

Unlike Hunter, 24-year-old Nicolas Cage was a veteran of eight movies, including three for his uncle Francis Ford Coppola, *Rumble Fish* (as Nicolas Coppola), *The Cotton Club* and *Peggy Sue Got Married*. Cage was more at ease away from the avuncular control, and his best performances had been in *Birdy* (Alan Parker) and *Moonstruck* (Norman Jewison), both in 1984. In *Raising Arizona*, Cage was able to emulate Jerry Lewis, whom he admired for "his freedom, his craziness." There is certainly something frantically demented about his Hi McDonnough, the doleful, maladroit thief trying to settle down with a lady cop and a kidnapped baby. Cage is a "leading man in a character role" as the Coens describe him.

However, Cage later complained, in *American Film Magazine*, about the Coens' "autocratic nature." Mainly, perhaps, because they stick rigidly to the written script. John Turturro compared the Coens' style on the set to that of a conductor working with a classical music score as opposed to the jazz-like approach of Spike Lee. "With Joel and Ethan, it's a little harder to improvise," Turturro explained.

Joel thinks that the "autocracy" is a function of economics. "You have to maximize the money. The way to maximize the budget is to be real specific about how you're going to direct the production elements ahead of time, as opposed to in the middle of the chaos on the set." Barenholtz contended that the Coens worried more about how the budget was being spent than he and his partners did.

The six-foot-three-inch, 300-pound John Goodman literally burst his way into the Coens' repertory company in *Raising Arizona*. For the dramatic escape from prison, which takes place during a raging storm, a deep hole was dug and covered with a mud-packed foam sleeve. Boards were placed in the hole for reinforcement. After John Goodman emerges, he reaches back down to grab the hand of William Forsythe, whose leg was attached to a cable, and as Goodman pulls him up, a crane helps lift Forsythe out of the mire.

It was Goodman's tenth movie, but the first in which he made much impact. The actor should be grateful to the Coens for giving him some credibility on the big screen away from such cartoonish inanities as *Revenge of the Nerds*, *King Ralph* and *The Flintstones*. Cartoonish as *Raising Arizona* may be, it was cinematically eons ahead of any other Goodman vehicle.

33   Baby Talk

WHEN W.C. Fields was asked how he liked babies, he replied, "Fricasseed!" The Coens might have agreed with him after the filming of *Raising Arizona*. The typically cryptic title means the raising of a baby, Nathan Arizona Jr., but could also imply a homophonic razing Arizona. The Coens recalled an unfinished furniture store in Minnesota called Plywood Minnesota, and thus Unpainted Arizona became a similar shop owned and run by the wealthy Nathan Arizona (Trey Wilson) in the film. He is the father of quintuplets, one of whom is kidnapped by petty crook Hi and prison officer Ed.

When asked what the vital ingredients of *Raising Arizona* were, Joel explained that the film contained all the essential elements of popular cinema: "Babies, Harleys and explosives." At that stage, neither brother had children. (Nine years later, Joel and Frances were to adopt a baby through legal channels, unlike Hi and Ed.) "The movie is about parenting, and neither of us is a parent. But we're really not intimately acquainted with murder either, and we made a movie about killing people," Joel commented at the time.

But the Coens had to direct a Babel of bawling babies, potential mini-Harry Langdons, 300 of whom they auditioned. Perhaps they could have used *Dr. Spock's Baby and Child Care*, the manual that is passed from hand to hand in the film as a circular joke. They were looking especially for crawlers. "We kept firing babies when they wouldn't behave. And they didn't even know they were being fired, that's what was so pathetic about it. Some of them took their first steps on the set. Ordinarily you'd be pretty happy about something like that, but in this case it got them fired. They'd make the walk of shame. The parents were horrified. One mother actually put her baby's shoes on backwards so he wouldn't walk."

THE COENS found themselves part of the Hollywood *zeitgeist* again in spite of themselves. Just as sexy and violent *films noirs* were regaining popularity when they made *Blood Simple*, and *Miller's Crossing* was released at the time mobster movies were busting out all over, babies had become rather fashionable in pictures of the mid to late 1980s. In the same year as *Raising Arizona*, there appeared *Baby Boom* and *Three Men and a Baby*, gooey coochie-coo films on the theme of coping with a tiny tot's wee-wees and poo-poos. Even worse were the sequels to *Three Men and a Baby*, as well as *Look Who's Talking*, and its sequels, plus the TV series *Baby Talk*. But the Coens' movie, which they claimed to have been the first film "from the baby's point of view," had little in common with the others, as it cynically viewed babies as both consumer goods, good publicity and as objects for kidnapping, not a subject one generally makes jokes about.

"We were worried about it a little. But we thought that as long as it was clear that there was never any physical threat to the baby and that the motives of everybody involved were pure, that even though it was a kind of taboo subject, we'd be able to put it over. The major obstacle was making the characters sympathetic to the audience so that it wouldn't be offensive. And also to make it clear that when the baby is supposedly in some kind of danger, he's enjoying himself. You can put a baby up on the handlebars of a Harley-Davidson as long as you have him laughing." The motorcycle was placed on a big trailer and there were people standing all around within inches of the baby.

In another scene, when Gale and Evelle realize they have driven off without the baby, having left him in the middle of the road, they return and stop the car just inches from him. The scene was shot in reverse, as the Coens could not have had complete confidence in even the best stunt driver. A few years later, when Ethan was a father, he admitted that he would not have liked to use his own baby.

Nathan Arizona Jr. was played by eight-month-old T.J. Kuhn, the son of a Phoenix detention officer and his nursing assistant wife. "T.J.

was the main baby. There were others for long shots. A baby is somewhere between an actor and a prop. You can't talk to it and tell it what you want it to do. And you can't just put it some place in a shot and reliably predict it'll stay there. The movie took three months to shoot, so we tried to get all his scenes in the first two months because we didn't want him to get too cranky—he was a placid and cheerful baby, but he did have his cranky moments. You just roll a lot of film to avoid that. Above all we didn't want him to age noticeably over a three-month shoot."

Hi: Lookahere, young sportsman. That-there's the kitchen area where Ma and Pa chow down. Over there's the TV, two hours a day maximum, either educational or football so's you don't ruin your appreciation of the finer things. This-here's the divan, for socializin' and relaxin' with the family unit. Yessir, many's the day we sat there and said wouldn't it be nice to have a youngster here to share our thoughts and feelin's . . .

—Raising Arizona

34   Shake, Rattle and Roll

RAISING ARIZONA was shot in the state of the title, at and near Carefree Studios (the home of the *New Dick Van Dyke Show*) in Greater Phoenix. Ethan, Joel and cinematographer Barry Sonnenfeld spent ten weeks before the shoot not only rehearsing actors but running through scenes on location, so they were able to storyboard the whole film based on the actual locations.

As with *Blood Simple*, Sonnenfeld was involved early on, and had a lot to say about camera set-ups, movements and lighting, because the Coens work out the look of the film as much as they work out the story. The script, which made it to the screen almost verbatim, was complete with camera directions and editing notations.

Sonnenfeld pre-shot Super 8 video to test the feasibility of the settings and camera movements. For example, they were hoping to use a lake with the "World's Tallest Fountain"—a man-made 250-foot spout—as backdrop to the picnic scene. They discovered that the fountain was invisible on film and the lake fired off too much glare, and were able to reconsider the setting in time.

In the extended prologue the directors worked with Sonnenfeld for a look that would be "colorful and beautifully lit." The dramatic desert sunset was filmed over the course of 40 minutes with motionless stand-ins. For an Arizona sunrise later in the film, they shot a far more spectacular sunrise upside-down and reversed the negative.

The Coens exemplify the concept of self-conscious camera, no more so than in *Raising Arizona*, which meant Shakicam, not Steadycam, which they avoided. "The Coens are control freaks," claimed Sonnenfeld. "With the Steadycam the camera just floats there out of control." However, when used with a wide-angle lens, the Shakicam is not all that shaky. It took a bit of persuading to get professional grips and gaffers, who are accustomed to doing things smoothly, to loosen their camera mounts, to allow a little vibration to add a sense of energy to the shots. Sometimes they even re-shot scenes that seemed too slick. The early dailies so worried the film's producers that they considered selling public shares in the picture.

The continuously experimenting Coens had the idea that when the Biker throws a punch at Hi, it should be seen from the recipient's point of view. For this shot, Sonnenfeld designed what he called a Barrycam, with which he and his camera were strapped to a wooden plank resting on a pivot. When the Biker unleashed his punch at the camera, the grips dropped the Barrycam to the ground, simulating Hi's point of view, reeling from the mighty blow. But even the Coens found the shot too weird-looking to use. Another shot that didn't make it to the screen was the camera itself punching Hi. Why this was abandoned one cannot judge without seeing the shot. But, as long ago as 1946, Robert Montgomery, directing himself as Philip Marlowe in *The Lady in the Lake*, used a "camera I" throughout, even being knocked out at one stage, seen from his point of view.

During the long chase sequence, when a dog is after Hi, the Coens thought of having Nicolas Cage holding a camera pointed at his face as he ran through the house. But it looked like a close-up with a bad back-projection. Elsewhere in the picture, when Hi is attempting to kidnap the quins, and they prove "more than he can handle," there is a sequence of shots from the infants' points of view. The goal was "to see the movie as much as possible from a baby's perspective, and low angles can be very dynamic."

AS ALWAYS the Coens played with the soundtrack. Subjective sound joins subjective camera as Hi takes a family portrait. He plants a camera on a tripod and sets the timer. The Coens' camera tracks in toward Hi's camera as the sound builds, creating farcical suspense. "Initially," recalled Joel, "we shot it static. We went back four weeks later and shot it as a tracking shot. It wasn't storyboarded as a tracking shot, it was something we decided to do after we shot the scene. We looked at it and said, 'Wouldn't it be nicer if it were tracking in?'" They asked supervising sound editor Skip Lievsay to create a mix of low-level beep (the timer), thunder, and the sound of a photo flash warming up.

One of the most spectacular sequences in the movie is when the mother of the quins discovers that one of them is missing. The camera races down the streets, through car windows and up a ladder toward the kids' bedroom window, ending with a shot of the mother's mouth, in close-up, screaming. It was achieved by two grips running like madmen with the Shakicam, lifting it over a car and approaching the house. They then stopped at the foot of the ladder as a remote camera rode up toward the bedroom window and came to a stop at the curtains. The Coens had to cut the "tail" of this shot, an astounding close-up of the vibrating epiglottis of the woman screaming at the window, because it came after the camera movement had ceased, and it diffused the excitement of the rapid motion.

35 Through a Lens Widely

Wide-Angle Lens: A wide-angle lens creates an increased depth of field, thus keeping in focus both foreground and background. For this reason this type of lens is especially effective in showing simultaneous planes of action.

Wide-Angle Shot: Such shots are effective for giving a wider panorama of a location, and for placing a character in the context of an area. Since objects in the rear are abnormally small and those close to the camera are abnormally large, the area between the various planes seems to be exaggerated and action to or away from the camera appears accelerated.

—The Complete Film Dictionary (Ira Koningsberg)

THE COENS have always favored the wide-angle lens, the most extreme example being in *Raising Arizona*, in which there is the kind of baroque distortion mentioned in the quote above. It is partly their use of the wide-angle lens that has led some critics to accuse the Coens of attempting to create a distance between the audience and the characters, producing an alienating effect. However, in the case of *Raising Arizona*, it was germane to the farcical and cartoon nature of the film.

The Coens are fast workers, but the chase scene after Hi robs the convenience store ate a large part of the shooting schedule. The night shooting with wide-angle lenses meant problems for Sonnenfeld. "A major pain of using wide angles is the lighting—there's nowhere to put the lights." But the Coens were willing to sacrifice lighting for depth of field, which meant Sonnenfeld needed the wider lens and fewer lights, and necessitated the use of high-speed Kodak 5294 film. The Coens also prefer to cover a scene with quick set-ups from several angles rather than fuss with lighting for one angle.

Raising Arizona also established what has become a cliché in Hollywood films of the 1990s: the floor-level chase sequence. "The lower the camera, the more dynamic it is. You get a sense of power from the legs, from the things on the floor," Sonnenfeld remarked in order to explain the many ground-level shots in the movie. When Hi is chased through the supermarket, Sonnenfeld wanted to raise the low camera six inches, because the fluorescent lights on the ceiling distracted the eye and caused a flare on the lens. The Coens said that a high camera wouldn't be as wacky. "Every time I put on a lens, Joel and Ethan would ask, 'Does it look wacky enough?' " No one disputed that the film was wacky.

"We're certainly not willfully different. We don't sort of say, 'Let's do something different.' Our tastes are actually fairly mainstream. We are struggling to get into the mainstream. I hope it's more mainstream, if mainstream means reaching a wider audience. But, I mean, if you're going to be real calculated about it, to make a mainstream movie that's going to go over big with everybody, you don't make a comedy about kidnapping."

36 Running Around in Circles

"THERE'S AN old Mack Sennett studio that used to bring someone in from the insane asylum to sit in on the story conferences and blurt things. They called them wildies. If it sounded good to the writers, they'd write it into the script. We make up our own wildies."

It is appropriate that Joel should evoke Mack Sennett in relation to *Raising Arizona*. James Agee described the Sennett comedy chase as a "majestic trajectory of pure anarchic motion that cops, dogs, cats, babies, automobiles, locomotives, innocent bystanders, sometimes what seemed like a whole city, an entire civilization, were hauled along head over heels in the wake of that energy like dry leaves following an express train."

In *Raising Arizona*, there is a spectacular slapstick chase that pays homage to the Sennett trademark while technically surpassing most chases of its kind. Ex-con Hi, with panty hose over his face, is holding up a convenience store where he has stopped to get some Huggies for the baby. His wife Ed waiting outside for him in the car is shocked by his recidivist action and drives away. The alarm goes off. Hi runs out of the store chasing the car. He leaves the Huggies in the middle of the road. The police are after him. He flags down a car and jumps in, getting the driver to take him home. They are faced by the young store cashier holding a .44 Magnum that blasts into the car which plows into a wall of a suburban house. Hi vaults a fence into a yard, where he is confronted by a vicious Doberman. The dog, whose POV we see, leaps and stops within inches of Hi's face, reaching the end of his chain. (The surprise of the yanked chain is comparable to the thump of the newspaper on the door in *Blood Simple*.) Hi runs through the house, a Shakicam tracking along behind him. The dog breaks loose and chases Hi, as do other dogs. He arrives back at the supermarket to get more Huggies, pursued by a trigger-happy cop and the store manager, who blasts away with a shotgun while a shopper screams through the aisles with her cart. He finds the original Huggies he abandoned in the road and picks them up.

The scene described could easily be one in any broad Hollywood comedy, but it is done with breathtaking skill and wit, as well as emphasizing the cyclical nature of the screenplay. The characters get nowhere very fast. At the beginning, Hi keeps returning to prison where he sees the same menacing convict mopping up in the same place, and he has to listen to the same boring tales of eating crow told by the prisoner in the bunk above him. He keeps re-offending and comes before the same parole board.

When Gale and Evelle hold up the "hayseed" bank, they accidentally leave Nathan Jr. in the middle of the road, as Hi left the Huggies, and so have to return to the scene of the crime. There are even repeated actions. Hi pulls a baby out from under a cot by his feet in the same action (and camera set-up) as the Biker pulls Hi from under a car. In the end, the baby is returned to his parents, and Hi and Ed are exactly as they began, in love but without a child, still living in the trailer, and Gale and Evelle return to prison down the hole from where they escaped.

DESPITE ITS cinematic maturity, *Raising Arizona* is a young man's film (Joel was 31 and Ethan 28 when they made it), demonstrating an unruly delight in film-making. It also displays a healthy distrust of institutions like work, prison, marriage and parenthood. If *Blood Simple* was considered by some as "anti-American," a catch-all phrase that means different things to different people, *Raising Arizona* has more claims to that label. "Un-American" might be a better description had it not another specific connotation.

Primarily, the film has at its heart an implicit censure of family values. Although Hi and Ed dream of having a child, the reality becomes too much for them to handle. Respectable married life is represented by Glen, Hi's cretinous boss, and his wife Dot (Frances McDormand), who come to visit with their brood of brats. Dot wants another baby, because her other children are now "too old to cuddle." As Dot rattles on with a litany of all the responsibilities and obligations toward a baby, from diphtheria injections to life insurance, Hi wants to opt out.

When Nathan Arizona, the father of the quins, is being interviewed by the media about the kidnapping, he can't resist cynically using the occasion as free publicity for his store. "If you can find lower prices anywhere my name ain't Nathan Arizona." The point is, it ain't his name; it's really Nathan Huffhines.

The underlying critique of Reaganite policies is also present. Asked by the police if he had any disgruntled employee who might have kidnapped the baby, Nathan Arizona says, "They're all disgruntled. My motto is 'Do it my way or watch your butt.'" Hi's blaming Reagan for his recidivism ("Not a pretty name, is it, Hi?") is double edged, because we are able to laugh at him and agree with him at the same time. "I tried to stand up and fly straight. It wasn't easy with that son-of-the-bitch Reagan in the White House. They say he's a decent man, so maybe his advisors are confused."

DOT:—and then there's diphtheria-tetanus, what they call dip-tet. You gotta get him dip-tet boosters yearly or else he'll get lockjaw and night vision. Then there's the smallpox vaccine, chicken pox and measles, and if your kid's like ours you gotta take all those shots first to get him to take 'em. Who's your pediatrician, anyway? . . . Well you just gotta have one! You just gotta have one this instant! . . . even if he don't get sick he's gotta have his dip-tet! You started his bank accounts? . . . That-there's for his orthodonture and his col-

lege. You soak his thumb in iodine you might
get by without the orthodonture, but it won't
knock any off the college. Anyway, you probably got the life insurance all squared away .
. . You gotta do that . . . What would Ed and
the angel do if a truck came along and splat-
tered your brains all over the interstate?
Where would you be then . . . Or you got carried off by a twister?

–**Raising Arizona**

37   *Arizona Dreaming*

"THE CINEMA is a dream we all dream at the same time," said Jean
Cocteau. For the Coens this is particularly pertinent. Since films
began for them as a means of escape while incarcerated in "Siberia,
USA," they would dream themselves out of prison, like George du
Maurier's Peter Ibbotson. The 1935 Henry Hathaway movie, *Peter
Ibbotson*, starring Gary Cooper, was taken up by André Breton and
the Surrealists as the cinematic embodiment of *l'amour fou* and the
thin membrane that exists between dreams and reality. Surrealism is
too precise and associative a term to apply to the Coens, but most of

their films aspire toward the condition of surrealism. This allows them more creative scope within the commercial structure that is American cinema. With experiments in color, high overhead shots, vertiginous tracking shots, superimposition, trick photography, and juggling with time and space, the Coens have been an important force in imaginative film-making without being accused of avant-gardism by cautious studio moguls. It is also, perhaps, a reason why their films hark back to earlier products of the Hollywood Dream Factory, where realism (not reality) was kept at bay.

Miller's Crossing sets its tone by beginning with a dream. *Barton Fink* moves further and further from reality into an apocalyptic nightmare, ending with Barton dreaming himself into the calming photograph of a girl on a beach looking out to sea that broke the monotony of the peeling wallpaper in his hotel room.

The Hudsucker Proxy is a magical fable and dreamlike in conception. Therefore, the dream that Norville has of doing a ballet with a woman representing his lover, is utterly redundant, and seems more of an excuse for the Coens to get in a musical number. Just as irrelevant are the crass dream sequences in *The Big Lebowski* that are tenuously related to the plot or the characters' own obsessions, and smack of the Coens showing off.

In *Raising Arizona*, Hi dreams of his nemesis, the Lone Biker of the Apocalypse, before he has ever seen him. There is a strong case to be made for Leonard Smalls being a product of Hi's imagination. When Gale and Evelle, the two dim-witted, giggling brothers, escape from prison, they emerge like some primordial creatures through the mud as thunder and lightning rages. They, too, have come to ruin Hi's life. Is it all a dream which Hi is having in his prison cell? If so, they are dreams within dreams. There is a clue: when Hi, who is the "I" of the film, is blissfully contemplating starting a family with Ed, he says, "This whole dream, was it wishful thinking? Was I just fleein' reality, like I know I'm liable to do?"

At the end of *Raising Arizona*, Hi has a sentimental dream of the future. He imagines Nathan Arizona Jr. becoming a high-school football hero, and that he and Ed would have a brood of children and grandchildren. It is a vision that could be taken at face value or as a send-up of a typical Hollywood happy ending. It's a pity, therefore, that the Coens destroy the ambiguity by undercutting it with a jokey reference to Utah, a state which borders on Arizona.

"The shades and shadows of the people in my life wrassled their way into my slumber . . . It seemed like us. It seemed real. And it seemed like . . . well, our home—if not Arizona, then a land not too far away, where all the parents are strong and wise and capable, and all the children were happy and beloved. I don't know . . . Maybe it was Utah."

DOUBLE CROSSING
VI

"It's about time at that point to shed a little

blood. The movie's in danger of becoming

tasteful, you know?'

ON THE night of the first New York screening of *Raising Arizona* at the Gotham Theater in February 1987, the Coens were on the other side of town to see a small screening of Sam Raimi's *Evil Dead 2: Dead By Dawn*. Someone noticed them there, and said, "I thought you guys would be at the other movie?" "Nah," said Joel. "We've seen that one." During *Evil Dead 2*, they "heh-heh-hehed" at the chain-sawings, shotgunnings and battles with demons from the Beyond.

The Raimi connection continued with *Darkman* (1990) when the Coens contributed, uncredited, to the screenplay. It starred Liam Neeson and Frances McDormand. One line that came from the brothers was McDormand's: "If you're not going to kill me, I have things to do."

"I should have had more fun with it, and embraced the damsel-in-distress thing," Frances recalled. "I was playing a character that has a masters in real estate law, but in the end I was still handcuffed to a building waiting to be rescued. I really should have gotten into that. I was really bored out of my mind just being a kind of prop, and a woman in an action film is a prop."

The comic-book type plot has Neeson as a scientist hot on the trail of a formula for cloning body parts by computer when his lab is burned down by thugs and he is left for dead. Horribly disfigured, he becomes Darkman and uses his invention of synthetic skin to take on the shape of other people in order to seek revenge.

Raimi wanted high-school friend Bruce Campbell (star of the *Evil Dead* trilogy) for the lead, but had to bend to studio wishes for the rising Neeson, and could only give Campbell a cameo at the end. Raimi was moving into bigger budget territory, and losing some of his edge and independence. The Coens, too, were given a much bigger budget for their next film, *Miller's Crossing*, the responsibility of which might have contributed to the writer's block they suffered while working on the screenplay.

Raising Arizona was made for about $5 million and grossed $25 million, which got the moguls sensing that the Coen brothers could become hot. So hot in fact that Warner Bros. offered them *Batman* with a budget they could never have dreamt of when they were going around cap in hand, or facing businessmen across large desks, only a few years before. Sticking to their principles of only doing original work on their own terms, they dauntlessly turned Warner Bros. down. One could amuse oneself in contemplating how different their *Batman* might have been from Tim Burton's. In fact, Sam Raimi might have been ideal as he had a collection of 25,000 comic books. The Coens were into comics and cartoons, but although there are elements of these in their first two features, fleshy and bloody characters interested them more.

For *Miller's Crossing*, they turned not to comic books but to Dashiell Hammett for inspiration, and to Fox for money. It was financed completely by Fox, but, according to Ben Barenholtz: "Fox did not have a say in cast, title—nothing. Do you think *Miller's Crossing* would have looked like that, would have had that ending, if Fox—or any major—had final cut? Of course not. They would have pigeon-holed it. Circle has the contract with the Coen brothers, but I don't have artistic control."

Barenholtz made a deal with Fox in which the studio paid for an option based on a two-line description of the project. Two lines! A summary of the convoluted plot would take almost as long as the film to recount. Did Fox go for something like the two lines below?

> Leo likes Tom, but hates Johnny. Leo loves Verna. Tom loves Verna.
> Tom loses his hat. There is much shooting and killing.

Once the script was presented to Fox, the studio had the option to either turn it down or accept it. If Fox refused, its money would have been returned and Barenholtz would have taken the film elsewhere.

If they accepted, they were not entitled to dictate anything, from the cast to the title. The only way Fox could intercede creatively during production was if the Coens had deviated substantially from the screenplay.

"It's a unique deal. And it shows that there is room to work within the system and get good films made," Barenholtz crowed. *Miller's Crossing* would cost $14 million, more than twice *Blood Simple* and *Raising Arizona* put together. If the definition of an indie movie means a low-budget picture made outside the system, then the Coens were moving away from the indie scene, despite their having no artistic restriction put on them.

39 Bigheads

SOMEONE ONCE said that the process of writing a screenplay was the solving of a series of problems. There seemed to be more problems than usual for the Coens on *Miller's Crossing*, even though they had ready-made models in Hammett's *The Glass Key* and *Red Harvest*, the latter giving them the idea of making a movie where everybody is a gangster; the good guys and bad guys are gangsters— even the cops. Also typical of Hammett is the enigmatic central character, here called Tom Reagan. "It's a wonder the Hammett estate didn't sue for plagiarism," wrote the critic John Harkness in *Sight and Sound*. Naturally, Raymond Chandler was not far away, and the girl's name of Verna echoes Velma in *Farewell, My Lovely*. In *The Big Sleep*, there is a bootlegger called Rusty Regan, "a big curly-headed Irishman . . . an adventurer who happened to get himself wrapped up in some velvet."

The screenplay took longer to write than their previous two scripts—about eight months—because they got stuck halfway through. Referring to the untitled film as *The Bighead*, a nickname they had given the Tom Reagan character, the writing brothers found the plot had become too complicated for them to figure out. They tried various techniques to overcome the block, including different locations. They remember banging their heads against the wall and wearing out the rug pacing the floor, but artistic *angst* isn't something either will admit to.

They spent two weeks with Sam Raimi. They talked at length to John Turturro. They called Barry Sonnenfeld. Nothing worked. They went to stay with their friend William Preston Robertson for a week during which, according to Robertson, they listened to Clancy Brothers records, drank coffee, ate doughnuts and watched *Jeopardy* on television. One night, having made no progress with *The Bighead*, they went to see *Baby Boom*, and left for New York the next morning.

They abandoned *The Bighead*, and wrote *Barton Fink* instead, which concerned a screenwriter with writer's block. Two months later, they returned undaunted to *The Bighead*, now called *Miller's Crossing*, "because we couldn't think of a better title," and attempted to solve the plot problems to their satisfaction. "*Barton Fink* sort of washed out our brain and we were able to go back and finish *Miller's Crossing*." However, when the shoot was delayed for two weeks, due to tragic circumstances, the Coens took advantage of the break and rewrote the entire second half of the screenplay.

The role of the Irish gangland boss, Liam "Leo" O'Bannion, was written for Trey Wilson, the actor who played Nathan Arizona, the father of the quins, in *Raising Arizona*. But a few days before rehearsals began, the 43-year-old actor had a stroke and died of a brain aneurysm. Luckily, the powerful British actor Albert Finney was available to take over. "Ironically, the character wouldn't have been written if it weren't for Trey," Ethan remarked. "Now it's impossible to imagine another actor than Finney in the part." Finney is out of the movie for most of the last two-thirds, yet such was his performance that he loomed large *in absentia*.

The dialogue was not rewritten for Finney, nor was it written with an Irish accent in the mind's ear of the Coens, despite the fact that

Leo O'Bannion and Tom Reagan (portrayed by the Dublin-born actor Gabriel Byrne) were Irish-Americans. But when Byrne read the script he found that it had an authentic Irish lilt and rhythm to it. In the event, Finney and Byrne's accents hover a little uneasily between American and Irish.

A description of the mobster Shad O'Rory in *The Glass Key* seems to fit the Finney character. "He wore a dark blue overcoat over a dark blue suit and carried a brown derby hat in a black gloved hand . . . His voice was a musical barytone [sic]. The faintest of brogues colored his words."

Another character in *The Glass Key* is described thus: "Bernie Despain was a small man, short and stringy, with a head too large for his body. The size of his head was exaggerated until it seemed a deformity by long thick fluffy waved hair. His face was swarthy, large-featured except for the eyes, and strongly lined across the forehead and down from the nostrils past the mouth."

This resembles Bernie Bernbaum, the slimy, small-time gangster, played by John Turturro, the most significant member of the cast in terms of his relationship with the Coens' work. Turturro first came to their notice as a double-crossing convict in *To Live and Die in LA* (1985). "It's extraordinary how he allows himself to be humiliated in front of the camera," the Coens commented. Turturro, who looks like an identikit portrait of both Ethan and Joel, and was born in the same year as the former, was to become a kind of talisman for the Coens. He was their quasi-surrogate in *Barton Fink*, would have an outrageous cameo as Jesus Quintana in *The Big Lebowski* and an important role as a dim escaped convict in *O Brother, Where Art Thou?*. For Turturro, "Bernie is a conglomerate of Joel, Ethan, people that I've met, and imagination."

Another actor who would become a member of the Coen repertory company was the short, around and bald Jon Polito, who plays Leo's hot-headed mobster rival. "I saw *Blood Simple* and *Raising Arizona* and I was in love. I read the script in August, and I said, 'I only want to play Johnny Caspar.' They weren't looking for anybody my age—I'm 38, and it's written for a 55-year-old man. They wanted me to read for all the other gangster characters, but I said no." Polito

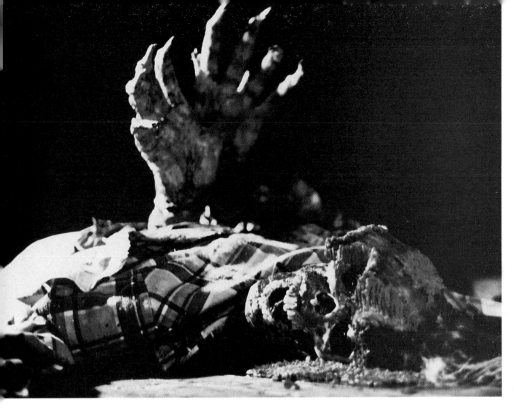

The gory end of one of the possessed students in *The Evil Dead* (1983), the slasher picture that was also the gory beginning of Sam Raimi's career as director. Joel Coen, in his first professional job in the movies, was assistant editor, which explains the conscious influence of Raimi and the film on *Blood Simple* the following year.

The illicit lovers, Abby (Frances McDormand) and Ray (John Getz), soon to become suspicious of one another after the murder of her husband in the noirish *Blood Simple* (1984).

The illicit lovers, John Garfield and Lana Turner in Tay Garnett's *The Postman Always Rings Twice* (1946), the third screen version of James M. Cain's novel, and the model for *Blood Simple*.

Dan Hedaya as Julian Marty the 'dead' husband being prematurely buried in a shallow grave. One of the eeriest and most blackly comic moments from *Blood Simple* (1984).

M. Emmet Walsh, the sleazy private eye, in agony as his hand is stabbed at the memorable but stomach-turning climax of *Blood Simple* (1984).

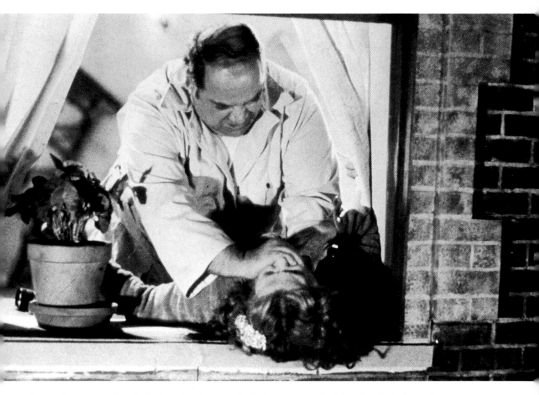

In *Crimewave* (1985), Louise Lasser is being strangled by Paul Smith after he has chased her through a series of doors, his arm having broken through one of the walls. The only Coen Brothers' screenplay directed by someone else (Sam Raimi), the movie contained variations on themes used in *Blood Simple*, and prefigured elements in *Raising Arizona*.

Joel (left) and Ethan on the set of *Raising Arizona* (1987), on location in the state of the title – young (thirtysomething) and trendy, with (significant?) phallic cacti in the background.

In *Raising Arizona*, John Goodman and William Forsythe as Gale and Evelle, the dim-witted, giggling brothers. According to the Coens, they were 'the Laurel and Hardy of the Southern penal society . . . They looked like grown-up babies'.

Stan Laurel and Oliver Hardy, the favourite comedians and a comic influence on many of the films by the Coen brothers, a pretty good double act themselves.

'Over there's the TV, two hours a day maximum, either educational or football so's you don't ruin your appreciation of the finer things.' A happy family – Ed (Holly Hunter), Hi McDonnough (Nicolas Cage) and Nathan Arizona Jr (T.J.Kuhn) in *Raising Arizona*.

The alarming figure of ex-boxer Randall 'Tex' Cobb as 'The Lone Biker of the Apocalypse', transporting kidnapped Nathan Arizona Jr (T.J. Kuhn) to claim his reward in *Raising Arizona*.

During the long, spectacular and bloody sequence in *Miller's Crossing* (1989), Irish-American gangster Leo (Albert Finney) shoots at his assailants from under his bed.

'You can't kill me. I'm praying to you! Look in your heart!' John
Turturro as Bernie Bernbaum, the Shmatte, pleading for his life in *Miller's
Crossing*.

'You're a sonofabitch, Tom . . . You got me to tell you where he was and
then you killed him.' Verna (Marcia Gay Harden) thinks Tom Reagan
(Gabriel Byrne) has killed her brother Bernie in *Miller's Crossing*.

'. . . Six, please.' Barton Fink (John Turturro) in the antiquated elevator with the superannuated elevator man (Harry Bugin) in 'The Hotel for A Day or A Lifetime', the slogan for the rundown Hotel Earle, in *Barton Fink* (1991).

Below The Coens go Hollywood. Ethan (left) and Joel pose uncomfortably on the set of *Barton Fink*. 'Our life in Hollywood has been particularly easy. The film isn't a personal comment.'

Above 'I respect your artistry and your methods, and if you can't fill us in yet, we should be kissing your feet, for your fine efforts . . .' Studio boss Jack Lipnick (Michael Lerner) humbles himself before an embarrassed Barton Fink (John Turturro).

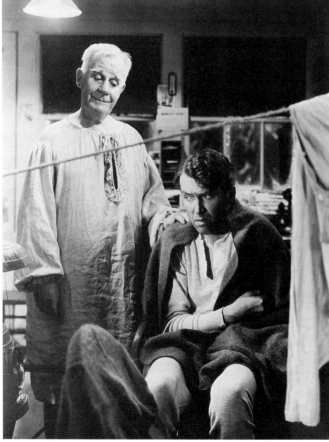

Above The revenge of the 'Common Man'. The likeable insurance salesman Charlie Meadows (John Goodman) turns out to be a serial killer called Karl 'Madman' Mundt in *Barton Fink*. 'Heil Hitler!' he yells.

Left James Stewart with Clarence (Henry Travers), his guardian angel in Frank Capra's *It's A Wonderful Life* (1946), which anticipates some of the more supernatural elements, including an angel, in *The Hudsucker Proxy* (1994).

'I used to think you were a swell guy – well, to be honest, I thought you were an imbecile.' The sappy Norville Barnes (Tim Robbins) is no match for the scheming journalist Amy Archer (Jennifer Jason Leigh) in *The Hudsucker Proxy*, a relationship not unlike that of Gary Cooper and Jean Arthur in Capra's *Mr Deeds Goes To Town* (1936).

'Once a newspaperman, always a newspaperman.' Ace reporter Hildy Johnson (Rosalind Russell) is welcomed back to the newsroom in Howard Hawks' *His Girl Friday* (1940). The character was one of the models for Amy Archer in *The Hudsucker Proxy*.

One of the longest desks in all the Coen movies, a launching pad for suicidal businessmen in *The Hudsucker Proxy*. 'I'm getting off this merry-go-round,' yells one of the board members, before attempting to emulate his former boss, Hudsucker, by hurling himself through the window, not realising it has been replaced by Plexiglas.

'Oh! Oh, geez!' William H. Macy as the miserably incompetent Jerry Lundegaard in his parka, in *Fargo*, discovers his father-in-law Wade's body.

'You fucking imbeciles!' At the scene of the drop, Carl Showalter (Steve Buscemi) has shot Wade Gustafson (Harve Presnell) on a snow-covered exterior parking garage in *Fargo* (1996).

Frances McDormand (Mrs Joel Coen) as Marge Gunderson gets her man at the climax of *Fargo*, and gained a Best Actress Oscar for her performance at the same time.

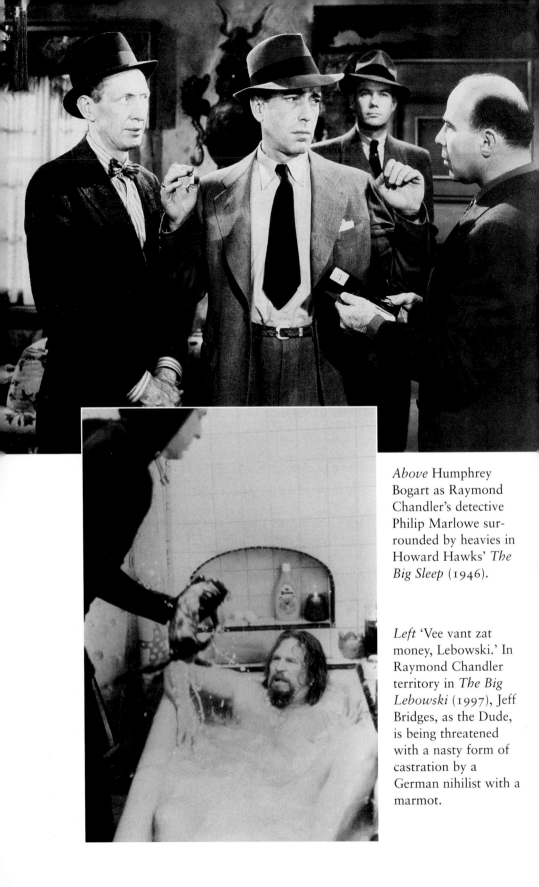

Above Humphrey Bogart as Raymond Chandler's detective Philip Marlowe surrounded by heavies in Howard Hawks' *The Big Sleep* (1946).

Left 'Vee vant zat money, Lebowski.' In Raymond Chandler territory in *The Big Lebowski* (1997), Jeff Bridges, as the Dude, is being threatened with a nasty form of castration by a German nihilist with a marmot.

Above The laid-back Dude (Jeff Bridges), spaced-out Donny (Steve Buscemi) and belligerent Walter Sobchak (John Goodman), in their favourite hangout, the bowling alley in *The Big Lebowski*.

Above Joel and Ethan in the cutting room while working on *The Big Lebowski*. Roderick Jaynes, the editor on the movie, refused to have his photograph taken.

Right A spoiled movie director, John Sullivan (Joel McCrea), tired of making fluff, takes to the road to see how the other half lives in order to be able to make the social drama *O Brother, Where Art Thou?* in Preston Sturges' *Sullivan's Travels* (1941), only to find himself working on a chain gang.

'I don't want to make *O Brother, Where Art Thou?* There's a lot to be said for making people laugh. That's all they've got in this cockeyed caravan.' Movie director Sullivan (Joel McCrea) returns to Hollywood in *Sullivan's Travels*, after suffering on the road and decides not to make 'the greatest tragedy ever made'.

George Clooney (Ulysses Everett McGill), John Turturro (Pete) and Tim Nelson (Delmar O'Donnel) as three cons on the run from a chain gang in the south in *O Brother, Where Art Thou?* (2000), the Coens' homage to Preston Sturges and to *Homer's Odyssey*. Left to right: John Turturro, Tim Blake Nelson and George Clooney.

had played racketeers before; the first part he won when he first came
to Hollywood was in the television series *The Gangster Chronicles*.
Polito was also Detective Steve Crosetti on the 1993–94 season of
Homicide: Life on the Street.

"The actors never changed one word of dialogue," Polito stated.
"We followed the scenario extremely faithfully. A large amount of
direction is already in the screenplay. I remember going through my
opening monologue at first and I got one word wrong. 'You've missed
that word.' They don't let actors change a single word. They sort of
giggle and make you laugh along with them, until finally you realize
you're going the way they planned years before. They have a wonderful way of catching you off guard."

The Coens flew Marcia Gay Harden, who plays Verna, and who was
making her screen debut, to the New Orleans location for an unsched-
uled costume fitting that went on "until the wee hours of the morning."
They redesigned her dresses to make them more clingy, had her spend
a week on make-up tests, had her eyebrows plucked and her hair cut.
"That was important to them. But they left me on my own concep-
tionally. They'd use words like 'smoky, sensuous, sexy'."

There are rare occasions when one feels that a little more "conceptual" directing might not go amiss, especially in the case of Polito,
who gives a hammy, eye-rolling performance. For Gabriel Byrne it
was, "Close the door after you, that sort of thing. It wasn't a fun set at
all. People were there to work really hard." Joel was surprised by
Byrne's comment. "Did he really say that? Well, I don't think you'll
find that to be a particularly widely held perception. Actually Gabriel
had a thankless task in that he was in practically every shot and was a
foil for the other characters." "Also he got hit a lot," Ethan pointed
out. "Yeh, I suppose you cannot really blame him for saying that. He
got up at five in the morning, went into make-up for an hour and
then spent twelve hours being hit."

Tom Reagan gets beaten up as much as the hero Ned Beaumont
in *The Glass Key*, who also keeps bouncing back. The gangster's
henchman Eddie Dane calls Tom "Little Miss Punching Bag." The
Coens found the character getting his face smashed up rather funny.
"Well, violence is frequently very funny. There is no funnier part of

The Apartment than when Jack Lemmon is smacking Shirley Maclaine when she has passed out," they claimed rather perversely.

40 Way Down Yonder

MILLER'S CROSSING was the Coens' first period piece—only three of their nine films are set contemporaneously—and was a break from their previous "hayseed sagas," which they would return to with a vengeance in *O Brother, Where Art Thou?*.

Like *The Glass Key*, *Miller's Crossing* is set in an unnamed American city in the 1920s, yet the city resembles Personville, nicknamed Poisonville, in *Red Harvest*. The film was actually shot in New Orleans, although almost nothing was shown that could identify the city. Only those local residents familiar with the office buildings and private clubs that were used would realize where the film was shot.

"We looked around San Francisco, but you know what that looks like: period but upscale—*faux* period." New Orleans was chosen for the location because of the late 1920s period architecture which meant it could pass for the generic Anytown. "There are whole neighborhoods here of nothing but 1929 architecture. New Orleans is sort of a depressed city; it hasn't been gentrified. There's a lot of architecture that hasn't been touched, store-front windows that haven't been replaced in the last sixty years." Some cosmetic restoration was done in some neighborhoods, but most of it remained the same, representing perfectly those Hammett cities festering with corruption.

For the scene in Leo's club, the members of the staid International House opened their doors for the first time to a film crew. During the days when the downstairs dining room was needed for filming, the members took their lunch in a smaller upstairs room, where little cards on the table informed them that they were being inconvenienced "to facilitate filming in New Orleans."

In Magazine Street several blocks looked like the 1920s, and Picayune Street was the location for an exterior scene between Tom and Verna. The place of the title was a tree farm 90 minutes from the city. All of the scenes there were shot in Fuji, because Fuji's greens are much more muted than Kodak stock.

The South was also chosen because the schedule necessitated shooting in winter, but the brothers didn't want to show any snowy exteriors. They would make up for it a few years later in *Fargo*, which had more snow and ice than any film since *Scott of the Antarctic*.

Because the Coens always want to work with the same people as far as possible, *Miller's Crossing* had the same team of Barry Sonnenfeld (cinematographer), Carter Burwell (composer), Skip Lievsay (sound editor), J. Todd Anderson (storyboard artist) and Richard Hornung (costume designer), all of whom had worked on the previous picture. Only the scene designer, Jane Musky, wasn't free, so David Gassner, who had worked with Francis Coppola, came in. He helped them in the choice of colors, which are more controlled than in the precedent films. Gassner had the idea of columns in architecture that corresponded to the trees of the forest.

41   Hats On!

"WE DIDN'T want to do another out-and-out comedy like *Raising Arizona*. We wanted to do something that was a little morbid. We've always liked gangster movies. Though, it's closer to a *film noir* than a gangster movie. But we're attracted to the genre more in the literary than the cinematic."

It just so happened that there was a revival in the late 1980s and early 1990s of gangster movies, sparked off by the success of Brian De Palma's unsubtle *The Untouchables* (1987). In the same year as *Miller's Crossing*, there appeared Martin Scorsese's amoral *Goodfellas* and Francis Coppola's conclusion (to date) to his mafia saga, *The Godfather Part III*. The Coens felt, quite rightly, that of all the gangster films on offer theirs was the most "mythical," although Ethan once generously confessed that he thought *Goodfellas* better. The opening of *Miller's Crossing* is almost a pastiche of the opening monologue in *The Godfather*. The final scene, however, between Leo and Tom after Bernie Bernbaum's funeral, harks back to the walk away at the end of *The Third Man*, though in reverse.

Hats are an essential part of the aesthetic of the gangster movie from the 1930s to the 1950s. Difficult to imagine James Cagney and Edward G. Robinson walking bareheaded in the streets when going off to blast someone to smithereens. A hat is also an important plot point in *The Glass Key*. In *Miller's Crossing*, a child comes across a dead man, Rug Daniels, in an alley, takes off his toupee and runs away with it. In *The Glass Key*, a man is found dead in an alley, but his hat has disappeared. "He won't need it now" is the remark, both about the rug and the hat.

The film had its genesis in the image of a black hat coming to rest in a forest clearing, then lifting to soar away again down an avenue of trees, an image that accompanies the main title.

"The hat thing, what can you say about the hat? It's not that there's any hidden mysteries or anything. It's just because, you know, it's there." Working on the principal that, "If you want to get ahead, get a hat," the Coens "wanted to make a film with people who were dressed in a certain manner, hats, long coats, and put them in an unusual context like a forest."

"The characters in this movie don't open up, don't reveal themselves at any point, so the Coens wanted brims very broad and down over people's eyes, often shadowing them," said the designer Richard Hornung. "People are very covered up in this."

The selection of Byrne's hat was a long process. Five identical hats were made for Byrne to wear during the filming. The one in the opening shot was filmed at high speed using a special lightweight hat that could be controlled with a fishing line. "The hat really becomes a big symbol in the film," Hornung continued. "Every time Tom gets knocked down, the hat falls off and people are always handing it back to him." A question of boy gets hat, boy loses hat, boy gets hat.

The Coens also remembered, in their childhood, attending the synagogue where they were surrounded by men wearing old-fashioned hats, while others wore yarmulkes. However, you couldn't have a gangster in a yarmulke, could you? Well, Albert Finney as Leo wears one at Bernie Bernbaum's funeral.

"Are any of your brother's hats missing? Paul says he had a hat on. There was none there when I found him. See if you can find out how many he had and if they're all accounted for—except the one I borrowed." . . . "Why are you so interested in the hat? Is it so important?" He shrugged. "I don't know. I'm only an amateur detective, but it looks like a thing that might have some meaning, one way or another."

–**The Glass Key** (Dashiell Hammett)

42 Shoot the Tenor

"BEFORE WE shot the movie, they were saying it should be like *Unbearable Lightness of Being* [shot by Sven Nykvist]," remarked Barry Sonnenfeld. "And I would disagree and tell them why not. And we would go back and forth and back and forth. Finally, and this is what's happened on every movie, I say, 'How about this: What if we just make it look nice?' And they'll go, 'Yeah, that would be great, that's exactly what we're talking about.'"

"It's about time at that point to shed a little blood. The movie's in danger of becoming tasteful, you know?" the Coens commented before the long, spectacular sequence in which four of Johnny Caspar's gunmen are sent to rub out Leo. The tightly-edited montage was shot over a period of several weeks in various locations, ranging from studio interiors to a residential street in the suburb of Metairie, to a house near the French Quarter, to a vacant house in the Garden District (now occupied by the novelist Anne Rice).

"Exactly which part was filmed when is hard to remember," said Joel, "with one exception. We burned down the house the night of the Academy Awards." This was on 29 March 1989, the night Barry Levinson's *Rain Man* won Best Picture, Best Actor, Best Director and Best Screenplay. Was it some kind of rebellion against the Oscar ceremony, from which so-called "indies' like the Coens were usually excluded, or a huge bonfire to celebrate this annual Hollywood rite? Six years later, however, Frances McDormand and the Coens would be on the podium at the Dorothy Chandler Pavilion accepting the gold-plated statuettes for *Fargo*.

THE HARDEST shot of the film to get right is the one in which Leo rolls under the bed to shoot. The Coens used an elevated set, about three feet off the ground, so the camera would be level with the bed. Two men played the second gunman, but the reverse shots required a stunt co-ordinator. "Thompsons are not light guns. It's difficult to hold one while it's firing and bucking, and also with squibs going up your back," Joel explained. "You have to sell all that body language, taking the bullet hits. What sells the hit is the dance. He shoots up the chandelier, the paintings, his toes. All kinds of fun things. It was a lot of fun blowing the toes off. The only regret is that it goes by so fast, you almost kind of miss it. They're a highlight.'

In the course of planning this scene, the peacenik-looking Coens became experts in the lore of Thompson guns, several of which they procured for the film. While they were enamoured of the gun's output—given sufficient ammunition, they can fire 800 rounds a minute—they had to accept its predisposition to jam, a drawback that forced innumerable retakes. "The gun is incredibly loud, and it does vibrate. You can see it sort of jingle. The whole thing was a very satisfying experience."

Towards the end of the segment, as Leo walks down the street firing the gun at the speeding getaway car, Finney had to maintain a cool demeanor while controlling the powerful weapon. As an added challenge, the Coens set up a bucket behind him to see how many expelled cartridges he could land in it. "He got a very high percentage," said Ethan. "Technically, he's a very good actor."

The Coens recruited Irish tenor Frank Patterson, who played the vocalist in John Huston's final film, *The Dead*, to perform *Danny Boy*, the song that Finney is listening to on the victrola when the gunmen burst in, and which continues throughout the entire sequence. After the scene was edited, Patterson went into the studio with an orchestra to record the song, tailoring his cadences to fit the action.

GABRIEL BYRNE helped in the selection of the music, including *Danny Boy* and *Come Back to Erin Carter*, an Irish tune which Carter Burwell used as the principal theme of the film. "My first preference is for variety," commented Burwell. "I would not like to do the same things again and again. One of the reasons I love working with Joel and Ethan is that they never ask me to do the same thing. In *Miller's Crossing*, we all agreed that it should be an orchestral score, but we also knew that I knew nothing about orchestral music! That didn't faze them at all; they were perfectly willing to give me the job. I figured I would learn orchestral film music and do it."

Although Carter Burwell (born 1955) learnt classical piano, his interest in music was first sparked when a friend taught him how to improvise blues in high school. It was soon after that he discovered his love for composition. As a fine arts major at Harvard, he continued this growing attachment to music by playing piano whenever he could. When he was about to graduate, he joined a band for fun and was serendipitously discovered in a club by Lee Orloff, the sound mixer on *Blood Simple*.

"Going into it, I wasn't sure what it was going to be like. I thought they were going to be breathing down my neck, but it was quite the opposite," recalled Burwell. "They were very supportive. They let me do what I wanted to do. I didn't get a lot of specific instructions from them. They told me what they liked and what they didn't like, but they weren't specific about what a piece of music should do. One thing they did say with some sections, though, was if they felt it was getting too dark, they would say, 'It's got to be fun; it's got to be fast!' If it got to be too much fun, they would say, 'There's got to be a dark side.'" In general, Burwell's music is characterized by gripping but simple melodies, incorporating touches of contemporary styles like jazz or heavy metal and quiet, somber, instrument sequences using guitar or piano. In *Blood Simple*, Burwell provided a haunting theme played on the piano, and other eerie music including chanting and drums. Burwell went onto do the music for all the brothers' subsequent movies.

43 Tutti Fruity

IT COULD be said that *Miller's Crossing* was the first of the Coens' films not to be "politically correct." An unusually hypersensitive Greek or Texan, just might have taken exception to *Blood Simple*, but *Raising Arizona* actually made an idiot out of a man who told Polack jokes. In *Barton Fink*, "kike" is thrown around without discrimination, but only by a fellow kike (Jack Lipnick), whereas there are references to potato eaters, eye-ties and sheenies in *Miller's*

Crossing. "It ain't right all this fuss over one sheeny. Let Caspar have Bernie—Jesus, what's one Hebrew more or less?" says police chief O'Doole.

The Irish and Italians don't come out too well, both being equally corrupt. The Jews, as represented by Bernie Bernbaum, come off worse. But Bernie is also a homosexual, which seems more contemptible in the characters' eyes (as distinct from those of their creators). The homosexuals are the most irredeemable people in the picture. The despicable Bernie is having an affair with Mink (Steve Buscemi), who is "Eddie's boy"—that is Eddie Dane, Caspar's vicious henchman.

"What's going on between you and Bernie?" Tom asks Mink. "Nothing, Tom, we're just friends, you know, amigos?" "You're a fickle boy, Mink. If the Dane found out you had another 'amigo'—well, I don't peg him for the understanding type." For Joel, the relationship of Bernie, Mink and Eddie was "just a mirror image of the central triangle" of Tom, Verna and Leo, a feeling for symmetry and counterpoint that is inherent in most of their screenplays.

The homosexuality was so obliquely treated that the film escaped the ire of gay groups who vociferously objected to two films the following year, which, they felt, treated gays in an extremely negative manner. In Oliver Stone's *JFK*, there is an implicit assumption of a homosexual mafia having been involved in the killing of President Kennedy, and the portrayal of a gay transvestite serial killer, who skins the bodies of his young female victims, in Jonathan Demme's *The Silence of the Lambs* was less than flattering. In *Miller's Crossing*, Eddie Dane is a woman-hater and, grabbing Verna, tells her, "I'll track down all you whores."

In *Barton Fink*, Jack Lipnick, head of Capitol Studios, says he has heard that Barton's play was "a little fruity, but I guess you know what you're doing." Later the two cops, when enquiring about Charlie Meadows, who turns out to be a serial killer, ask Barton, "You two have some sick sex thing?" "Sex! He's a *man*! We *wrestled*!" "You're a sick fuck, Fink."

In *The Big Lebowski*, it is not spelled out whether Jesus Quintana (John Turturro) is a homo or heterosexual "paedophile," or whether it is only in Walter's imagination. "Yeh, he's a fucking pervert, Dude

. . . Your man is a sex offender. With a record. Spent six months in Chino for exposing himself to an eight-year-old."

In Ethan's gangster story *Cosa Minapolidan*, a rumor starts about how, in the prison showers, a gangster "got his throat slashed by a homo . . . Joe de Louie had rebuffed the homosexual advances of a man convicted of soliciting sex from a state trooper." The "persevering homo" then steals a spoon from the mess and spends two months honing it, and "used it on the throat of the by now unsuspecting de Louie."

In another story, *Red Wing*, a couple have a gay son, Kyle, living in Minneapolis. When the husband is not in the mood for sex one night, the wife accuses him of being gay as well. "Well, I guess it's true what they say . . . that the fruit don't fall far from the tree . . . Maybe you prefer sticking your thing into Norm Wollensky's big old butt," she says.

But the Coens have no *parti pris* or "hidden agenda." It is part of the maturity of their approach to their characters that they recognize the existence of racism, anti-Semitism and homophobia.

44 "I'm Talkin' about Ethics"

Although most of Raymond Chandler's and Dashiell Hammett's novels are written in the first person, *Miller's Crossing*, unpredictably, does not have a narrator. Instead it starts with a long speech delivered by Johnny Caspar to an impassive Leo. "I'm talkin' about friendship. I'm talkin' about character. I'm talkin' about—hell, Leo, I ain't embarrassed to use the word—I'm talkin' about ethics." This from a brutal hoodlum. It echoes the equally ironic opening monologue of *The Godfather*, in which a minor Mafia figure intones, "I believe in America. America has made my fortune. And I raised my daughter in the American fashion . . ." It is a typically audacious thing for the

Coens to do, leaving audiences wondering whether it is a homage, a rip-off or a take-off.

A more rarefied allusion is the playing of the tune "Runnin' Wild" in the background, the song sung by Marilyn Monroe in *Some Like It Hot*, the Billy Wilder movie set in the same gangster era. But could there possibly be any deliberate reference to Alan Parker's kiddie gangster movie, *Bugsy Malone*, especially in the scene at Miller's Crossing? Parker claims that he was inspired to write the movie while watching *The Godfather*. Another frivolous reference in what is essentially a dark and violent film, is one to the Keystone Kops.

It is in the nature of the Coens that they are willing to shift gear at any moment from drama to comedy, sometimes sacrificing the dramatic impact for the sake of a joke. After Tom has told Leo that he was sleeping with Verna, an enraged Leo follows Tom (and so does the camera in a flowing long take) out of the Shenandoah Club, punching him as he does so. Tom falls down the stairs, and is punched again. As Tom rises bleeding, he grabs the skirt and bodice of a fat lady, who screams and hits him vigorously on the head with her handbag.

The characters, articulate phrase-makers no matter how stupid, sometimes move into Damon Runyon territory: "I was just speculating about a hypothesis," says a cop. But, no matter how much spoofery there is in the film, it does not undermine the intrinsic melancholia of the subject or the treatment, reflected in the autumnal colors. It is about betrayal (as most gangster movies are), but also, as Johnny Caspar says, "friendship, character, ethics."

TOM: Do you always know why you do things, Leo?

LEO: Course I do. It was a smart play. Jesus, Tom! I'd give anything if you'd work for me again. I know I've made some bonehead plays!

I know I can be pig-headed but, damnit, so can you! I need your help, and things can be like they were, I know it! I just know it! As for you and Verna—well, I understand, you're both young, and—well, damnit, Tom, I forgive you!

TOM: I didn't ask for that and I don't want it . . . Goodbye Leo.

–Miller's Crossing

HOLLYWOOD NUTS

VII

"*Barton Fink* is very far from our own experi-

ence. Our life in Hollywood has been particu-

larly easy."

45 Fade In

FOLLOWING *MILLER'S* Crossing, the Coens went almost immediately into production on *Barton Fink*, which started shooting in June 1990 in Los Angeles. They hired an office above a nondescript car rental agency near the beach, where hand-lettered cardboard signs, bearing the word "Fink" and an arrow, pointed the way to their makeshift production offices. Most of the film was shot in LA. The New York bar and restaurant at the beginning of the film was shot on the liner *Queen Mary*, and the last scene near Zuma Beach. Despite the relatively poor showing at the box-office of *Miller's Crossing*, the faithful Circle had the same deal with Fox as for the previous film, but this time retained the foreign rights.

The brothers wrote *Barton Fink* in three weeks before returning to *Miller's Crossing*. "Perhaps because it was a relief from *Miller's Crossing*, it came easily. Certain films come entirely in one's head. You know how it will look. Even if you don't know the ending. You have an intuition about the conclusion. In contrast, other scenarios are like a voyage where you don't know exactly where you're going. We just sort of burped out *Barton Fink*.

"It makes things much easier if you know in advance where the characters are leading you. It also helped because we knew the actors very well. We wrote the part of Charlie Meadows for John Goodman, because of his warm and likeable image, so the public are at ease with him. We exploited that image. There is something menacing and worrying about the character." The Coens did the same again with Goodman's cuddly bear image in *O Brother, Where Art Thou?*, in which he plays a crooked bible salesman and member of the Ku Klux Klan.

In case anyone would associate their bilious view of Hollywood with their own experiences, the Coens were quick to dissociate themselves from the Barton Fink character. *"Barton Fink* is very far from our own experience. Our life in Hollywood has been particularly easy. The film isn't a personal comment. We don't have any rejected scenarios in our drawers. There have been projects on which we started work, but we didn't finish them for one reason or another. Artistic problems that we were unable to solve or the cost was prohibitive." Thus, they give the lie to the belief that artists must suffer to understand the suffering of others. Much to the frustration of other struggling film directors (and of biographers thirsting for drama and tragedy), the Coens have been given a comparatively easy ride by the industry.

The dictionary meaning of "fink" is a blackleg, strike-breaker or unpleasant person. Like his surname, "Barton is in a lot of respects a shit, but it's not as if we're not interested in the audience having some access to him as a human being. We have a lot of affection for our characters. Even the ones that are idiots! There's comedy in idiocy, just like there can be comedy in violence, but that doesn't necessarily mean you're condescending. People get very uncomfortable when the main character in the movie is not sympathetic in a Hollywood formula way. And what's irritating about that is the implication that the only stories you can tell are stories about sympathetic characters, which is an absurd idea."

"I felt I could bring something more human to Barton," John Turturro remarked of the role written for him. "I felt I could bring a little something extra. Joel and Ethan allowed me a certain contribution. I tried to go a little further than they expected." Turturro spent a month with the Coens in LA before the shoot, just to get in sync with them. He also learned to type, although with Barton Fink having writer's block he didn't need to do much. (There are two slightly facile cuts from Barton, unable to put words down on paper, to the rapid typing of a secretary.)

Although Barton spouts about the common man, he doesn't really give a hoot about them. When Charlie Meadows tells him he has stories to tell, Barton doesn't listen but talks about his own theories. At the USO dance, Barton refuses to let a sailor cut in while he's dancing. "I'm a writer! Celebrating the completion of something good! Do you understand that, sailor! I'm a writer! . . . This is my uniform (*tapping his head*). This is where I serve the common man."

As if to compensate for Barton's egotism, Ethan gave the "common man" a voice in his story *There is an Ancient Mariner*, in which a man, probably a salesman, bends the ear of a fellow customer in a bar, telling him a tale of how a man was stabbed in the neck by his wife while on the bar stool occupied by the listener.

> BARTON: I've always found that writing comes
>
> from a great inner pain. Maybe it's a pain that
>
> comes from the realization that one must do
>
> something for one's fellow man—to help
>
> somehow to ease his suffering. Maybe it's a
>
> personal pain. At any rate, I don't believe
>
> good work is possible without it.
>
> —**Barton Fink**

46　*1941 and All That*

BARTON FINK, the second in the Coens' chronological period trilogy, was set in Hollywood in 1941 on the eve of the USA entering the Second World War. It was the year both John Huston and Orson Welles made their feature film debuts; Huston with his version of

Dashiell Hammett's *The Maltese Falcon* and Orson Welles with *Citizen Kane*. It was also the year of Preston Sturges' Hollywood satire, *Sullivan's Travels*, which was to inspire *O Brother, Where Art Thou?* and, marginally, *Barton Fink*.

At the end of the preceding year, F. Scott Fitzgerald and Nathanael West, authors of two of the great Hollywood novels, *The Last Tycoon* and *The Day of the Locust*, had died within 24 hours of each other. West's novels are strange fables of innocence and corruption in which naïve heroes, not unlike Hi, Barton and Norville, are invariably crushed by the world's pitiless indifference to their good intentions.

The great novelist William Faulkner had left Hollywood disillusioned with the industry after working as a script doctor at MGM and Fox. "I'm a motion picture doctor," Faulkner said. "When they run into a section they don't like, I rework it and continue to rework it until they do like it . . . I don't write scripts. I don't know enough about it."

Faulkner returned to Hollywood in 1946 to work on *The Big Sleep* mainly as an act of charity by Howard Hawks. He went there in the first place to earn more money than his novels made. Clifford Odets, the hero of the left-wing Group Theater in New York, was also doctoring scripts in Hollywood and being accused by his erstwhile colleagues in the theater of having sold out—in fact, of being a fink. Odets tied himself into psychological knots trying to justify writing for Gary Cooper and Joan Crawford, and, much later, Elvis Presley. "Great audiences," he proclaimed in 1937, "are waiting now to have their own experiences explained and interpreted for them." Compare this with Barton Fink's language. "We have an opportunity to forge something real out of everyday experience, create a theater for the masses that's based on a few simple truths . . . The hopes and dreams of the common man."

In 1941, Harry Cohn, Louis B. Mayer and Jack Warner were the most powerful moguls in Hollywood, hiring and firing, making and breaking people. The Coens' fictional Capitol Studio boss Jack Lipnick (Michael Lerner) is an amalgam of Cohn, Mayer and Warner. His girth resembles Mayer but he has many of the vulgar traits of Cohn. (Lerner, who was in Bob Rafelson's *The Postman*

Always Rings Twice, had played both Jack Warner and Harry Cohn in
TV movies previously.) The scene in the film when Lipnick puts on
an army uniform derives from Warner. After the US entered the war,
Warner used to strut around in a uniform borrowed from the costume
department. It was Warner who described scriptwriters as "schmucks
with Underwoods," as demonstrated by Barton struggling to write his
script on an Underwood typewriter.

The writer W.P. Mayhew (John Mahoney) is plainly based on
William Faulkner. He is a novelist of repute, wears a white suit, has a
Southern accent and drinks. And for eagle-eyed spectators, the words
"Slave Ship" written on the door of Mayhew's office in the Writer's
Building at the studio is not only an ironic description of the writer's
position at the studio, but was also the title of a 1937 Tay Garnett
movie, on which Faulkner was one of four writers credited. The film
was about a rebellion on a slave ship, with Wallace Beery as one of the
leaders, which could be seen as emblematic of a writers' strike.

Faulkner also contributed to *Flesh* (1932), an unusual picture
from John Ford, which starred plug-ugly Beery as a German wrestler
who is thrown into a mire of corruption in America. It was a film
obviously influenced by German Expressionist cinema and the films
starring Emil Jannings, similar to "Devil on the Canvas," the
wrestling picture, directed by "Victor Soderberg" in *Barton Fink*. The
name of the director is meant to remind audiences of the great
Swedish director Victor Sjöström, who made nine films in
Hollywood under the name of Victor Seastrom. The fact that
Sjöström's last American film was in 1930, eleven years before the
action in *Barton Fink* takes place, did not deter the Coens from making the film-buffy reference.

The Coens were alerted to *Flesh* by reading *City of Nets* ("City of
Nuts," as one critic called it) about Hollywood in the 1940s, in which
the author, Otto Friedrich, mentions that Faulkner worked on a
wrestling picture with Wallace Beery. "It was mostly about German
expatriates in Los Angeles in the Forties, and not exclusively about
the movie business. It started us thinking about that location and that
period as a context for a story."

"Wrestling pictures were a weird sub-genre," commented Ethan.
"There were all sorts of reasons in seeing two guys in their underwear

grappling with one another. The whole sort of queasy homoerotic thing. The weird connection between the characters. Barton is a self-important figure, wrestling with his problems, reduced to writing a vulgar genre movie." When Barton finally delivers his script of "The Burlyman" to Lipnick, the mogul says, "This is a wrestling picture; the audience wants to see action, drama, wrestling and plenty of it. They don't wanna see a guy wrestling with his soul—well all right, a little for the critics—but you make it the carrot that wags the dog . . . We don't put Wallace Beery in some fruity movie about suffering . . ."

Wrestling obviously fascinated/amused Ethan, because seven years later, without Joel, he co-wrote *The Naked Man*, the first feature directed by J. Todd Anderson, the Coens' storyboard artist. It was about a man who is a respected chiropractor by day but becomes a masked super wrestler, in a body suit, by night.

As the allusion to *Flesh* and Victor Sjöström indicate, the Coens, for all their knowledge of Hollywood history, seem to be rather out of sync with the time in which *Barton Fink* is placed. By 1941, the brave new socially-conscious theater that Fink burbles about had already erupted. Clifford Odets' *Waiting for Lefty*, about a taxi drivers' strike, had blazed the trail six years earlier. And by 1941, Wallace Beery was too old at 56 for wrestling movies—a genre which Hollywood never really cultivated, though any actor can be taught to wrestle, just as every wrestler is taught to act. When Lipnick tells Barton that the wrestling character needs someone to care about—"a girl, a little orphan boy"—he could be referring to King Vidor's *The Champ*, a maudlin 1932 movie about ex-prizefighter Beery and his small son (Jackie Cooper), trying to scrape a living in Tijuana.

THOUGH PHYSICALLY he was made to resemble George S. Kaufman, a commercially successful Broadway playwright, the character of Barton Fink was loosely based on Clifford Odets. Barton's play called "Bare Ruined Choirs: Triumph of the Common Man," was a brilliant pastiche of American realist drama of the 1930s, such as Odets' *Awake and Sing* (1935), which concerned a financially embarrassed Jewish family's frustration and revolt. (Coincidentally, Frances McDormand appeared in the latter play on Broadway.)

"I'm blowin' out of here, blowin' for good. I'm kissin' it all goodbye, these four stinkin' walls, the six flights up, the el that roars by at three A.M. like a cast-iron wind. Kiss 'em goodbye for me, Maury! I'll miss 'em—like hell I will!" "Dreaming again!" "Not this time, Lil! I'm awake now, awake for the first time in years. Uncle Dave said it: 'Daylight is dream if you've lived with your eyes closed.' Well my eyes are open now! I see that choir, and I know they're dressed in rags! But we're part of that choir, both of us—yeah, and you, Maury, and Uncle Dave too!" "The sun's coming up, kid. They'll be hawking the fish down on Fulton Street." "Let 'em hawk. Let 'em sing their hearts out." "That's it, kid. Take that ruined choir. Make it sing!" "So long, Maury." "So long. We'll hear from that kid. And I don't mean a postcard." "Fish! Fresh fish!" "Let's spit on our hands and get to work. It's late,

Maury." "Not anymore, Lil. It's early."

–Barton Fink

"Did Jake die for us to fight 'bout nickels?

No! Awake and sing, he said. Right here he

stood and said it. The night he died, I saw it

like a thunderbolt! I saw he was dead, and I

was born! I swear to God, I'm one week old! I

want the whole city to hear it—fresh blood,

arms. We got 'em. We're glad we're living."

–Awake and Sing (Clifford Odets)

The Coens must have been aware of a 1946 *film noir, Deadline at Dawn,* the only movie directed by Harold Clurman of the Group Theater, in which a sailor on shore leave in New York wakes up to find the woman he was with the night before murdered. He believes he must have killed her while he was out cold. It was written by Odets, and based on a novel by William Irish (Cornell Woolrich), the *noir* writer who lived a reclusive life in seedy hotels.

Barton Fink, like Odets, Faulkner, Chandler and Aldous Huxley, is convinced that Hollywood is beneath him. *The Big Knife* (1949) was Odets' melodramatic indictment of the Hollywood film industry. In *Sullivan's Travels,* the situation is the opposite of the artist reduced to a hack. John L. Sullivan (Joel McCrea) is a successful Hollywood director who has made nothing but lightweight pictures such as "So

Long, Sarong," but suddenly gets the notion that he wants to make a searing drama about deplorable social conditions and human suffering called "O Brother, Where Art Thou?" However, he discovers that to make people laugh is a greater social function. Sturges, in his autobiography, *Between Flops*, wrote: "I wanted to tell some of my fellow filmwrights that they were getting a little too deep-dish, and to leave the preaching to the preachers." Getting "a little too deep-dish" is what the Coens always wanted to avoid without being superficial. "We're not trying to educate the masses. Does that make us bad people?" they said.

47   Down the Plug-hole

"WE MADE a detailed storyboard. But there were changes when we were on the stage. It was simpler to do than *Miller's Crossing* and the budget was a third of the cost. The time of the shooting was eight weeks as against twelve. In *Miller's Crossing*, we had lots of film we didn't use. It wasn't the case with *Barton Fink*. We used almost everything we shot. We *did* shoot some scenes of the life in the Hollywood studio, but we found them banal."

Barry Sonnenfeld, the Coens' cameraman on their first three films, was busy launching a lucrative career as a director with *The Addams Family*, and would go onto make mindless mainstream movies such as *Men in Black* and *Wild Wild West*, and become very much part of the Hollywood establishment. The brothers turned to British cameraman Roger Deakins, because "we loved the night images and interiors in *Stormy Monday*, *Sid and Nancy* and *Pascali's Island*."

Deakins, who grew up in Torquay, Devon, was a painter before he turned to photo-journalism and then film, studying at the National

Film School in London. His first features were *Another Time, Another Place* and *1984*. Deakins' agent sent him the script of *Barton Fink* but advised against accepting it. Deakins rejected the recommendation and met the Coens to discuss it in a café in Notting Hill, where they hit it off immediately.

"I remember the first day of the shoot. I hadn't worked with them before. It was the theater scene [shot at the Orpheum Theater in New York]. They had storyboarded a few set-ups. We wrapped at 11:30 in the morning. We had nothing else to do for the rest of the day. That was rare."

Deakins proved an ideal collaborator, doing almost anything the brothers asked of him. "There was only one moment when we surprised him," Joel remarked. "It was when we asked him to track down a plug-hole." The shot comes when Barton is in bed, about to make love to Audrey (Judy Davis). The camera moves from the bedroom into the bathroom and down the drain and through an endless shaft that leads to a wailing underworld.

"The shot was a lot of fun and we had a great time working out how to do it," the Coens commented. "After that, every time we asked Roger to do something difficult, he would raise an eyebrow and say, 'Don't be having me track down any plug-holes now.' " There has been no shot of a plug-hole to equal it since the last shot of the shower sequence in *Psycho*. It is also the most blatant sexual metaphor since Hitchcock's train in the tunnel at the end of *North by Northwest*.

Besides the modesty of putting their names only on the end credits, the Coens discreetly avoid the obligatory sex scenes that are found in most adult films. In *Blood Simple*, there is a long shot of the lovers in bed, otherwise there is no bonking in any of the other films, excepting a comic and unerotic scene of the two kidnappers strenuously having sex with two hookers in *Fargo*.

48   The Ghost Hotel

THE PRODUCTION designer, Dennis Gassner, who had designed *Miller's Crossing*, got to work on the hotel, the pivotal set of *Barton Fink*. Joel explained: "We spent three weeks shooting in the hotel, where half the film takes place. We wanted an art deco style. It had to be organically linked to the film. In a way, it was an exteriorization of the John Goodman character. The sweat falls from his brow as the wallpaper falls from the walls. At the end, when Goodman says that he's a prisoner of his mental state, that it is like hell, the hotel should suggest an infernal place." Ethan added: "We used a lot of green and yellow to suggest putrefaction."

"Ethan always describes most hotels as ghost ships," said Joel, "where one notes signs of the presence of the other passengers, without ever seeing them. The sole indication are the shoes in the corridors. One imagines that it's peopled by unsuccessful traveling salesmen, with a sad sexual life, and who are crying alone in their rooms."

It was in Austin, Texas, during the shooting of *Blood Simple* that they saw the sinister hotel that stayed in their minds when it came to writing *Barton Fink*. "We thought, 'Wow, Motel Hell.' You know, being condemned to live in the weirdest hotel in the world. On presenting the hotel, we suggested on Barton's arrival in Hollywood that it was not totally normal."

THE CLIMAX—the conflagration of the hotel, when John Goodman runs down the flaming hallway—proved to be the most complicated part of the film to set up. It was originally going to be done in the cutting room, with flames placed around the actors by an optical process. But the Coens wanted real heat. So the corridor was built in a disused aircraft hangar at Long Beach, which had once housed *The Spruce Goose*, Howard Hughes' giant seaplane.

The wallpaper was scored and perforated and a system of gas plumbing was set up behind the walls, using a gas which burns cooler than normal. There was a master switch which could cut off the gas in a second. There was also the problem of getting the fire to follow the running Goodman without getting ahead. For this they employed a man on a catwalk above the corridor, turning on each jet as Goodman passed it. The whole thing was lit for a cameraman by wall sconces. After each take the whole corridor had to be rebuilt, so there was a spare one without the gas equipment to which they could retire and do pick-up shots. "Actually, we just set it up very crudely and burned lots of stuntmen to death . . . Just kidding," Joel commented. "It's a very considerable fire. A very philosophical fire," Ethan added.

"THE IMAGE of the woman on the beach came early. We asked ourselves what would be in his room. We wanted the room to be sparsely decorated. That the walls were bare and that there was no particular view from the window. We wanted the only opening on the outside world to be this image. It was important to create a feeling of isolation. Our strategy was to immediately establish the protagonist's state of dislocation. The image on the beach gives a sense of relief. Perhaps it contrasts with the oppression of the room or accentuates it. We like the idea of the woman in the picture. In a weird kind of way it's emotional, evocative, rather than having a specific kind of meaning."

The strange but overly neat conclusion has Barton on the beach he had seen in the photo in his room, sitting with the box that most likely contains the head of a woman. The girl from the picture in his hotel room walks toward him. She says something but her voice is lost in the crash of the surf. She repeats herself. "I said it's a beautiful day . . ." (Marge Gunderson says exactly the same words toward the end of *Fargo*.) She sits down on the sand. "You're very beautiful. Are you in pictures?" Barton asks. She laughs. "Don't be silly," she says, proving herself untainted by Hollywood. She then takes up the same posture as in the photograph.

This scene cannot but evoke the last scene of Federico Fellini's *La Dolce Vita*, when Marcello encounters an innocent young girl on a beach after a night of orgies. She is not part of his "sweet life" world, but works as a waitress. She shouts something to him. But he cannot hear her because her voice is lost in the crash of the surf.

There were two open-grille elevators but only

one seemed to be running and that not busy.

An old man sat inside it slack-jawed and watery-eyed on a piece of folded burlap on top of a wooden stool. He looked as though he had been sitting there since the Civil War and had come out of that badly . . .

In the lobby of the Belfont Building, in the single elevator that had a light in it, on the piece of folded burlap, the same watery-eyed relic sat motionless, giving his imitation of the forgotten man. I got in with him and said, "Six." The elevator lurched into motion and pounded its way upstairs.

–The High Window (Raymond Chandler)

49 Kafka Who?

BARTON FINK is again a richly allusive film, with Hammett, Chandler, West, Fitzgerald, Faulkner and Odets, all American classics, thrown into the creative pot. However, Franz Kafka has to be summoned up, even at second hand. Joel predictably, but probably truthfully, deflected the latter influence on the movie.

"It surprises me that some critics have mentioned Kafka, because I haven't read him since I was at university where I devoured works like *Metamorphosis*. Some people have evoked *The Castle* and *The Penal Colony* which I've never read." Ethan concurred. "As some journalists have suggested that we were influenced by *The Castle*, I'm keen to read it."

Perhaps this Kafkaesque element was filtered through another influence on the film — Roman Polanski. "There is no doubt we have been influenced by Polanski's films. *Barton Fink* doesn't belong to any genre, but it's in the line of Polanski," admitted the Coens. Like the figure of K in Kafka's novels, the victim in most of Polanski's films uncomprehendingly believes himself to be partly responsible for his or her fate. *Repulsion* (1965), *Rosemary's Baby* (1968) and *Chinatown* (1974) create an atmosphere of evil, gradually turning the realistic settings of the cities of London, New York and Los Angeles into horrifying death-traps. There are similarities to *Chinatown* in *Blood Simple*, *Miller's Crossing* and *The Big Lebowski*, all of which reconstruct a *film noir* plot. Polanski himself played the tormented K character in *The Tenant* (1976), perhaps one of the most Kafkaesque films ever made. *Barton Fink* was called by one critic *"The Tenant* and *Cul-de-sac* meets *Repulsion."*

Providentially, Polanski headed the jury at the 1991 Cannes Film Festival at which *Barton Fink* carried off the Golden Palm, the direc-tor's prize and best actor award (John Turturro), an unprecedented achievement. However admired the movie was, several critics felt that making it a triple winner was going a bit too far, especially as it was in competition with Jacques Rivette's *La Belle Noiseuse* and Krzysztof Kieslowski's *The Double Life of Véronique*. Also in competition, all of which had some connection with the Coens, were Spike Lee's *Jungle Fever* (also with Turturro), David Mamet's *Homicide* (with William H. Macy, later to appear in *Fargo*) about a cop questioning his Jewish identity, and Alan Parker's *Mississippi Burning* (starring Frances McDormand). "We didn't know that it would be shown at Cannes or that Polanski would be on the jury. We don't want to give the impres-sion that we were licking his ass," the Coens insisted.

Barton Fink went to Cannes fresh from the laboratory. It was an unfinished "answer print" (a first print to which changes are made) without the final color gradings. In 1979, Francis Coppola had decided to risk entering *Apocalypse Now* in competition at the Cannes Festival as "a work in progress." The risk paid off, and it shared the Golden Palm with *The Tin Drum*.

"What's your name?" K asked as they were

proceeding. "Block, a commercial traveler,"

said the little man turning around to intro-

duce himself, but K would not suffer him to

remain standing. "Is that your real name?"

went on K. "Of course," came the answer,

"why should you doubt it?" "I thought you

might have some reason for concealing your

name," said K. He was feeling at ease now, at

ease as one is when speaking to an inferior

of some foreign country.

–The Trial (Franz Kafka)

50   Second Sighting

I'M ONE of the many barnacles sticking to the bottom of the Good Ship Cannes in May 1991. The Coens are giggling through another of a long line of interviews on the terrace of the Carlton Hotel. I'm having a kir at the next table. I've been nursing it for 20 minutes. I'm pretending not to notice or listen to the conversation. Needless to say, I'm not staying at the Carlton but at a dump off the rue d'Antibes. A woman comes up to the Coens and tells them that Krzysztof Kieslowski is at another table, and asks them if they would like to meet their rival for the Palm d'Or. "Who's Kieslowski?" one of the brothers asks. I choke on my kir and nearly fall off my chair. "Come on," I think. "Your film is in competition with one of Kieslowski's films and you've never heard of him!" That's the difference between American and European cinema. It's far more likely that someone like Kieslowski would have heard of the Coens than vice versa, discounting any qualitative comparisons. Ethan mentions that the only film he has had a chance to see has been Jean-Pierre Jeunet and Marc Caro's *Delicatessen*, one of the few co-directed movies, and found it "wonderfully wacky."

In Hollywood, the screenplay is written by a salaried writer under the supervision of a producer, that is to say, by an employee without power or decision over the uses of his own craft, without ownership of it, and, however extravagantly paid, almost without honor for it . . . As a result there is no such thing as an art of the screenplay, and there never will

be as long as the system lasts, for it is the

essence of this system that it seeks to

exploit a talent without permitting it the right

to be a talent. It cannot be done; you can only

destroy the talent, which is exactly what hap-

pens—when there is any to destroy.

–**Raymond Chandler** (*The Atlantic Monthly*, November 1945)

CapraCoen VII

"In a weird kind of way, *Hudsucker* is almost an

exception to the other movies we have made. It

was almost calculated to prove what people

thought about our previous movies . . .

Hudsucker truly is a comment on the genres it

draws from."

51　Hi, Yo, Silver!

IMMEDIATELY AFTER making *Blood Simple* in 1984, the still unknown Coen brothers went to Los Angeles and shared a house with Sam Raimi, where they wrote *The Hudsucker Proxy*. Sitting down together, the three of them took two to three months to complete the screenplay. In a 1985 interview, the brothers spoke of a forthcoming project which "takes place in the late Fifties in a skyscraper and is about big business. The characters talk fast and wear sharp clothes." Almost a decade later, *The Hudsucker Proxy* was dusted off, revised and ready for production. As far as most of the critics were concerned it should have been left in the proverbial bottom drawer. Why did it take so long to make?

"The script was written with Raimi before most of the technology that we used existed," Joel explained. "We don't really think of how we're going to do it in a technical sense when we're writing. We were lucky that we couldn't get the money to do it at the time because the sequences would have been a lot cruder if we had shot it then eight or nine years before. There are certain movies that just won't die. And *Hudsucker* was one of them. *Blood Simple* was another which took us forever to get a distributor."

Having completed their four-picture contractual obligation toward Circle Films, the Coens began to look elsewhere for financial support. They found it in the London-based Working Title and in Hollywood producer Joel Silver. Although *Barton Fink* met with meager commercial success, the critical praise was enough to convince Silver that the Coens should be given the chance to work with an even bigger budget for their next film.

The Coens haven't connected with the right piece of commercial material yet [Silver explained]. But one day they will, and they'll hit it out of the park. I've been a fan of theirs for many years. I thought that their style and aesthetic are so articulate and so impressive. Their agent is a close friend of mine and he always knew about my feelings. When they came up with this problem of putting *Hudsucker* together, because it's such a big budget movie, he said, "Well, Joel, here's your chance." I read the script and I thought it was the most accessible of their movies. The key to this, and I want to make this clear, this movie is very funny. I really thought that it could potentially be a big hit movie. I happen to like big hit movies. I always try very hard to make them happen.

On the set of *The Hudsucker Proxy*, the hirsute Silver's expensive gear made a striking contrast with the Coens' casual wear. At the time, the brothers commented: "Joel just really sold himself to us. He said, 'I want you to do your movie and I want to help you to make it, do whatever you want.' And we kept wondering if there was a catch, as you would, and so far there hasn't been a catch." The Coens' autonomy remained, though the budget soared to $25 million.

Joel Silver and the Coens seemed to make strange bedfellows. Silver was stereotyped as The Hollywood Philistine Producer, and he bears more than a passing similarity in his shape and manner to the mogul-producer in *Barton Fink*. On the surface, Joel Silver, a contemporary of Joel Coen's at New York University, did not seem the ideal producer for a Capraesque screwball comedy by two independently-minded, idealistic film-makers. Silver had risen rapidly in the movie business after graduating. He had made his name and fortune from brainless action movies: three *Lethal Weapons*, two *Die Hards*, *48 Hours*, and a couple of Arnold Schwarzenegger pictures, *Predator* and *Commando*. Perhaps Silver wanted a break from the kind of action movie with which he was associated. Once, on *Commando*, he was heard to say, "What's a bunch of Jewish guys doing trying to make this big Teutonic guy look good?"

"Joel Silver's got this reputation for being a Hollywood vulgarian, a producer of big, glass-shattering action movies. But his interests are much more wide-ranging than his press allows," insisted the Coens.

"He was great. He's a very funny guy, a great raconteur and he knows what he's doing. If he's interested, we'll work with him again," Joel said after the *Hudsucker* experience. (To date, they have not worked together again, which could have something to do with the movie being one of Silver's rare box-office disasters, and the Coens' biggest commercial flop.)

Perhaps there is no conscious connection between Joel Silver and a character mentioned *en passant* in Ethan's short story, *Have You Ever Been to Electric Ladyland?*. "There's Nathan Silver, Head of Monsoon. I signed one of his acts, the Hasta La Huega Sunshine Band, back in the eighties. Well, by then it was his only act. That was much the end of Monsoon, uh—Silver's fallen on hard times . . . He lives in the Marina now, Jesus . . . He's probably sitting in his little fucking condo in the Marina, brooding . . . and he's probably very fucking angry with me. Very fucking angry. But this is the business we're in."

Obviously, Joel Silver is a good sport. His temperamental outbursts were caricatured in *Who Framed Roger Rabbit?* (1988), in which he played himself, and for the introduction to the screenplay of *The Hudsucker Proxy* he allowed himself to be interviewed by one Dennis Jacobson, professor of cinema studies at the University of Iowa.

During the interview, Silver, in his rather blunt manner, was able to put the pretentious Coen brothers in their place, and encapsulate much of what they're about. "They would *kvetch* about—say, when I suggested they use Paul Newman. 'No, he's too big, he's iconic—he represents a larger—' a whole line of bullshit . . . Like it's a sin to use a movie star. God forbid someone should actually be enticed into the theater to see one of their movies." He went onto complain that Ethan insisted on playing the leading role, actually doing a screen test. "It was goddamned embarrassing," said Silver. "I suggested Tim Robbins . . . Ethan sulked and things were never right between him and Tim. He never made peace with it. They'd be shooting a scene and you'd see Ethan off in the corner, mouthing the lines as Tim spoke. It was pathetic . . . On the set they just sort of retreat into their storyboards. Don't talk to the actors . . . Joel looks through the camera, looks at the storyboards, walks in and shoves Paul Newman a couple of steps to the left. Just shoves. This is Butch Cassidy here! This man is iconic! You don't shove!"

JACK LIPNICK: I'm taking an interest. Not to

interfere, mind you—hardly seems necessary

in your case. A writer—a storyteller—of your

stature. Givveta me in bold strokes, Bart.

. Gimme the broad outlines. I'm sitting in the

audience, the lights go down, Capitol logo

comes up . . . you're on!

–Barton Fink

52   *You Know . . . for Kids!*

THE HUDSUCKER *Proxy* begins (and ends) on New Year's Eve 1958/1959, when Joel was four years old and Ethan fifteen months. Yet, the film is imbued with the atmosphere of certain Hollywood films of the 1930s, in both the screwball comedy/fantasy screenplay and the art deco sets, while the buildings are from the Twenties, the clothes from the Thirties and Forties, and the furnishings from the Fifties. This could only have a disorienting effect, purposeful as it was, and the only reason for this dislocation seems to be the need to include the invention of the hula hoop.

"Ostensibly we state that the movie is set in New York in the 1950s, but it is not historical—everything is cheated," the Coens stated. "This is a mythical 1950s. We wanted everything to be unspecific, like a fable. A lot revolves around the hula hoop and the Frisbee, both of which did come out in the '50s, but we also play with the invention of the flexible plastic drinking straw, and we have no idea when that came."

Six designers and 200 assistants worked on the sets some three months prior to shooting. *The Hudsucker Proxy* was shot in Chicago as well as in North Carolina because Dino De Laurentiis had built a big sound stage complex there. The film takes place inside Hudsucker Industries, a gigantic office building and factory which has much in common with the soulless, monolithic organization in *Brazil* (1985), which its director Terry Gilliam called "Walter Mitty meets Franz Kafka," a description that could be applied to *The Hudsucker Proxy*, another design-led movie.

Production designer Dennis Gassner, who won an Oscar for his Forties art direction on Warren Beatty's *Bugsy* in 1991, explained his aims. "It is a matter of an emotional state and an illogical state that have to be in sync. My job is to create with those two attitudes in mind, so that the audience feels comfortable with all those different feelings." Something of the grab-bag nature of the conception came out in Gassner's further statements.

"We wanted everything to be big. We wanted Mussburger's office to be like Mussolini's ['30s?]. The table in the conference room is based on a photo from the 1950s [sic]. We transformed a really long room with a 90-meter long corridor into the mailroom, which looks like it could have been designed by Albert Speer ['40s?]." Even more confusing is the "executive toy" that Mussburger has in his office—you know, for adults!—"a perpetual motion gizmo of the swinging ballbearings going click-click-click"—that was introduced in the 1960s. One of the better jokes in the film is that they obediently stop clicking when Mussburger shouts "Wait a minute!" when confronted with Norville's circle on a page.

"The whole circle motif was built into the design of the movie," remarked the Coens. "The tension between vertical lines and circles, you have these tall buildings and these circles everywhere that echoed the plot. It starts at the end and circles back to the beginning. The hula hoop just seemed perfect." (This might also have been a subconscious valedictory homage to Circle Films, who financed their first four movies.) The motif even extends to the halo that the Angel Hudsucker wears when he descends from heaven at the end. "How d'ya like this thing? They're all wearin' 'em upstairs. It's a fad."

"We had to come up with something that this guy was going to invent that on the face of it was ridiculous. Something that would seem, by any sort of rational measure, to be doomed to failure, but something on the other hand the audience already knew was going to be a phenomenal success."

The hula hoop, "you know, for kids," can also be used as an emblem of the movie. A rather useless commodity that serves no moral purpose other than to amuse, despite much of its satire on big business methods. As Georg Seessien has noted: "The hula hoop is an invention that is both inspired and idiotic, the most simple thing in the world, but also something that could only function in a tremendously complicated society."

Allowing Norville to invent the hula hoop, at first called the Extruded Plastic Dingus, is probably the most original and inspired notion in the film. The whole long hula hoop sequence takes the movie beyond its rigidly referential dimension. It begins with the manufacture of the colored hoops, with interjected scenes of the admen trying to come up with a name for it, and the accountants costing it. Finally, piles of the hoops reach the shops, where they lie unsold while a montage shows the prices being reduced from $1.79 to "free with any purchase."

Then the film takes on the tone of the classic French children's film, *The Red Balloon* (1956), which tells of how, on his way to school one morning, a little boy comes across a bright, red balloon hanging around a lamppost. The balloon takes a fancy to the child and attaches itself to him. In *The Hudsucker Proxy*, a red hula hoop follows a little boy down the street, rolls up to him, circles around him before falling down. The boy picks it up, steps inside it and starts hula hooping. Other kids see this and rush to the shop, and it becomes a sensation nationwide.

"Arthur Bridges, the kid, was a real artist," Ethan enthused. "We had a lot of kids come in and audition with the company hula hoop we provided, but Arthur brought his own! He had a lot of charisma, but I never actually heard him say a word on the set."

In order to make the hoop roll by itself, it had water in it to make it more stable, and there was also a ramp release contraption for its movement. It was done by the special effects co-ordinator Peter Chesney, who also did the earlier scene where the newspaper follows Tim Robbins. The newspaper was on a wire, while another wire pulled it into Robbins, with air movers agitating it to give it a natural windy action.

During the end credits, we learn that it was not Norville Barnes or the Coen brothers who invented the hula hoop or the Frisbee. It was a company called Wham-O — "A true American success story," as the title has it.

NEWSREEL ANNOUNCER: As Old Man 1958 hobbles toward his finish, "Barnes' is the name on every American lip—Norville Barnes, young president of Hudsucker Industries, a boy bred in the heartland, but now the toast of New York, Barnes is the brainy inventor of America's latest craze, the hula hoop. Reaping untold profits for his company, the hula hoop is winning a place in the hearts— and hips!—of all American youngsters—Whoa-ho! Did I say youngsters?! Here's Mom, taking a break from her household chores . . .

–The Hudsucker Proxy

53   *Mr. Barnes Goes to Town*

THE HUDSUCKER Proxy is a distillation of Frank Capra's *It's a Wonderful Life* (1946), *Meet John Doe* (1941) and *Mr. Deeds Goes to Town* (1936), with elements of Howard Hawks' *His Girl Friday* (1940), and Preston Sturges' *Christmas in July* (1940), a satire on big business, advertising and the success ethic. In the latter, a young impecunious clerk (Dick Powell) is tricked into believing that he has won $25,000 in a coffee company's slogan competition with his terrible slogan, "If you can't sleep, it isn't the coffee, it's the bunk." The unemployed Norville Barnes is tricked into believing that he is elected President of Hudsucker Industries, when he is merely a stooge to inspire panic in the stockholders.

Norville hovers between being a Capra hero and a Sturges one. Sturges, unlike Capra, never suggested that guileless virtue may defeat entrenched corruption. In his films, the victory is more likely to go to silliness and gullibility. Capra's hick heroes or "wise fools' such as Longfellow Deeds and Jefferson Smith (*Mr. Smith Goes to Washington*, 1939) cling onto their idealism. Capra's comedies from the mid-1930s, glorify the "little man" fighting for what's right and decent and losing the battle until the hectic rush to achieve the happy ending. However, Coens' heroes such as Norville, Hi, Barton Fink, Jerry Lundegaard and the Dude, who are thrown into a situation which forces them to confront violence and corruption, usually act from egotistical motives and are drawn into the system and become tainted themselves.

Norville as played by Tim Robbins is a simple sap, with elements of Gary Cooper's "Cinderella Man" in *Mr. Deeds Goes to Town*, and Henry Fonda in Sturges' *The Lady Eve*, made suckers by strong "career" women—Jean Arthur in the former and Barbara Stanwyck in the latter. Norville arrives from Muncie, Indiana, to look for a job in New York, and accidentally succeeds in business without really trying. Country boy Mr. Deeds comes to town to collect his inheritance and is made to seem ridiculous by a hard-bitten woman journalist. Norville is exposed as a fool by journalist Amy Archer (Archer—Arthur?) played by Jennifer Jason Leigh.

The scenes in the newspaper office are a pastiche of every similar one in Hollywood movies of the 1930s, particularly *His Girl Friday*— fast-talking editor clashing with top reporter, though they know they need each other. "There's a lot of the *His Girl Friday* kind of pace. It was something we were consciously trying to do."

However, the Coens denied having watched any of these films specifically before embarking on *The Hudsucker Proxy*, although they knew them well. "We don't tend to do a specific screening with the purpose of making an upcoming movie, except for really narrow technical reasons. But never for genre reasons. Spielberg used to show *It's a Wonderful Life* to an entire cast and crew and say, 'I want to make a film this good.' We don't have any inspirational film we play for everybody."

AMY ARCHER: Why won't they let us interview him? Genius my eye—why won't they tell us a single solitary thing about him? And just take a look at the mug on this guy—the jutting eyebrows, the simian forehead, the idiotic grin. Why, he has a face only a mother could love—on payday! The only story here is how this guy made a monkey out of you, Al.

–The Hudsucker Proxy

BABE (JEAN ARTHUR): That guy's either the dumbest, the stupidest and most imbecilic

idiot in the world or he's the grandest thing
alive. I can't make him out . . . I'm crucifying
him. Who says we're right? Here's a guy
that's wholesome and fresh and looks to us
like a freak.

–Mr. Deeds Goes To Town

54 Icoens

IT WAS a change of pace for Tim Robbins to play a *naïf*, as he had just come from portraying two smiling, cynical bastards, the cold executive in Robert Altman's *The Player* and the manipulative politician in his own film, *Bob Roberts*. Norville has a similar nerdish name to that of Norval Jones, played by Eddie Bracken, the epitome of nerdishness, in Sturges' *The Miracle of Morgan's Creek* (1944). It is also the sort of name Jerry Lewis used to adopt in his movies. He was always a Seymour, Virgil, Wilbur, Homer or Harvey.

There is a Jerry Lewis-like moment when Norville tries to put out the fire in the wastebasket with the water cooler in the office of his boss, Sidney J. Mussburger. "This came out of rehearsing the scenes with Tim before we started shooting. We had a clear idea of what the sets were going to be like, and the distance he had to cover, what the action was in terms of the fire. The specifics of how he moved and what he was doing with the water jug came out of rehearsal. Tim is also a great improviser, so if you give him a prop or situation he goes off on his own."

Like Robbins, Jennifer Jason Leigh had recently been in an Altman movie, *Short Cuts*, in which she played a housewife who supplements the family income by working as a phone-sex performer, while sitting in her living room changing diapers. According to Joel Silver in his interview with Professor Jacobson, "Joel and Ethan's dream cast was Ethan as Norville, Jeanne Moreau as the girl . . . He had some line of shit of how it had to be a powerful woman . . . an iconic strong feminine—you wouldn't believe the line of shit on this guy. He said he wanted the equivalent of Rosalind Russell. I said fuck, *get Rosalind Russell*—she's younger than Jeanne Moreau!"

Here, in the Rosalind Russell role, Jason Leigh's voice is a curious blend of Jean Arthur's emotionally-charged croak, which gave a new meaning to the word wisecrack, and Katharine Hepburn's celebrated quaver that she herself described as "a cross between Donald Duck and a Stradivarius." Unfortunately, Jason Leigh's portrayal comes over as an irritating impersonation rather than a performance, reflecting the film as a whole—a smart imitation rather than the genuine article. "Jennifer just came in with that voice when we first started, and we liked it so there it was. It wasn't a big point of discussion," Joel remarked.

Paul Newman, who was first choice for Sidney J. Mussburger, has a gruff voice, and is cast against type as a Machiavellian business tycoon. Newman was the first really big Hollywood star in the Coens' movies. None of the other actors they had used up to then or were to use in the two following films, were big stars. It was only with the entry of George Clooney in *O Brother, Where Art Thou?* and Brad Pitt in *To The White Sea* that one was aware of creeping staritis.

"They obviously have a very perverted vision. Perverted, yes, I think it's a good word," said Newman, referring to the Coens. "They don't tell a story directly, they move like crabs and it's just refreshing to find something so original and eccentric." His biggest adjustment was learning their language. "Well, they don't use Stanislavsky language. They don't speak in the word of the active verb. They are not interested in the psychology. They are more interested in the pacing—'faster, faster'. But they have very good eyes. They may not express it in a way I'm accustomed to, but that's alright. In this case it's up to the actor to accommodate their style rather than them to accommodate my style."

Newman, who had been serious for so long, told the Coens that he had not enjoyed himself more in any movie since *Slapshot*. The only thing he was concerned about was showing his legs. In one scene where he is being fitted by the tailor, he is standing there in his boxer shorts and he thought he had knobbly knees. There is a wonderfully eccentric moment when Mussburger is dangling upside down out of the 44th floor window ("not counting the mezzanine") like Harold Lloyd while Norville holds him up by his trouser legs. Mussburger suddenly has a flashback in which the Italian tailor offers to put a double stitch in his trousers for strength, which Mussburger declines. But the tailor puts one in anyway, and his life is saved.

55   *Technophilia*

LIKE CAPRA'S *Meet John Doe*, which begins atop a skyscraper where Gary Cooper is contemplating suicide, *The Hudsucker Proxy* opens with Norville about to throw himself from the 44th floor. When Sam Raimi and the brothers started the script, they began with the idea of Norville jumping off a building. "But then you're at the end of the script and you have to figure out how to save him. That stumped us for a while. And we had to resort to the ridiculous extreme of stopping time."

Norville jumps off the building at the stroke of midnight on New Year's Eve, but Moses, the mystical clock-keeper, stops the huge clock that dominates Hudsucker Industries, under which reads the legend, "The Future Is Now," thus freezing him in mid-air. However, the evil Aloysius (Harry Bugin) starts the clock again, until something jams it. "We had the problem of stopping the clock but didn't know how. It was the co-producer [Graham Place] who said, 'What about dentures?' The only problem was whether the actor playing the part of Aloysius wore dentures, because we didn't suppose he would let us extract his teeth for the scene. But he had absolutely no teeth and said, 'I'll be happy to take them out for you boys.' It was a happy coincidence. Teeth are always funny. When in doubt use dentures."

THE MOST memorable image in the film is the suicidal jump from the skyscraper by Waring Hudsucker, played by Charles Durning. "We cast Durning on the idea that a fat person falling 40 floors is a lot funnier than a thin person falling 40 floors," Joel explained. "Charles actually used to be a dancer, and all that stuff he does at the beginning where he gets up and digs his heel and shakes the tension out of his body was all Charles. He choreographed all his movements."

Hudsucker's fall, and later Norville's, was achieved by using the blue screen process. Characters are shot against a blue backing, and these images and those of a separately shot background are scanned into a computer. In this case, the actor was shot flying by wire in white light against a blue background which was removed later—blue is used because the "bleeding" of color onto the rest of the picture is less troublesome. Then a scale model of the skyscraper was filmed and the two brought together.

"Essentially the falling sequence was done on a long miniature of the building that was lying on the floor of the studio and we would shoot plates of tracking down the length of the building and we composited that on a computer with shots of the actors who were suspended from wires with huge air guns hitting them."

The Hudsucker Proxy certainly had more technical problems than any of their other movies. "It was a learning process for us and the making of the movie was an introduction to a whole new world. We've always been interested in problem solving, whether it's visual effects or other kinds of effects."

The Coens have admitted to being technophiles, but they insist that their technophilia is all in the service of telling a story. "What is interesting about making movies are the new technological problems that each one poses, though we have no technical training. We did not learn about all this stuff—the compositing and the effects work—for the sake of learning about it."

On *The Hudsucker Proxy*, they had the first unit working, plus the miniature unit, plus the blue screen unit shooting the actor in front of the blue screen, plus Sam Raimi's second unit overlapping, and sometimes all shooting at the same time. Roger Deakins, the cinematographer, had to oversee all the four different units, making sure they would work.

The opening shot when the camera pans through Manhattan in the snow combined matte-painting, live action and miniatures. The "techni" Coens explained:

> The first shots you see in the movie are all of the models clustered together ... The camera was on a crane that moved through the miniatures. The biggest problem was how to figure out how to do the snow. Since we were doing it in real time, on miniatures, we essentially needed miniature snow that fell at the right speed. We ended up using little mini-fibres ... and after a lot of experimentation we got it to fall at a slow rate that looked like snow. The last shot in this sequence is actually a combination. We got off the miniatures and we shot Tim coming out onto a full-scale set ... We snowed him live, so we had to get out of this previous snow and seamlessly get to real snow ... We sort of papered over the difference with a little computer-generated snow to smooth the seam between the two. The two snows are different in that they fall at different rates ...

56   Parodies Lost

THE HUDSUCKER *Proxy* was the Coens' most expensive film and their only box-office disaster. "In a weird kind of way, *Hudsucker* is almost an exception to the other movies we have made. It was almost calculated to prove what people thought about our previous movies . . . *Hudsucker* truly is a comment on the genres it draws from. It is very self-conscious, which is not the case with, say, *Miller's Crossing*. It shows you how hard it is to second-guess these things. If we'd had to predict in the abstract which would be the more successful, *Fargo* or *Hudsucker*, we would have certainly bet on *Hudsucker*. *Fargo* seemed like a very obscure regional exercise. In fact, *Hudsucker* made less than any other film we've released, and *Fargo* made the most. It's just very, very hard to predict, but you have to try, because you have to make some sort of estimation to justify the money you're going to spend."

No matter how brilliant *The Hudsucker Proxy* is technically and conceptually, the movie cannot help but suffer from being a too self-conscious pastiche. The Coens have tried to butter their toast on both sides, and ended up with neither. Those who know their 1930 and 1940 screwball and/or fantasy comedies consider that Howard Hawks, Frank Capra and Preston Sturges, to whom palpable allusions are made, did it better. Those for whom the references mean nothing, lose an essential component in the appreciation of the film. The Coens, therefore, lost their audience.

57   Third Sighting

JOEL AND Frances, with their newly adopted baby Pedro, and Ethan have arrived at the Edinburgh Festival in August 1995. The brothers have come to be interviewed on stage by Mark Cousins, the director of the Festival. They made sure that they flew in (standard class) some days before the interview, so they could do a bit of touring in Scotland. They rented a car with a kiddie seat, and off they went.

They're now back in Edinburgh, and Joel and Ethan are waiting in the bar of the huge MGM cinema drinking a few Becks beers with Mark Cousins, who is dressed like Norville Barnes in a 1940s suit, dicky, suspenders and bow tie. They are amused, flattered and impressed by this gesture, although they seldom go overboard emotionally. I knock back a beer, and listen to Joel telling Mark that he and Frances love Scotland so much that they are seriously considering buying a house there.

The staff of the cinema had arranged to close off the small bar to all but invited guests. However, a few young Coenheads have managed to find their way into the bar and are welcomed in by the brothers, who answer their questions politely. A little while later, on stage, they are pretty relaxed, but talk more easily about the technical aspects of making *The Hudsucker Proxy* than about plot development, social or political themes and character motivation.

We're now around a long table at the restaurant in the ultra-modern Point Hotel. Frances and Pedro have joined us. There is a noisy family atmosphere. Frances asks Mark Cousins who the woman sitting on the other side is. He tells her it is Suso Cecchi D'Amico, the celebrated Italian screenwriter, who wrote a number of Luchino Visconti's films, as well as having contributed to Vittorio de Sica's *Bicycle Thieves*, one of Joel's favorite movies. Frances leans over to Joel and indicates D'Amico. Joel is delighted and an animated conversation takes place between Joel and D'Amico above my head, physically speaking. I am busy speaking to Leslie Caron, who is sitting beside me, and whom I had met previously in Paris while researching my Jean Renoir biography. On my other side is Dianne Ladd, who asks me my star sign, and declares her belief in astrology. I never get to say very much to the Coens. It is a pity that I don't ask Dianne Ladd what my future holds, because if I knew that I was going to write this biography a few years later, I might have forced myself upon the brothers a little more.

YAH! YAH!

IX

"If a movie like *Fargo* succeeds, then clearly

nothing makes much sense, and so, you know,

you might as well make whatever kind of movie

you want and hope for the best."

"FAILURE SHOULD never lead to despair," says Charles Durning as Waring Hudsucker. This could have been a message to the Coens after *The Hudsucker Proxy*'s negative critical and commercial reception. There seemed a lesson to be learned. They had aimed at making a big, expensive Hollywood movie of sorts, as they had with *Miller's Crossing*, and it bombed.

According to William Preston Robertson, "Joel and Ethan were contemplating, with considerable ill ease, just what the point of things was—you know: moviemaking wise. The broad artistic license the movie industry had granted them for so many years in the hope that such patience might someday be rewarded with a box-office hit in addition to a merely critical one was, the Coen brothers believed, swiftly narrowing. The clock was ticking. The heat was on." The answer seemed to be to return to the world of low-budget movies with *Fargo* ($7 million) and to their Minnesotan roots.

"It was nice doing *Fargo* after *Hudsucker*. *Hudsucker* was quite a big picture. *Fargo* was a small picture so we could be more flexible. A smaller crew and a much more intimate production are advantages in many ways. It was fun for all of us and a relief in a way," commented the Coens.

FARGO OPENS with the following text: "This is a true story. The events depicted in this film took place in Minnesota in 1987. At the request of the survivors the names have been changed. Out of respect for the dead, the rest has been told exactly as it occurred."

Could it be that the Coens, whose genre films echo other genre films, and are full of cross-references and self-reflection, should now be offering a faithfully reconstructed true story? After the failure of the fantastical *The Hudsucker Proxy*, they seemed to be going in the opposite direction in desperation. Who were they kidding? There cannot be a spectator who, by the end of *Fargo*, believed that it "has been told exactly as it occurred." The Coens later admitted: "The film is based on a real event, but the details of the story and the characters are pure invention. What didn't interest us was to make a documentary film so we didn't have to do any research on the nature of the murder. By informing the public that it was based on fact, we prepared them not to see the film as an ordinary thriller. But there was a kidnapping of a wife in Minnesota in 1987. We're not big on research. We just didn't care at a certain point. We found the story compelling, and beyond that, we were not interested in rendering the details as they were." At the end of his tangential introduction to the screenplay of *Fargo*, Ethan gives the game away. "It aims to be both homey and exotic, and *pretends* to be true."

59 You Betcha!

There were two or three things that attracted us to the subject. It took place in a region with which we were very familiar. Also it involved a kidnapping, which we like to shoot. There was also the possibility of shooting a crime film with characters away from stereotypes of the genre. It would have a specific background and not a fictional one. Paradoxically, what is closest to home can seem exotic. We can't read about the South Seas without comparing it to Minneapolis, and can't describe Minneapolis, even to ourselves, without it seeming like the South Seas.

That specific Minnesota atmosphere was where the juice was for us. *Fargo* evokes the abstract landscape of our childhood—a bleak, windswept tundra, resembling Siberia except for its Ford dealerships, and Hardee's restaurants.

One forgets that within the stereotype of the midwest there are pockets of different cultures and idiosyncratic accents. When we were growing up we weren't conscious of the Scandinavian heritage that marked our region. Our parents still live in the region, and we return often, so we didn't have to do research into the manner of speaking, the expressions, the cadences. After all, this culture formed us. We felt as though we had been divorced a little from this environment where we were brought up.

Time magazine wrote that the Coens' attitude toward the Minnesotan characters was condescending. "I'm sure—and I know Joel and Ethan well—that they were not making fun of the people," Frances McDormand declared. "And many of the actors are from that area—the kidnapped wife is from Fargo itself, for example—so the regional mannerisms were very familiar to them."

"It's very easy to offend people. There's always going to be someone who feels affronted for regional, ethnic, or whatever sorts of reasons. In Minnesota the public was split in its reaction to the film," remarked the Coens. "The locals who liked it saw in it something specific that could not have been made by someone who does not or has not lived there. But there were others who were deeply insulted. It's hard to make something without somebody misunderstanding it. People who are not from that region think we're somehow exaggerating the behavior or the accents, but most of the actors in the movie are Minnesotans, and they're using their own accents. [Frances McDormand, William H. Macy and Harve Presnell had dialogue coaches to teach them the accent of the region.]

60 Margie

"WHEN YOU write a character for someone, it's not because the actor resembles the character. It's like you have a suit of clothes and you feel a certain actor's going to fit them. In fact, if someone we've written a part for can't do the movie we'd just as soon not make it." (They did break this rule on *Miller's Crossing*, after having to replace Trey Wilson with Albert Finney.)

Joel certainly had to pacify his wife by writing a part for her. "Fran's the only one of that group who consistently says, 'Are you writing for me?', 'When are you going to write me another part?' I don't get that from John Turturro, you know, I don't get that from him at home."

"I love their movies," Frances stated. "But on the other hand I had to have my own career, not only because it makes for better stories when you come home at night, but also just pride-wise. It was important, especially when I was younger, that people couldn't say that I got a role because Joel was my boyfriend. Now it doesn't matter. If people want to say I slept with him for thirteen years to get the part in *Fargo*, let them!"

The Coens have always written strong parts for strong women: Prison Officer "Ed" (*Raising Arizona*), Verna Bernbaum (*Miller's Crossing*), Audrey Taylor (*Barton Fink*), Amy Archer (*The Hudsucker Proxy*), Penny McGill (*O Brother, Where Art Thou?*) and the two roles created by McDormand, Abby (*Blood Simple*) and Marge Gunderson (*Fargo*), twelve years apart. In contrast, Ethan's short stories have very few women in them. They tend to concentrate on an almost exclusively masculine world. In Marge, the brothers had written possibly their best female part, and the warmest. It does help when the director is in love with the star, as one can witness in other examples such as the Marlene Dietrich—Josef Von Sternberg, Vincente Minnelli—Judy Garland, Jean-Luc Godard—Anna Karina, Woody Allen—Diane Keaton/Mia Farrow collaborations.

Since making her film debut in *Blood Simple*, McDormand had gone from strength to strength on stage, and on big and small screens. She gained a Tony nomination for her Stella in *A Streetcar Named*

Desire on Broadway, appeared regularly on TV in *Hill Street Blues*, played the fearful wife of a Klan-minded sheriff in Alan Parker's *Mississippi Burning*, for which she was Oscar-nominated, and she was in Ken Loach's *Hidden Agenda*. She had played a German Jew in *Paradise Road* and an Irish nanny in *Talk of Angels*, rivalling Meryl Streep in her range of accents.

But, with *Fargo*, despite around twenty films to her credit—or debit, as the case may be—McDormand emerged into real stardom. Before the Oscar enabled this metamorphosis to take place, she was only recognized from role to role.

"After *Blood Simple*, everybody thought I was from Texas. After *Mississippi Burning*, everybody thought I was from Mississippi and uneducated. After *Fargo*, everybody's going to think I'm from Minnesota, pregnant, and have blond hair. I don't think you can ever completely transform yourself on film, but if you do your job well, you can make people believe that you're the character you're trying to be. I'm a character actress, plain and simple. Who can worry about a career? Movie stars have careers—actors work, and then they don't work, and then they work again."

Fargo was the brothers' first significant collaboration with McDormand since *Blood Simple*, and there were a few awkward moments in the first week of shooting. "I assumed I knew what Joel was going to say before he finished his sentence. Which isn't unlike our relationship the rest of the time. On *Blood Simple*, when Joel said cut after a take, the way he and Ethan laughed either meant it was good or it wasn't. It was the same on *Fargo*, except for one scene—the last meeting between Marge and Jerry when I went crazy and didn't know what to do. I had to find my way through it myself."

Joel and Frances did, however, stay in adjoining hotel rooms during the shoot. "I know what he's like when he's making a movie. He's a slob. And I'm kind of neat. And especially if you only have one room. I didn't want him coming in, leaving his dirty clothes everywhere. So we made my room the living room, where we could invite people over, and his room was the bedroom and laundry room."

The Coens wrote the part for McDormand, not only because Joel was being nagged by her but because "one of her strengths as an actor is that she has a lack of vanity when she's playing a character. She's not looking for what makes her look good, but what's right for the character. Frances read the script and suggested she should throw up because she's got morning sickness."

"I looked like a huge turd out there in the snow, waddling around. Joel said, 'You know, the character does not have to be as unattractive as you're making her.' But I love the way I look as Marge." However, would even this simple-minded police force allow a woman in such advanced pregnancy to do such dangerous work? "You betcha!" according to McDormand. Apparently it is not a rarity. "In St. Paul, I met Officer Nancy, who was seven months pregnant and still working. She was on the vice squad doing search and seizure. She was going to go into the office and do a desk job in the middle of her eighth month, but until then, she was still out there doing it." One has to take McDormand's word for it, but without that knowledge, it seems merely one of the Coens' perverse needs to find something quirky to add to the character.

Not since *Raising Arizona* had the Coens depicted a marriage, happy or otherwise. Neither Tom Reagan, Barton Fink nor Norville Barnes ends up with the girl, as is the Hollywood custom. In *Fargo*, the marriage between Marge and the non-demonstrative, well-named Norm, dull and habitual as it may be, rings true. It also has the first genuinely happy ending, as distinct from the postmodern resolutions of *Raising Arizona* and *The Hudsucker Proxy*, with only a hint of condescension. "I'm so proud a you, Norm. Heck, we're doin" pretty good, Norm." "I love you, Margie." "I love you, Norm." "Two more months." "Two more months."

MARGE (ON A PUBLIC PHONE): Yah, this is Marge

Gunderson from up Brainerd, we spoke—Yah.

Well, actually I'm in town here. I had to do a

few things in the Twin Cities, so I thought I'd

check in with ya . . . Oh, yah? Well, maybe I'll

go visit him if I have the . . . No, I can find

that . . . Well, thanks a bunch. Say, do you

happen to know a good place for lunch in the

downtown area? . . . Yah, the Radisson . . .

Oh yah? Is it reasonable?

–Fargo

61   Family Values

BESIDES FRANCES McDormand, the Coen "family" were gathered together again for *Fargo*. Principally Roger Deakins, the cinematographer, and their regular composer Carter Burwell, who came up with the central theme, which he based on a popular Scandinavian melody. Unfortunately, Richard Hornung, their costume designer since *Raising Arizona*, was dying of AIDS, but he recommended Mary Zophres, his one-time assistant, to take over, and she has been with the Coens ever since. Also on the team was Tricia Cooke, the assistant editor, now married to Ethan, who had divorced Hilary.

Steve Buscemi, among the brilliant cast, had appeared in only small roles previously for the Coens: in one scene as the talkative and nervous Mink in *Miller's Crossing*, and as the hotel clerk ("My name is Chet") in *Barton Fink*. As Carl Showalter in *Fargo*, a role written specifically for him, Buscemi expertly switches from the menacing to the comic, echoing the tone of the film itself.

Among the new members of the "family" was William H. Macy as the nerdish husband Jerry, whose sudden solitary fits of anger are

miniature comic gems. Macy made his name in David Mamet's theater company and in Mamet's films, while Harve Presnell, as Macy's
despotic father-in-law, made his reputation in musicals. "He actually
did a 'dancin' in the snow' musical number, but we cut it out for
length," joked Joel.

The actress Kristin Rudrüd, as the kidnapped wife, actually came
from the area, and is the most mistreated of all the characters.
Although she is the fulcrum around which the plot revolves, nobody
(including the Coens) really gives a damn what happens to her, not
even her father, who is willing to risk her life to save the ransom
money. Once she is kidnapped, the actress was replaced by a double
with a hood on her head.

Among the final rolling credits, there is one that aroused the
curiosity of those that bother to stay and read them. There is no name
beside the credit for Victim in the Field, but a sign that looks like the
logo for the Minneapolis musician formally known as Prince, turned
on its side with a smiley face drawn on it. When asked, the brothers
refused to reveal who played the man seen at the window of a car
wearing a red cap and jacket who witnesses the shooting of the state
trooper and is then shot while running away. It was, in fact, the storyboard artist formerly known as J. Todd Anderson. "It's top secret if I
tell you," Anderson whispered to a reporter. "I'll have to kill you.
Besides I want to work with those guys again."

CARL: Look at that. Twin Cities. IDS Building,

the big glass one. Tallest skyscraper in the

Midwest. After the Sears, uh, Chicago. You

never been to Minneapolis?

GRIMSRUD: No.

CARL: "No." First thing you've said in the last

four hours. That's a, that's a fountain of con-

versation, man. That's a geyser. I mean, whoa,

daddy, stand back, man. Shit, I'm sitting here

driving, man, doin' all the driving, whole fuck-

ing way from Brainerd, tryin' to, you know,

tryin' to chat, keep our spirits up, fight the

boredom of the road, and you can't say one

fucking thing just in the way of conversation.

–Fargo

62 *Whiteout*

FARGO HAS certain resemblances to *Blood Simple* and *Raising Arizona*. The three films were made on a modest scale, they treat crime and kidnapping and are very specific in their geographic location. But *Blood Simple* was influenced by horror movies and the novels of James M. Cain, and *Raising Arizona* had cartoons and slapstick comedy as models.

"We approached *Fargo* from a different stylistic viewpoint. In a very dry manner. We also wanted the camera to report the story as an observer. We didn't want any diversions and digressions. Each incident was at the service of the intrigue. Except the interpolated scene between Frances and her old [Japanese] friend from school. We even permitted the heroine to enter halfway through the film. [Actually, a third of the way through.] It was also a way to signify to the audience that it wasn't a typical genre movie." This is the converse of *Psycho*, where the heroine (Janet Leigh) exits a third of the way through.

Another curiosity is that the principal action takes place in Brainerd, which is in Minnesota, and not in Fargo, which is in North Dakota. Fargo is the town where Jerry Lundegaard (William H. Macy) first meets the two hoods (Steve Buscemi, Peter Stormare), to arrange the kidnapping of his wife, but is not where the main events take place. "We liked the sound of the name. There is no other significance. There is a Western connotation with Wells Fargo, but it wasn't voluntary, and it's a pity that some people thought it was. We just felt Brainerd was not cool enough."

The trouble is that Minnesota wasn't cool enough. The plan was to shoot entirely in and around Minneapolis. The shoot began in a record high temperature winter in Minnesota. They worked for a while with artificial snow, but when the snow didn't come they had to chase the migratory snowfall into North Dakota for the large exteriors. "We went to Minneapolis in the winter hoping for snow. As a rule, the winter is ridiculously cold and snowy. But predictably, since we were going there to shoot a movie and looking for snow, it turned out to be warm. The second warmest winter in a hundred years. And very dry. We ended up shooting about two weeks in North Dakota.

"There we found what we were looking for. A cloudy sky without direct sunlight, no visible horizon, and a neutral and diffuse light. It was a dramatic and oppressive landscape. There were no mountains and no forests. It was flat and desolate. That's what we wanted to appear on screen."

"FIRST OF all, we were trying to reflect the bleak aspect of living in that area in the wintertime—what the light and this sort of landscape does to one psychologically. It was very important to us to shoot on non-sunny days. We talked early on with Roger Deakins about shooting landscapes where you couldn't really see the horizon line—so that the snow-covered ground would be the same color as the sky—

on these sort of slight gray or whiteout days that you get in Minnesota. We scheduled the show so that we could be able to avoid blue skies as much as possible."

"They wanted the look of the exteriors to be quite bland," explained Deakins. "Difficult to do something that's bland but not boring. They wanted it very real, very middle America. I think the Coens would probably make a blank white wall interesting."

"The whole idea of the car emerging ghostlike out of the snow—the whiteness and weirdness—was important to us. We talked with Roger about these landscapes where you couldn't really see where the horizon was, where the ground melted into the sky. We put everything else aside and didn't shoot until we got that feeling. It was nerve-racking."

"On Fargo they talked about making it like a documentary," said Deakins, who came from documentary films. "The camera as an observer. In the end, even the first shot was a 50—60 foot dolly track. But it was much more observational. We used longer lenses. We shot the night scenes black rather than illuminating them with Moscow lights. The day would be all white." The Coens told the production designer Rick Heinrichs to find the most soul-deadening, flattened locations. "He'd find some dumpy café, and we'd say, no, it's too good . . . Less color, less design, less kitsch. Now that can be hard. We wanted no design. Absolutely nothing."

However, the art department was allowed to break the monotony by designing and building the statue of Paul Bunyan, the giant hero from American mythology, wielding his axe. It was his mighty footprints that are said to have created Minnesota's 11,000 lakes. On the plinth is the legend: "Welcome to Brainerd, Home of Paul Bunyan." The joke is that Heinrichs and his team have given Bunyan madly staring eyes so that he looks like an axe murderer. In fact, he resembles the kidnapper Grimsrud, who buries an axe in his partner's neck and then chops him up at the end.

63   *Roger's Grandmother*

"WE DON'T look through the viewfinder that much. We believe in our cameraman. When you work regularly with someone you have more and more confidence in them. There is a sort of telepathic communication between you."

Early on, the Coens had discussions with Roger Deakins to establish the visual style of the film. "We always involve Roger very early. After we finish the script we sit down with him and talk in general terms about how we were thinking about it from a visual point of view. Then, in specific terms, we do a draft of the storyboards with Roger, then refine those ideas scene by scene. Frequently storyboards can be tossed out of the window when we get on set and the three of us see something we'd prefer to do, given the location or whatever. But they're there as a guide, a point of departure for us to start talking about the movie with Roger."

On set, Deakins and the Coens will work out the dynamics of a given scene, with Joel and Ethan frequently switching roles. "Either of them will be talking about the shot, lenses or whatever," Deakins explained. "They just swap around duties. I think having a relationship on a couple of films before this made it easier to do a project on a small budget and get more out of it. Once you've got a pattern of working, you know how to cut corners, and what each other's wants are. We don't have as much discussion on the set anymore about shots. We basically block the scene in the morning. And go through the shots. It's quite a quiet set."

WITH ITS limited budget, all of the film, save for two small bathroom sets, was shot on location, using available exterior light through windows when they could. "I was very much working off natural sources," Deakins explained. "A lot of the film was shot in bars and clubs. If there wasn't daylight we couldn't do the shots. Most of the interiors, which were mainly small bedrooms, houses and offices as opposed to big spaces, were lit by window-light during the day. The impulse here was to de-dramatize things rather than dramatize them."

The Coens elected to shoot the scene of the drop, when Wade Gustafson (Harve Presnell) comes to pay the kidnappers, on a snow-covered exterior parking garage. "We chose that location because there was a smokestack belching away on the roof of a nearby building, and we wanted to use that as a background for part of the scene. The special effects people had to snow that entire area because there was no snow."

"I worked with a lot more colors on *Fargo* than I have on either of the Coens' other films," said Deakins, a paradoxical statement—when one thinks of *Fargo*, one thinks white. "Photographically, I wouldn't say that I've been more bold on *Fargo*, but I did play around a bit more. It's actually one of my favorite projects, though I don't think anything shouts out, 'Wow, this is great photography!' If you've got a huge amount of money and great big sets, it's actually not hard to make it look good. It's often more of a challenge to try to give a film a coherent style from start to finish, one that remains interesting and feels real." In fact, those members of the Academy Awards did say "Wow, this is great photography!" by nominating Deakins' work on *Fargo* for an Oscar.

Working with Deakins has rewarded the Coens with a kindred collaborator and a close friend. "We're lucky we found Roger. He understands what we are after, and frequently comes up with stuff on the spot that reflects what we want to do in the scene."

But Deakins, like his predecessor Barry Sonnenfeld, has had a long-standing debate with the Coens about their affinity for wide-angle lenses. "We've gotten better actually partly because of Roger's influence. He has been quietly bringing us around to longer lenses. It's a joke between the three of us. We're now up to 32mm and 35mm lenses!"

Deakins retorts: "On *Hudsucker* I'd put on a 28mm and they'd say, 'Shouldn't this be an 18mm?'" But after three films, Deakins' cajoling seems to have taken root. "On *Fargo* we shot longer lenses than the Coens have ever shot before. Our main lens was probably a 40mm or a 32mm, whereas normally it would be 25mm."

"I think it's still a prejudice with us, wanting to go wider more often," the Coens remarked. "It has to do with wanting to enhance the camera moves. For instance in *Hudsucker*, a lot of the effects stuff, the falling shots, were quite wide in the interest of making the moves and the falling more dynamic. In *Fargo* we moved the camera far less and used a lot more over-the-shoulders.

"Whenever we fret about some kind of detail in the frame, or start looking too closely at something, Roger simply says, 'Well that could be my Gran in the shot and she's been dead for twenty years. Don't worry about it.' Actually, there's a lot of discussion about Roger's grandmother on the set. It's an important part of his work and it shouldn't be overlooked."

64   Chip off the Old Block

ON THE surface, *Fargo* is perhaps the Coens' most conventional film and therefore their most popular. It is unflashy—there are no flash-ins, flashbacks or flashforwards. There are no dream sequences. Unlike *Blood Simple* and *Miller's Crossing*, its plot is lucid. It avoids the broad strokes and humor of *Raising Arizona* and *The Big Lebowski*, and is less allusive than *The Hudsucker Proxy* and *O Brother, Where Art Thou?*. Though one can find a plethora of cross-references and postmodern ironies in their other films, critics have found it difficult to use the dreaded word about it. The Coens are always *kvetching* about the way critics find influences from other movies or novels (i.e. those of Kafka) that they have not seen or read or even heard of.

However, in order to continue the critical convention, one could suggest that *Fargo* does evoke, at a pinch, whether intentional or coincidental, François Truffaut's *Shoot the Pianist* (1962), which has a kidnapping, a snowbound hideout, a couple of semi-comic gang-sters, and a death in the snow. It also contains a visual joke of which the Coens would approve. When the sleazy nightclub owner exclaims to another character, "If I'm lying, may my mother drop dead!," Truffaut cuts to a shot of an old woman dropping to the floor. The Coens used a similar flash-in in *The Hudsucker Proxy*, as Paul Newman remembers his tailor while dangling outside the skyscraper window. *Shoot the Pianist* also happened to be based on a pulp American *noir* novel, *Down There* by David Goodis, of which the Coens were certainly aware.

Yet *Fargo* has the Coens' fingerprints all over it. Like the other movies, it manages to move seamlessly back and forth between black humor, violent crime drama and genial comedy, while telling a good yarn. The semi-stylized dialogue, so important to the films, is here given another dimension by the "yah-yah" rhythms of the local dialect. And it is superbly photographed, with the white acting as a blank canvas on which are painted memorable images such as the stunning high overhead shot of Macy walking to his car through the snow.

The only jarring note is the unnecessary pandering to the horror crowd—a remnant of the *Evil Dead* days—when Buscemi is being fed into the mechanical wood-chipper, although we only see some of his leg sticking out of it. To illustrate how props in films can take on talismanic properties, the wood-chipper, owned by Milo Durben, a Delano farmer who acted as dolly grip on the film, had its own float in the 1996 Delano Fourth of July parade and was in the window of Dayton's store in downtown Minneapolis as part of a movie display. Milo and his wife have continued to use the machine to chip wood on their farm, presumably now cleansed of bits of Buscemi.

65 *Pedro Coen*

JOEL AND Frances live in an Upper West Side apartment, while Ethan and Tricia live in Kips Bay, on New York's East Side. The brothers' office is in an apartment building on the Upper West Side. High on a shelf looms a replica of the statue of Paul Bunyan, who represents tall stories, of which they are masters.

Just before filming began on *Fargo*, Frances and Joel, who had been married for twelve years, adopted a Paraguayan baby boy, Pedro. Ethan and Tricia's son Buster was born during the filming in January 1996. The personal changes in the brothers' lives might have caused their mellowing toward marriage and parenthood in *Fargo*.

Having a child changed the two families' schedules somewhat. It was more difficult for Joel, Frances and Pedro to stay together, because of McDormand's acting commitments. "Joel only leaves to go away to work once every two years," Frances explained. "I'm the one who goes off every few months. I've been planning to be a mother most of my adult life, so this is the way it happened. I'm not planning to have any other children. I started too late. I can barely keep up with Pedro now. But I don't know what I'll be doing in five years."

Frances loves children and spends much of her spare time as a volunteer with the 52nd Street Project based in the Hell's Kitchen district of Manhattan. "I've been involved with it for twelve years. It's basically recreational for kids from seven to fourteen and takes place in the world of the theater. We do playwriting classes with the kids and in the summer we take ten of them away for the week to work on plays. The adult volunteers come in and help kids who are having trouble in school." She also claimed that "One of the best things that happened to me—and I mean this most sincerely—was doing this *Sesame Street* video, *Big Bird Gets Lost*, which helps kids if they get lost."

After completing *Fargo*, the family went to Australia, and Joel and Pedro spent time on the beaches of Port Douglas, in Queensland, while Frances was making *Paradise Road* nearby. "Oh, it was fantastic," said Joel. "Four weeks in Port Douglas. I just hung out on the beach with our little boy. Great beaches. We went up to Cooktown and all that." The relaxation was necessary for all the tiring publicity that was to come.

66   Roderick Jaynes

FARGO WAS up for seven Oscars at the 1997 ceremony: Best Director (Joel Coen), Best Actress (Frances McDormand), Best Supporting Actor (William H. Macy), Best Screenplay (Ethan and Joel Coen), Best Cinematography (Roger Deakins) and Best Editing (Roderick Jaynes).

Roderick Jaynes, you will recall, was the mysterious and reclusive Englishman who emerged from his home in Sussex into the world to edit *Blood Simple*, *Barton Fink* and *Fargo*, and to write the introductions to the published screenplays of *Barton Fink* and *Miller's Crossing*. Besides the Coens' movies, he was said to have edited a British comedy called *The Mad Weekend*, starring Alastair Sim and Basil Radford, *Beyond Mombasa* and *Operation Fort Petticoat*. (There is no record of a film with this exact title. Jaynes was probably confusing *Guns of Fort Petticoat* and *Operation Petticoat*.) Jaynes, a member of BAFTA (British Academy of Film and Television Arts), won a British Academy Award for *Barton Fink*, and enrolled the Coens in the Academy.

"I'm not sure why the lads called me on their fourth picture, *Barton Fink*; our last conversation had ended with sharp words on both sides." However, Jaynes accepted, but found that the footage he had been given had "the Borstal sensibility of the boys' earlier efforts—entire scenes covered without a proper camera angle, tattiness of setting and wardrobe, and actors once again encouraged to bellow and banshee." He was taken off the picture, although, masochistically, the Coens decided to ask him to edit *Fargo*. Because of it, Roderick Jaynes had gained an Academy Award nomination. His main rival for the award was Walter Murch for *The English Patient*. The question was, would Jaynes turn up at the ceremony? The Coens insisted that he would be there. They told the press that Jaynes was very excited about the prospect of winning and would make a "thank you" speech if he did.

Unfortunately, on the big night, Jaynes didn't show. When asked where Jaynes was, the Coens replied, "Oh, he's back at home in Haywards Heath watching cricket on TV."

However, Jaynes was soon to get a terrible shock. He would discover, on the eve of the Oscars, that he didn't exist. The Coens never told him. *Daily Variety* had been informed by a mole that the Coens had invented Jaynes when they were working on *Blood Simple*, over a decade earlier, because they thought there were enough Coens on the credits already. Nobody had bothered to question Jaynes' existence before the nomination came up. Who cares about editors?

"When we got an editing nomination, we were going to have Albert Finney in disguise, as a friend of Jaynes," to accept the award on his behalf, but the Academy wouldn't let us do that, because of Marlon Brando." In 1973, Brando, who won the Best Actor award for *The Godfather*, used his non-appearance at the ceremony as a platform for airing a personal grievance. Spurning the award on his behalf was a native American girl called Sacheen Littlefeather, who came on stage to read a letter from Brando, to complain about his country's treatment of her people. Proxy acceptances have been proscribed ever since.

Actually, Jaynes was not the first pseudonymous nominee. In 1957, during the Hollywood blacklist, Pierre Boulle accepted the Oscar for Best Adapted Screenplay for *The Bridge on the River Kwai*, based on his novel. However, the screenplay was written by blacklisted writers Michael Wilson and Carl Foreman.

67 Oscar Wildies

FOR THE Best Director Oscar, Joel (who had won the Best Director award at Cannes the year before) was up against Anthony Minghella (*The English Patient*), Milos Forman (*The People vs Larry Flint*), Mike Leigh (*Secrets and Lies*) and Scott Hicks (*Shine*). If Oscars were won on artistic and auteuristic merit, then Mike Leigh would have been Joel's only serious rival. But the Oscars being the Oscars,

Minghella, the least interesting director of the least interesting film, won.

Another anomaly was the nomination of William H. Macy as Best Supporting Actor, though he played one of the leading roles in the movie, almost as long as McDormand's. (Macy lost to Cuba Gooding Jr. in *Jerry Maguire*.) The Academy sometimes finds it difficult to overcome the notion that certain players are supporting actors whatever the length of their roles.

Deakins' cinematography was felt to be less worthy than John Seale's on *The English Patient*, and Roderick Jaynes was pipped at the post by Walter Murch. The Academy played it safe by giving Murch his second Oscar. (He won Best Sound Editing for *Apocalypse Now*.) *The English Patient*, a film that will soon pass into oblivion, won nine Oscars.

Justice, however, was done with the Best Screenplay award going to the Coen brothers over *Jerry Maguire*, *Lone Star*, *Secrets and Lies* and *Shine*, and the Best Actress award to Frances McDormand. Certainly her performance was superior to those of Diane Keaton in *Marvin's Room*, Kristen Scott-Thomas in *The English Patient* and an irritating Emily Watson in *Breaking the Waves*. Only Brenda Blethyn's portrayal in *Secrets and Lies* could be said to have carried equal weight to McDormand's Marge.

"What am I doing here?" Frances asked in her acceptance speech. "Especially considering the extraordinary group of women with whom I was nominated. We five women were fortunate to have the choice, not just the opportunity, but the choice to play such rich, complex female characters, and I congratulate the casting directors for making casting decisions on qualifications and not just market value." She went onto thank her brother-in-law for "making me an actress," and her husband for "making me a woman."

Following the show, which ran for three hours and thirty-seven minutes, making it the longest awards show in American television history, Frances was widely photographed between a stunned Joel and Ethan. "It was weird," said Ethan. "Everyone was beaming at you; it was like a nightmare and was very disconcerting in a way. Jodie Foster kept smiling at me." "I won't be able to afford her anymore," Joel quipped, looking at his wife. The next day, the two Oscars were in a box ready to be taken back to New York, where they would stand on a little trophy shelf in the Coens' office. "Now I've got more to dust in the office," Frances commented. "Hollywood is a cultureless environment. The awards season is their social season, so it goes on for two months. The amount of time and money spent is incredible."

No doubt some cynicism may have balanced the euphoria the Coen family felt on Oscar Night. Perhaps, Ethan and Joel's guardian angel Raymond Chandler was whispering in their ears on the night.

> If you can go past those awful idiot faces on the bleachers outside the theater without a sense of the collapse of the human intelligence; if you can stand the hailstorm of flashbulbs popping at the poor patient actors, who, like kings and queens, have never the right to look bored; if you can glance out over the gathered assemblage of what is supposed to be the elite of Hollywood and say to yourself without a sinking feeling, "In these hands lies the destinies of the only original art the modern world has conceived"; . . . if you can stand the fake sentimentality and the platitudes of the officials and the mincing elocution of the glamor queens; if you can do all these things with grace and pleasure, and not have a wild and forsaken horror at the thought that most of these people actually take this shoddy performance seriously; and if you can then go out into the night to see half the police force of Los Angeles gathered to protect the golden ones from the mob in the free seats . . . if you can do all these things and still feel next morning that the picture business is worth the attention of one single, intelligent, artistic mind, then in the picture business you certainly belong, because this sort of vulgarity is part of its inevitable price. (*Atlantic Monthly* 1950)

A year later, Frances recalled: "Waiting for the opening of the envelope on Oscars night last year was kind of numbing. But we were all riding on this euphoria, not just because of *Fargo* being recognized in so many categories, but because so many independent features which we had seen and liked were in there, too . . . More importantly, what's surprising and gratifying about the acknowledgment is we have established ourselves, as Joel and Ethan have, outside the community. We don't live here [in LA], we don't work here unless we're doing work on location. We're not members of the community in the social sense. So the value of that kind of choice was being acknowledged. Also, it was never our goal—Joel and Ethan never set out to make a characteristically Academy Award-nominated movie. That's just not what they're interested in, nor what they're good at. Neither am I. I've never, ever been a part of the public-relations machine, other than promoting the work I've done. That whole thing was kind of odd, kind of a weird aspect of a movie that none of us even expected an audience to see. Isn't it astonishing? *That's* the best part. It cemented an audience for their films that I think is only going to escalate."

The Oscar figurine—described by screenwriter Frances Marion as "a perfect symbol of the picture business; a powerful athletic body clutching a gleaming sword with half of his head, that part which held the brains, completely sliced off"—is emblematic in Hollywood of success. The Coens had truly arrived. They had largely made their names as *Wunderkinder*, brash youths who took from old movies to make something new. But they were no longer kids. They may be iconoclasts but, with Oscars, six films to their joint credit, and a firm place in the movie industry, they had become established iconoclasts.

COOL DUDES

X

It's the world of drug takers. The noise of

bowling is also a drug for the Dude. In the

minds of most people, the psychedelic culture

is associated with Southern California.

STRANGELY, THERE are more elements that are actually true in *The Big Lebowski* than in *Fargo*, which was allegedly based on real events but, "in truth contains mostly made-up stuff." *The Big Lebowski*, though influenced strongly by Raymond Chandler, is based on real people and events.

The film seems to have been sparked off by a visit to a friend, Pete Exline, a rather bitter Vietnam vet. Whenever the subject of Vietnam came up, he would say things like, "Well, we were winning when I left." In order to cheer him up, the brothers complimented Pete on his apartment, which was actually "a kind of a dump." He was really proud of this "ratty-ass little rug" he had in the living room and told them how it "tied the room together." This expression was put into the mouth of aging hippy Jeff "The Dude" Lebowski (Jeff Bridges), after his threadbare rug has been peed on by one of two heavies, an action which ignites the plot.

Pete also regaled the Coens with the misadventures of his friend Walter, a fellow vet who had knocked around the movie business. Walter's car was stolen by teenage joyriders. When it was found, it was discovered that one of the thieves had inadvertently left behind his school homework that bore his address. So Pete and Walter tracked the kid down and confronted him. This incident was integrated into the screenplay of *The Big Lebowski*.

One would think that the seemingly gentle Coens would have little in common with Peter Exline or the director John Milius, whose macho interests include surfing, the martial arts, hunting, guns and motorcycles, many of which he has put into his bombastic films. The self-styled "Zen anarchist," who was denied entry to the US Marines on grounds of health, found compensation by making will-to-power allegorical movies like *Conan the Barbarian* (1982). Yet, Coens the Barbarians are (un)healthily attracted to the representation of bloody violence as in *Blood Simple* and *Miller's Crossing*—during the making of which they became fascinated by the Thompson gun.

"We met John Milius when we were in LA making *Barton Fink*. He's a really funny guy, a really good storyteller. He was never actually in the military, although he wears a lot of military paraphernalia. He's a gun enthusiast and survivalist type. Whenever we saw him he'd invite us out to his house to look at his guns—although we never took him up on it." Elements of Peter Exline and John Milius came together to constitute the character of Walter Sobchak (John Goodman), the Dude's Vietnam vet buddy.

The character of Dude, "quite possibly the laziest man in Los Angeles County," was based on a guy named Jeff Dowd, whom the Coens met on one of their first trips to Los Angeles in the 1970s. Dowd called himself the Pope of Dope, and was actually known as the Dude. He was a member of the Seattle Seven during the Vietnam years—he used to program the Seattle Film Festival—and did time in jail for conspiracy to destroy federal property. Later he moved to California, and hung around film people. (Today he's a respectable producer's rep.) In order to research his role, Jeff Bridges met this ex-Dude. "I took stuff from him for the Dude, and also from some of my own friends like that. But to be honest, it's mostly just me," Bridges remarked.

"The physical thing is one of the first things you do to figure out a character," said Bridges, who put on weight for the part. "The Dude is not the kind of guy to be doing a lot of sit-ups, and he gets most of his nutrition from kahlua, vodka and milk, so he doesn't mind looking the way he does with a pot belly. He eats pretty much whenever and whatever he wants. And I drew on myself a lot from back in the Sixties and Seventies. I lived in a little place like that and did drugs, although I think I was a little more creative than the Dude. But then maybe the Dude went through a creative period and just grew out of it. During my Dude period, I painted a lot and made music."

The role of the Dude is related to Bone (also played by Bridges), the complacent beach-bum buddy of a bitter, mutilated Vietnam vet in *Cutter's Way*, Ivan Passer's updated *film noir*, sixteen years previously. The Coens liked the character of the Dude because "We're pretty lazy. We're slow. That's why we tend to make a movie once every two years. The Dude has so little ambition that he's not a failure. There is a laid-back subculture in LA that draws on the surfing lifestyle. It's partly the weather that makes that kind of stoner culture possible." The Dude is one of the first pot-head heroes that movies have seen in years.

One critic called *The Big Lebowski* "a remake of *Cutter's Way* strained through *The Big Sleep*, a poison-pen love-letter to LA and all the movies made about it, a cowboy's opium dream of life at the end of the trail, and a bowling movie about Desert Storm." Ethan described the movie, with some element of seriousness, as "a Cheech and Chong movie with bowling." Thomas Chong and Cheech Marin were crude, irreverent pot-head comedians of the 1970s. "You go to our movies for four reasons: to laugh, cry, get scared, get a hard-on. If you can do all four at the same time, hey, it's the ultimate pizza combo, man."

69 Bowling Alley Cats

PETE EXLINE belongs to an amateur softball league, but the Coens thought the sport visually uninteresting so they changed it to bowling, which had the retro connotation they were looking for. "It's a very social sport where you can sit around and drink and smoke while engaging in inane conversation. It's not an active sport, which goes against the health and fitness thing of Southern California. Ten-pin bowlers have the same physique as dart players," they explained. "It's also a decidedly male sport, which is right because *The Big Lebowski* is kind of a weird buddy movie."

Bowling is not a sport to feature greatly in movies, but it does have an image as the game for the "average Joe." Homer Simpson goes bowling and, in *The Honeymooners*, the classic blue-collar sitcom of the 1950s, Ralph Kramden, played by roly-poly comedian Jackie Gleason (who bore some resemblance to John Goodman), was a bowling fanatic. The sport features in two celebrated 1940s *films noirs*: Fred MacMurray goes bowling after realizing that he is being drawn into a murder plot in Billy Wilder's *Double Indemnity*, and a bowling center is the locus of Jean Negulesco's *Road House*. In a memorable moment from Howard Hughes' *Scarface* (1932), Boris Karloff is shot while bowling, his death symbolized by a wobbling then falling bowling pin.

However, the Coens insisted that the *noir* element in the script didn't really seem to dictate anything stylistically in the movie. So, while *noir* seems to be the flavor of the narrative, with all these characters trapped by their pasts, it is essentially a comedy, and does not have the look of a *noir*. "Consistent with the whole bowling thing, we wanted to keep the movie pretty bright and poppy. Since the bowling alley is sort of a linchpin, visually speaking, we discussed it with Rick [Heinrichs—Production Designer] more than any other set— although it was a practical location, not a set. The exterior of the place was just one big, solid, unbroken wall. So we talked about what to do with that. Rick came up with the idea of just laying free-form neon stars on top of it and doing a similar free-form star thing on the interior." This led to the star motif of the film.

"Both dream sequences involve star patterns and are about lines radiating to a point. In the first dream sequence, the Dude gets knocked out and you see stars and they all coalesce into the overhead nightscape of LA," explained Heinrichs. "The second dream sequence is an astral environment with a backdrop of stars. The name of the bowling alley is the Hollywood Star Lanes. Stars were a Fifties thing, as well as being appropriate to LA." There was a rapport between the rich, saturated colors of Roger Deakins' photography and that of Heinrichs' designs of the bowling alley, which was lit by fluorescent lights.

On the day when they were supposed to shoot the bowling scenes, Goodman had torn some ligaments in his foot, was in a cast and on crutches. Ethan had minor surgery on an old knee problem and was walking with a cane. So both Ethan and Goodman were limping around, and they only had to reschedule one day. Goodman then used his limp in the movie after he falls out of a moving car.

THE BIG Lebowski was an eleven-week shoot with a lot of location shooting in and around LA. Therefore, the Coens took a house in Santa Monica. Tricia Cooke, Ethan's wife, was employed as co-editor with Roderick Jaynes, who, despite the scandal of Oscars, decided to prove his existence once more.

The locations were so varied, from the Dude's Venice beach cottage to the Big Lebowski's mansion to Jackie Treehorn's glass and concrete Malibu pad, that obtaining a unified look to the film was a challenge. This was mainly up to the cinematographer Roger Deakins, and the art department.

The Lebowski mansion was an empty house that was used mainly for filming. The Dude's second visit to see his wealthy namesake, is what the Coens call "a great room scene." "We like great room scenes for some reason: guys sitting in front of fires with blankets over their knees. This is a tycoon. He's in retreat." As Rick Heinrich recognized, "We needed it to have that grand feeling you get when you're looking, for example, at General Sternwood's place in *The Big Sleep* . . . You want a bit of a *Citizen Kane* feeling, to make a strong statement about this pitiful guy in a wheelchair with all his magnificent art work staring down at him."

> This room was too big, the ceiling was too high, the doors were too tall, and the white carpet that went from wall to wall looked like a fresh fall of snow at Lake Arrowhead."
>
> **–The Big Sleep** (Raymond Chandler)

70 Dude and Co.

THE BIG *Lebowski* was written about the same time as *Barton Fink*, but neither John Goodman, who was occupied on *Roseanne*, nor Jeff Bridges, committed to Walter Hill for *Wild Bill*, was available at the time. As the Coens try to make it a rule to work only with those actors for whom the roles were written, they decided to wait and embarked on *Fargo* instead.

Pauline Kael once wrote that Jeff Bridges "may be the most natural and least self-conscious screen actor that ever lived." Excusable hyperbole, perhaps, as Bridges is easy, relaxed, effortless, always himself and yet, paradoxically, always convincing as the character he is playing. In a way, Frances McDormand's Marge in *Fargo* paved the way for less artificial or stylized playing in the Coens' movies.

"The only time we ever directed Jeff," recalled Joel, "was when he would come over at the beginning of each scene and ask, 'Do you think the Dude burned one on the way over?' I'd reply 'yes' usually, so Jeff would go over in the corner and start rubbing his eyes to get them bloodshot. That was the extent of our direction."

Neither did the Coens explain much to Julianne Moore, who played Maude Lebowski, the avant-garde artist.

They don't really talk a lot, which I love, I don't like to talk a lot when I'm working. It gets in the way. They do seem to communicate in some symbiotic way. I really loved it because you have this duality that becomes the vision on the set. You get a larger breadth of artistic vision. There's always an eye there. Which I really enjoyed. So if you have any questions, you can go to either one of them. Yeah. Which I thought was extremely odd. I didn't discover that until the first day on the set, when Ethan came over, and the line was "Jeffrey, tell me a little about yourself," and Ethan said, "Lose the 'little,' " and he never told Joel, "I told Julie to do this," which would take obviously an incredible amount of time. That's when you realize that they just do that. But Joel will come over and say something, and they just balance it that way."

Maude, who swings on a rope spraying paint on a canvas while suspended naked in a harness, tells a bemused Dude, "My art has been commended as strongly vaginal." "I had no idea what they were going to do," Moore said. "I assumed I was going to be upright. I didn't know I was going to be like Superman. That was terrifying. And I was pregnant, and it was three in the morning, and I was 30 feet in the air, and they had to bring me up really fast. It was really strange, but it was worth it in the end."

The character was largely based on Carol Schneeman, who worked naked from a swing, and Yoko Ono. It was in 1961 that Ono realized her *Kitchen Piece*. She smashed eggs, jello, and sumi ink against a canvas on the wall and smeared them across the canvas surface with her hands, then set the canvas on fire. "I think it is possible to see a chair as it is. But when you burn the chair, you suddenly realize that the chair in your mind did not burn or disappear . . ." commented Yoko Ono in a line which the Coens would have been happy to invent.

Bridges, though giving out the usual guff about working relationships on a picture, i.e. "It was so great to work with the Coens," was sincere enough in what he had to say about them.

They're so relaxed. And the way things are set up, it works well. They know what they want and how to get it without a lot of hysteria. It's not like those big studio movies where everybody feels the tension of the money and the studio executives breathing down the neck of the director and producer. Here, the money-people are so happy to be working with them, it's kind of the other way round. The Coens are laid-back and easy, and they like other people to be that way. They low-ball everything, so instead of stretching it, they do what they can do on a smaller budget and, frankly, they're creative enough to do that. Not everybody can be that creative. They're kind of unusual guys. They've got a great sense of humor, but they're not out cracking jokes at the time. They're almost like straight men.

John Goodman said his time in the bowling alley was his best experience on a film. "There's something about those guys—they make me laugh. I'd say *The Big Lebowski* was the most fun I ever had on set—I laughed every day. I'd love just showing up for work." Actors who work with them say their sets are completely harmonious and that their films rival those of Woody Allen in terms of the enjoyment factor. Only

Nicolas Cage and Gabriel Byrne have struck a discordant note, and have not worked with the Coens since.

John Turturro had a broad cameo as Jesus Quintana, the "spick" bowler in a mauve outfit.

It was an early element in the script and we knew that we wanted John to play him [Joel said]. I had seen him about ten years ago in a play at the Public Theater called *Ma Puta Vita* in which he played a pederast. Well, maybe that's taking it a little too far, saying he was a pederast, but he had a scene where there was this little boy on his lap and he was kind of bouncing him up and down and there was a kind of lewd section with weird overtones. I was very impressed by it. So we thought, let's make Turturro a pederast. It'll be something he can really run with. I guess you could say it's just our attempt to bring John's *Ma Puta Vita* character to a wider audience. We shot a lot of his stuff in extreme slow motion. The Quintana scene was fun to do. We hadn't done a movie with Turturro in a long time. [Not since *Barton Fink* in 1991.]

Steve Buscemi, unfortunately, got the fuzzy end of the lollipop on this one as Donny, the nebbish bowling companion of Walter and the Dude. He can hardly get a sentence out without Walter saying, "Shut the fuck up, Donny!" In the end, Donny doesn't have the satisfaction of being shot by the anarchists after bravely standing up to them, but dies of a heart attack. He then has the humiliation of his ashes being put into a coffee jar, and having them scattered, not in the Pacific Ocean, but blown back onto the Dude, a rather creaky black joke.

71 *California Dreaming*

"I KNOW there is a real world and a dream world and I shan't confuse them," Judy Garland says in *The Pirate*. The Coens have not been so fastidious, and many of their dream sequences have bled into the main body of their films. Because *Fargo* was meant to be the most realistic of them, a dream sequence was cut from an early draft involving, as they insist, Marge and a Native American foetus. Their typically facetious explanation for dropping it was because "we couldn't agree on the spelling of foetus."

Miller's Crossing has the recurrent hat dream, and *The Hudsucker Proxy*, which might have worked better as a musical, has a dream sequence of Tim Robbins doing a ballet with a Dream Dancer (Pamela Everett) to an aria from *Carmen*, her dress blown by a wind machine as in the Gene Kelly–Cyd Charisse duet in *Singin' in the Rain*.

The Coens sometimes give the impression that inside them is a musical straining to get out. *The Big Lebowski*'s big dream sequence contains a hackneyed Busby Berkeley pastiche. Ever since the 1940s there have been imitators of Busby Berkeley's kaleidoscopic numbers, none of whom have ever come near the master in any way. Ken Russell made a reasonable attempt to do a couple of Berkeley-type routines in *The Boy Friend*, Mel Brooks in *The Producers* had a witty overhead shot of jackbooted chorus girls forming the shape of a swastika, and there is a spectacular animated Berkeley number in Walt Disney's *Beauty And The Beast* (1991). The Coens should have left it well alone. Firstly because it is another reductionist view of Berkeley's genius, and secondly, it is not the Dude's fantasy but the Coens imposing their own images on the character. "We've always loved Busby Berkeley, but it was more us trying to imagine what a pot-head who was slipped a Mickey Finn would dream about, what form it would take. That gave us freedom to do just about anything we wanted, so we came up with Busby Berkeley, Saddam Hussein and Kenny Rogers."

Among the images the Dude sees is Maude Lebowski, with braided pigtails, dressed in an armored breastplate and horned Norse headgear, and carrying a trident, the philistine's first image of what operatic prima donnas look like. Whether it is the Dude's or the Coens' philistinism is unclear; as is whether it is merely a recognition of the cliché as seen unforgettably in the Marx Brothers' *Duck Soup*, with Margaret Dumont singing an operatic song of victory, and Chuck Jones' cartoon *What's Opera, Doc?*, in which Bugs Bunny dons the Brünnhilde gear.

The Dude, on his back, is launched like a bowling ball down the lane straddled by a line of chorus girls, their legs turning it into a tunnel in imitation of the famous shot in the "Young and Healthy" number from *42nd Street* where the camera moves through a tunnel of female legs, ending with a close-up of a leering Dick Powell.

Jeff Bridges recalled the shooting of the sequence. "That day on the schedule was the dream sequence, and I thought it would be where I dance down the steps. That seemed cool, so I invited my wife and kids to come on set that day 'cause they like to see us making the movies and all, you know? But the Coens switched it and did the other imaginary sequence, and I thought oh God, what are my kids going to think when I turn over and I'm staring up these girls' dresses? So I didn't know it, but all the girls—the dancers got together and pulled this trick on me. As I float through there and turn and look at a dress, I see this big, well, tufts of hair coming out everywhere—and it's the same under the next girl's skirt. It turns out they'd put these big wigs under their leotards between their legs, hidden by their skirts, so only I would see them. Fortunately my wife had been told and she was waiting to see the look on my face, and now everybody was in on it. It was really funny, but I couldn't laugh. But that's why I had that weird smile on my face in the picture. But the expression on my twelve-year-old daughter's face was just as weird. She didn't know what to make of it."

You just had to be there!

72 The Past is Another Country

THE BIG Lebowski is set in 1991, at the time of the Gulf War. In fact, only the Coens' first two pictures were set in the year they were made. The "period" settings, like the wide-angle lenses, and the various allusions and asides, help provide the distance between the film and the audience that the Coens seem to require.

While so many Hollywood movies try to wring the emotions and, as if holding up cue cards, heavily signal to the audience when to laugh and cry, the Coens' cooler approach is refreshing. This cannot only be put down to their "Minnesotan reserve," but to a determined creative policy. While being poles apart in many ways, it may not be invidious to make a comparison between their strategem and Bertolt Brecht's celebrated (and often misunderstood) theory behind the basic aims in his theater. The "alienation" (*Verfremdung*) theory was an attempt to alienate the subject-matter of the drama by destroying the illusion, interrupting the course of the action, and lowering the tension, so that the audience could remain emotionally disengaged during the performance, in order to allow them to take an intelligent and objective view of what is before them.

Although they might repudiate this, it is very much what the Coens do in their films. Black humor often undercuts violence, preventing any danger of wallowing in it. Visual or verbal jokes deflate the drama. Unexpected POVs, such as a dog's (*Blood Simple*, *Raising Arizona*), unconventional narrators (*Blood Simple*, *The Hudsucker Proxy*, *The Big Lebowski*) and allusions to other films, shift the audience's focus away from identifying too much with one character or another.

THERE IS no compelling reason for *The Big Lebowski* being set seven years previously at the time of the Gulf War, unless it is to supply Vietnam vet Walter with a bellicose cause, and provide the opportunity for a Saddam Hussein gag. He pops up in one of the Dude's dubious dreams at a bowling alley, where he works at the bowling shoe hire counter. He hands over a special pair of shoes to His Dudeness.

Politics has been part of the period decor of many of the Coens' movies. In *Raising Arizona*, Hi rails against Ronald Reagan, and a picture of Barry Goldwater decorates the wall of the office of the parole board. When Gale and Evelle rob the "hayseed bank," they say that they got a tip that it was worth robbing from "Lawrence Spivey, one of Dick Nixon's under-secretaries of agriculture." (There is also a corrupt politician called Spivey in *O Brother, Where Art Thou?*.) In *Miller's Crossing*, both the mayor and the police chief are puppets of gangsters, and the coming war and the Depression are significant backgrounds to *Barton Fink* and *O Brother*.

The Big Lebowski has moved into the George Bush era, and Walter apes the president's macho stand against Saddam. "We're talking about unchecked aggression here;" "This aggression will not stand;" "I'm talking about drawing a line in the sand, Dude. Across the line, you do not . . ." "Let me point out, pacifism is not—look at our current situation with that camel-fucker in Iraq—pacifism is not something to hide behind."

ALL THE characters in The Big Lebowski live in the recent past, as do the Coens to a certain degree. Walter defines his experience by Vietnam, and his marriage that ended five years before. The Dude, who is an aging hippie, accuses Walter of living in the past. "Three thousand years of beautiful tradition, from Moses to Sandy Koufax— you're goddamn right I live in the past!" Porn producer Jackie Treehorn (Ben Gazzara), a Hugh Hefner type, has something of the 1970s about him. Maude Lebowski is a throwback to the Fluxus artists of New York in the 1960s. They are all defined by the music they listen to.

The Dude constantly listens to Creedence Clearwater Revival (he somewhat resembles the Fogerty brothers himself), his favorite band, and plays "Lookin' Out My Backdoor" in his car. Treehorn listens to 1960s mainstream jazz, and the millionaire Lebowski has Mozart's Requiem on the turntable. Maude has Kraftwerk's "Autobahn" ("Their music is sort of—ugh—techno-pop") among her vinyl collection, which includes Pink Floyd and Roy Orbison.

The nihilists, a bunch of European art-rockers who have taken to kidnapping to pay the rent, are trapped in the 1980s. "There are these kind of fringe rock'n'roll guys in LA. You'll see them in late-night diners on Sunset dressed in black leather with long stringy hair, and you can't quite figure what they're about," commented Joel.

DUDE: You brought a fucking Pomeranian bowling?

WALTER: What do you mean "brought it bowling"? I didn't rent it shoes. I'm not buying it a fucking beer. He's not going to take your

fucking turn, Dude.

DUDE: Hey, man, if my fucking ex-wife asked

me to take care of her fucking dog while she

and her boyfriend went to Honolulu, I'd tell

her to go fuck herself.

–The Big Lebowski

73 · The Big Goodbye

JUST AS the plot of *Blood Simple* was filched from *The Postman Always Rings Twice*, and that of *Miller's Crossing* from *Red Harvest*, so *The Big Lebowski* owes much to *The Big Sleep*, as reflected in the title.

"We wanted something that would generate a certain narrative feeling—like a modern Raymond Chandler story, and that's why it had to be set in Los Angeles. We live in New York and feel outsiders in LA. We wanted to have a narrative flow, a story that moves like a Chandler book through different parts of town and different social classes. That was the backdrop that interested us when we wrote the screenplay. There are lots of references to Chandler novels. More than one book in our minds. I think the story about the rich old guy in Pasadena who sparks off the entire plot, is typical Chandler. In *The Big Sleep* it's the two daughters who set everything in motion, here it's the fake kidnapping."

The Big Lebowski (David Huddleston), in his wheelchair, recalls the equally paralyzed General Sternwood, while his wife Bunny and daughter Maude are reminiscent of the two Sternwood daughters, Vivian and Carmen. Bunny's maiden name is Knutsen, whereas the name of Eddie Mars' wife in the Howard Hawks film is Knudsen. (In-joke: Bunny comes from Minnesota.) Jackie Treehorn resembles the suave owners of nightclubs in Chandler. The private eye (Jon Polito) called Da Fino, who tails the Dude in a redundant episode, is a variation of the snoop in *The High Window.*

The novels of Raymond Chandler deal with all social classes in Los Angeles. But, like the eponymous character in *The Big Lebowski,* there is always a dominant all-powerful figure who serves as a catalyst. He represents Money. He is also present in Roman Polanski's *Chinatown.* He is the man who has contributed to the construction of the city. He symbolizes the old order, and, at the end, he discovers it's all a sham.

The Coens also acknowledge their debt to *The Long Goodbye* (1973), Robert Altman's updating of the Chandler novel with Elliot Gould as Philip Marlowe, played as a laid-back, shambling slob, out of touch with the LA of the Seventies, just as the Dude is alienated from the LA of the Nineties. It is not too surprising that *The Long Goodbye* is the Coens' favorite Altman movie, although in the pre-postmodernist era of the Seventies, it seemed to reduce Chandler to an elaborate Hollywood party game.

The Cowboy Stranger narrator (Sam Elliott) helped them to create a certain distance. "We always like those devices—narration, voice-over. Also it's a [Philip] Marlowe thing, since all the Chandler novels are told in the first-person narration. But it would be too corny just to have the Dude narrating."

The grizzled, rough-necked Sam Elliott, with his distinctive gruff voice and lanky physique, who had played Virgil Earp in *Tombstone* a few years back, seems to have wandered onto the wrong set from a Western, bringing with him the tumbleweeds. But this is exactly the kind of incongruity that the Coens delight in and manage to carry off. However, the word "dude" is a cowboy's pejorative description for someone from the East or a big city, not used to the ways of the West. In Howard Hawks' magisterial Western *Rio Bravo* (1958), the alcoholic character played by Dean Martin (whom Peter Gallagher takes off in *The Hudsucker Proxy* singing "Memories Are Made of This"), is called the Dude.

At the happy ending, the folksy Cowboy addresses the audience directly to camera, summing up the story (and the film). "Whelp, that about does her, wraps her all up. Things seem to have worked out pretty good for the Dude 'n Walter, and it was a purt good story, dontcha think? Made me laugh to beat the band. Parts, anyway. Course—I didn't like seein' Donny go. But then I happen to know there's a little Lebowski on the way. I guess that's the way the whole durned human comedy keeps perpetuatin' itself, down through the generations, westward the wagons, across the sands a time—aw, look at me, I'm ramblin' again. Wal, uh hope you folks enjoyed yourselves . . . Catch you further on down the trail . . ."

ODD ODYSSEY

XI

"One of our favorite books is Homer's *The Odyssey*, and one of our favorite movies is *Sullivan's Travels*. Can't you see the connection?"

THE COENS had many subjects floating around for years that have not as yet, or never will, come to fruition. Some ideas take root ages before they surface in a screenplay. *The Hudsucker Proxy* was written before *Blood Simple*, *The Big Lebowski* before *Fargo*. In 1987, nine years before *Fargo*, the brothers had the following exchange:

JOEL: "Did you hear about the guy in Connecticut who put his wife in the wood chipper?"

ETHAN: "Heh, heh, heh."

Joel: "The cops said that one good rainfall would have washed her away, and they never would have found her."

ETHAN: "That was a good one."

JOEL: "That was a good one."

At about the same time, they explained that being suburban kids their imaginations were fired by empty American landscapes like those in Texas and Arizona in their first two films. "A movie about Minnesota people running around in snowsuits killing each other wouldn't be any fun."

For a while in the late 1980s, they talked about a number of other films they would like to make, imagined or otherwise. "We've been working on a screenplay about a barber in Northern California in the 1940s who wants to go into the drycleaning business," they told journalists, perhaps seriously. They also expressed a desire to remake Stanley Kramer's *Guess Who's Coming to Dinner?*. "It's a dream project we've talked about a lot. I think we could bring a new twist to that." What possible "new twist" could they bring to the plot about an ostensibly liberal middle-class WASP couple coming to terms with their daughter's wish to marry a black man? Perhaps they were considering introducing a kidnapping into it.

There was also another unlikely project about a Kim Philby-like figure, an idealistic British spy, who ends up in Moscow during the Cold War era. "It's so miserable it would have to be a comedy," the Coens remarked. More in the realm of the possible was a completed screenplay based on Elmore Leonard's novel *La Brava*, also involving a kidnapping. It would have been the first film adapted directly from someone else's work, before *To the White Sea* became a reality. Based on James Dickey's final novel, set during the Second World War after the bombing of Tokyo, the latter is about a B-29 tailgunner (Brad Pitt) shot down while flying over Japan, who is forced to embark on an epic journey across Asia to return home. The film will have virtually no dialogue.

Of the movie genres, most of which they have tackled, including the musical and Western *en passant*, science fiction has no attraction for them. "We're not really sci-fi fans. We've never really thought of doing one of those. Something about space suits. It's not up our street."

AFTER *THE* Big Lebowski, there was an unprecedented rupture. Ethan showed his independence by co-writing (with J. Todd Anderson) the screenplay of a quirky comedy called *The Naked Man*. It was the first feature directed by Anderson, the Coens' faithful storyboarder. Michael Rappaport portrays a guy who, as a nerdish child, had been bullied in the school playground. Thus he learns wrestling. As an adult, he becomes a chiropractor by day and a masked wrestler by night. When a pharmaceutical kingpin moves into his town to cause some real trouble, and his parents are murdered, he walks around town in his leotard, beating up and killing anyone who gets in his way to avenge their murder.

The film flopped justifiably, and Ethan has not strayed since, except for his well-received book of short stories, *Gates of Eden*, which appeared in 1998. The collection surprised many people, mainly because, while established novelists and short-story writers have moved into films, moves in the other direction are very rare.

The dialogue-dominated stories, some of them short plays, fall roughly into two categories: those that revolve around a murder or a violent act, usually perpetrated in a bizarre manner, and those that have an autobiographical basis. The latter stories deal with a bittersweet Jewish childhood in Minneapolis, the former are closer to the Coens' screenplays. However, only the gruesome final scene of *Blood Simple* can compete in gruesomeness with the playlet called *Johnnie Ga-Botz*. A character called Johnnie asks Monk on the phone to kill someone for him, but "first I want you to cut off his dick . . . and then I want you to stick it up his ass . . . Then you say, 'Johnnie Ga-Botz wants to know how you like it' . . . He says, ya know, I don't like it, you shoot him inna fuckin' head."

There then follows a discussion as to the practicalities of the scheme, revolving around the problem of his victim either having passed out or died from the amputation, and not being able to receive the fatal message from Johnny. The conversation spirals on in a more and more convoluted manner, ending with an everyday chat between Johnnie's wife and a friend. An example of how Ethan is able to take extreme situations and treat them in a matter-of-fact manner, or transfer the humdrum into the fantastic.

Ethan doing his own thing creatively, helped the public to appreciate that the Coen brothers were not, in fact, joined at the hip. They now had different families and different sets of friends. "We spend all day together in the office," they commented. "So we don't exactly need to go out for a beer."

IN MAY 1998, while the brothers were still writing their new film, Joel and Pedro, Ethan, Trish and Buster packed themselves off to Dublin to stay in John Boorman's house while Frances was performing as Blanche DuBois in Tennessee Williams' *A Streetcar Named Desire* at the Gate Theater. Just over a year before, after she won her Oscar, Gate director Michael Colgan met Frances in New York and asked her to come over to Ireland to play Blanche, a role he felt she was particularly suited for. This was McDormand's second *Streetcar* on stage. In 1988, she played Stella, earning a Tony nomination for her performance in the Broadway production which featured Blythe Danner as Blanche and Aidan Quinn as Stanley.

"I'm really interested in the idea of Blanche as this woman whose only tools to get through life are feminine wiles," she said. "How limiting those tools end up being and how in the end, just as Stanley pushes her to the edge, she ends up destroying herself. Just technically, I have to deal with the fact that I'm not a moth, I'm not a butterfly and that physically I'm not easy to lift and swing around the stage. So I think that this Blanche is going to be more of a survivor."

An intelligent actress like Frances McDormand, despite her Oscar-winning performance in *Fargo*, needs the stage to show what she can really do, and she brought an unusual range and strength to Blanche DuBois, who came across as more of a victim of her own doing than of others. "There are always roles waiting in the theater for actresses—huge chunks of bloody red meat to get hold of, whereas in film there's mostly just cocktail peanuts."

Frances, therefore, was not waiting for another "chunk of bloody red meat" from Joel and Ethan. "The parts they write are all character roles with quirks to them. But they're enthusiastic theater-goers and they have respect for the mystique of acting." However, whenever she is mentioned, "Oscar-winner" always appears in parenthesis after her name, so she specifically chose not to use it in the program notes for *A Streetcar Named Desire*. "My name's long enough," she explained.

BLANCHE: I never was hard or self-sufficient enough. When people are soft—soft people have got to court the favor of hard ones, Stella. Have got to be seductive—put on soft colors, the colors of butterfly wings, and glow—make a little—temporary magic just in order to pay for—one night's shelter!

–A Streetcar Named Desire (Tennessee Williams)

75 *Ants in their Pants of 2000*

"O BROTHER, Where Art Thou?" is going to be the greatest tragedy ever made. The world will weep, humanity will sob," says the movie director John L. Sullivan (Joel McCrea) in Preston Sturges' *Sullivan's Travels*. He tries to tell Veronica Lake that in a suffering world a director ought not to be making "Ants in their Pants of 1941." But she insists, "There's nothing like a deep-dish movie for driving you out into the open." The Coens, in agreement, have taken the portentous title from the 1941 movie, and made it into a comedy.

In *Sullivan's Travels*, Sullivan is falsely accused of murder and finds himself in a chain gang in the South. In *O Brother, Where Art Thou?*, Ulysses Everett McGill (George Clooney) and his two simple-minded companions, Pete (John Turturro) and Delmar (Tim Nelson), have already escaped from the chain gang at the beginning of the picture, and continue to be one step ahead of the law throughout.

The key scene in *Sullivan's Travels*, when the prisoners file into an old Baptist church to see a Mickey Mouse cartoon and Sullivan discovers that his destiny is to make people laugh, is almost replicated in *O Brother*, but for a less significant purpose. Everett and Delmar are in a movie theater, when a line of chained men, with much clanking of chains, file in and take up a row. Among them is Pete, who has been recaptured. He contacts his mates to warn them of an ambush the police have ready for them, thanks to Pete's spilling some beans to them about where they were heading.

Another reminder of *Sullivan's Travels* is the scene where a little boy of about eight years old helps the three cons escape the sheriff by picking them up in a car. He has wood blocks strapped to his feet so that he can reach the accelerator, brake and clutch, and sits on a Sears Roebuck catalog to see over the dashboard. In the Sturges film, Sullivan, pretending to be a hobo and trying to escape his Hollywood minders following him in a trailer, is picked up by a thirteen-year-old boy driving a coupé convertible, which speeds away until it crashes into a haystack.

There are also elements from other Preston Sturges movies, particularly in the portrayal of the scallywag politicians. In *The Great*

McGinty (1940) the hero is a tramp, who becomes Governor by initially ingratiating himself with the boss of a local political machine by voting forty times, at two dollars a time. Even more contiguous is *Hail the Conquering Hero* (1944) with its political shenanigans in which Raymond Walburn, as the bombastic rascally incumbent mayor, and his dim-witted son, vie with Woodrow Truesmith (Eddie Bracken), the false hero, in the mayoral race. In *O Brother*, there are a number of Sturgesian politicians, such as Pappy O'Daniel, the Governor, with his dim-witted son, whom Pappy keeps hitting with his hat, and his opponent Homer Stokes, who turns out to be a member of the Klan.

Apart from the Sturges film, *O Brother* contrives to encapsulate every cons-on-the-run picture one has ever seen, especially Mervyn LeRoy's chilling *I Am a Fugitive from a Chain Gang* (1932), Southern period crime dramas such as *Bonnie and Clyde* (1969), with its progenitors and successors, and hayseed sagas. The characters are a cross-section of mythical Deep South types: conniving politicians, a black blues singer, Ku Klux Klansmen, a radio DJ, a country prophet, Baptists, and a local-yokel posse complete with shotguns and hound dogs. But, yet again, the Coens' alchemy has worked.

EVERETT: How ya doin', boy? Name's Everett, and these two soggy sonsabitches are Pete and Delmar. Keep your fingers away from Pete's mouth—he ain't had nothin' to eat for the last thirteen years but prison food, gopher, and a little greasy horse.

–O Brother, Where Art Thou?

76 Geeks Meet Greeks

BUT SOFT, what's this? The first title that appears in O *Brother, Where Art Thou?* reads:

> Sing in me, Muse, and through me tell the story
> Of that man skilled in all the ways of contending,
> A wanderer, harried for years on end . . .

These are the opening lines of the *Odyssey* by Homer, upon which the Coens based the film. Or so they announce on the screenplay. It must have seemed their ultimate "postmodernist" joke. "Based upon the *Odyssey*" is putting it rather strongly, to say the least. Anyone other than the Coens might have put "suggested by Homer's *Odyssey*" or "from an idea by Homer."

But the two works do have enough in common to almost merit the attribution. The ancient Greek epic poem, the second work of Western literature after the *Iliad*, is an exciting story—not written down to be read, but to be recited to listening audiences, like the difference between a screenplay and a finished film. In fact, the *Odyssey* incorporates a lengthy flashback—during which Ulysses recounts his adventures while trying to return to his homeland of Ithaca, and his wife Penelope. The Coens eschew Homer's flashback technique for a straightforward narrative which recounts the adventures of Ulysses Everett McGill while trying to return to his home town of Versailles (pronounced Vur-Sallies), Mississippi, and his wife Penny. Both works are picaresque, if that it not too anachronistic a term for the *Odyssey* and O *Brother, Where Art Thou?*

At the moment of Ulysses' return in disguise as a beggar, Penelope announces her intention to marry one of her suitors. When Everett returns, disguised as a bearded "old-timey" country and western singer, Penny is preparing to marry Vernon T. Waldrip (the Eddie Bracken role), a political agent. However, both heroes manage to prevent the marriage in the nick of time.

There are other parallels. Ulysses consults the blind prophet Tiresius, who tells him his fate; Everett and his two pals meet a blind black seer on a flatcar, who tells them, "You must travel a long and difficult road—a road fraught with peril, uh-huh, and pregnant with adventure. You shall see things wonderful to tell. You shall scc a cow on the roof of a cottonhouse . . ." Like some of the miracles Homer's Ulysses witnesses, the Coens' Ulysses sees the cow at the end, but it is only taking refuge on a roof because of the flooding of the Tennessee Valley.

In addition, Pete is seduced by three women ("sigh-reens") washing clothes in the river, singing in unearthly voices. He then disappears, although Delmar believes he has been turned into a toad, because they find one hiding in his abandoned clothes. In the *Odyssey*, every traveler must beware of the Sirens, "who bewitch everybody who approaches them. There is no homecoming for the man who draws near them unawares and hears the Sirens' voices."

On the road, the three cons meet Big Dan Teague (John Goodman), a bible salesman, who wears an eye-patch. Big Dan robs them of the money they had gained from robbing a bank with "Baby Face" Nelson. He later appears in a Ku Klux Klan hood with only one eye-hole. He is, of course, a reflection of the dreaded Cyclops, the one-eyed giant, who eats a number of Ulysses' men. Governor Menelaus "Pass the Biscuits, Pappy" O'Daniel might like to compare himself with Menelaus, "son of Atreus, favorite of the gods, leader of his people."

"I read the *Odyssey* after I read the screenplay, and it was amazing to discover the connections between the two," said George Clooney.

THE COENS first approached 38-year-old George Clooney with the *O Brother* script while he was in Phoenix working on *Three Kings*. "I was nearing the end of a very tough five-month shoot, really ready to go home, and Joel and Ethan flew into Phoenix and handed me the script," recalled Clooney. "They told me they'd written it with me in mind and asked me if I'd do it. I said yes without even reading the first page. They both started laughing and asked me if I wanted to read it before agreeing, but I told them that wouldn't be necessary. I get about five scripts a week, and that's after a large screening process by two agents and the studio. And out of those, I rarely get even one really good one."

Clooney, who had only just ended his five-year run on NBC"s hit show, *ER*, in order to concentrate on his film career, was amazed that the Coens had thought of him.

When you first get here, you think they're both going to direct at the same time. Then you discover that they don't direct you a lot. They'll come over and say, "Yeah, um, let's do it again. Yeh, you know . . . Yeh." They play dumb a little, but they let you figure it out, because the writing's so good. In the morning you get the storyboard so you know how it'll look. The script didn't change since I first read it four months before we started shooting. They're open to trying things and you can suggest things and they say, "Okay, you can try that," but they've already covered all the bases. I recently asked my aunt Rosemary [Rosemary Clooney] why she is a better singer now than ever, and she said it's because she doesn't have to show off anymore. The Coen brothers don't have to show off.

Clooney got to lip-sync a version of the folk standard "Man of Constant Sorrow," which he and his fellow cons record as the Soggy Bottom Boys, and it becomes a hit throughout the region. Other singers who appear in the movie are Emmylou Harris and bluegrass acts Ralph Stanley, Alison Krauss and Union Station, the Cox Family, and blues musician Chris Thomas King.

The role of Ulysses Everett McGill cleverly plays upon Clooney's rather vainly handsome persona, while having him unshaven and dressed in hobo's clothes for most of the film. Even while on the run, he uses Dapper Dan pomade on his hair, for which he will not accept substitutes. "It didn't look like a one-horse town, but try getting a decent hair jelly," he complains. Everett also likes the sound of his own voice, speaking in an inflated one. It is not surprising, with his gift of the gab, to find that his crime was practising law without a license.

In a way, he is the Moe to John Turturro and Tim Nelson's Larry and Curly, especially in the moments when they black up, or put on false beards and pretend to be the Soggy Bottom Boys, one of the episodes that is definitely not in Homer.

Filming of *O Brother, Where Art Thou?* took place throughout Mississippi—from the Delta to Vicksburg, but mainly around

Jackson—and was followed by studio work in Los Angeles. It was completed in October 1999.

When the Coens first talked to Roger Deakins about the movie, they explained how they wanted it to look "brown and dirty and golden like a period picture book of the Depression." But when Deakins was told that the film was being shot in Mississippi, he said that it was "one of the greenest parts of the States." So, to get the look the brothers were after, the whole movie was digitized in order to take the green out of it. "We gave it an ocher feel," said Deakins. "I kept having to say to them, 'Just imagine it'll be all yellow.' "

The production designer Dennis Gassner also attempted to give it the desaturated look of an old photograph of the period. "Because it's loosely based on the *Odyssey*, we discussed classicism in the South as being a definitive aspect," Gassner remarked. "A kind of metaphor, an illusion of antiquity. Classic images of the South taken to the extreme."

77 *Mississippi Burning*

THE STATE of Mississippi, home of William Faulkner, Eudora Welty, Tennessee (sic!) Williams, Richard Wright and Bessie Smith. The Coen brothers are preparing the opening shot of *O Brother, Where Art Thou?*. It is of a chain gang of black convicts, wearing faded striped uniforms, swinging picks in unison against rocks at the side of a road in the middle of the flat delta countryside. They chant "Po' Lazarus" as they work under the broiling noon sun.

A few miles from the location, scores of black extras are clustered in a tent in their striped uniforms and leg irons. Some are drinking Cokes, while others are sitting patiently as a make-up woman, a blond girl in shorts, passes among them, smearing them with "sweat" and "dirt." A few of them walk over to look at the storyboard titled *Po' Lazarus Boys*, which has photos of all the convicts on cards. Then a signal is given for all the extras to get up and file out onto a coach that is to take them to the location. There is a great similarity between them and real convicts.

The men arrive at the location. It is on a levee on the Delta in about 100 degrees Fahrenheit. The sun is beating down. There is no need for a make-up person to add sweat to their bodies. The production managers have to try to keep two hundred people from dehydrating. There are little canopies around to protect many of the crew from the sun. Ethan and Joel are wearing straw hats and sunglasses. Joel is wearing a gray T-shirt and shorts. Sweat is staining their shirts. They look along the line of extras like prison warders. There is a man with a gun on a horse patrolling the chain gang. Joel briefly explains to the convicts what they're going to do. The woman assistant director shouts, "Playback!" and the singing of "Po' Lazarus" fills the air, as the extras swing their picks, mouthing the words. Joel watches impassively. Roger Deakins, in a black fedora, dollies along beside them on a special track built for the camera.

The assistant director shouts "Cut!" The extras are handed water bottles to slake their thirst. Then the water bottles are taken away from them, and they line up again to break rocks. Ethan grins to himself and strokes his ginger beard. He speaks rarely. The playback of the song as well as the sound of rocks being hammered starts up again. The picks swing in rhythm. There is no faking. They are really breaking rocks in the heat. Before the next take, Joel tells them, "The rhythm really has to be on." "Okay, chain gang, one more time," shouts the assistant director. Nobody believes the "one more time." Suddenly she notices that they are missing a convict. "There's a hole in the line. We have an escapee," she laughs. "Go without him for this take," says Joel.

Everybody in the crew, including Joel and Ethan, is drinking a lot of water out of plastic cups. While a crane shot is being prepared, Joel sits down in the shade on his director's chair, which is beside Ethan's, both of which are marked with their names and the title of the movie. Ethan takes over the direction for a while or, at least, he is indicating to some of the extras where to move.

After another take, the assistant director shouts to the "prisoners," "You can sit down if you want. We'll bring you water." Ethan, Joel and

Roger Deakins watch the rushes on the monitor and laugh a lot. Joel, with his glasses, hat off and hair flowing, looks like a mad professor.

78   Star Gazing

THE LOCATIONS are spread out. The cockeyed caravan moves on. There are wheatfields on either side of the road on the way to the next location. Sunflowers stare up at the blue sky. The team arrives at the next location, a burnt-out forest area. A few trees have been brought in. The scene, about ten minutes into the film, takes place outside a lone farmhouse. Everett (George Clooney), Pete (John Turturro) and Delmar (Tim Nelson), chained together, are advancing on the farmhouse, which belongs to Pete's cousin, Wash Hogwallop. "If your cousin still runs this-here horse farm and has a forge and some shoein' impedimenta to restore our liberty of movement . . ." says Everett, before a rifle shot rings out. On the porch is a grimy-faced boy, about eight years old, in tattered overalls, holding a gun almost as big as he is. "Hold it rah chair!," he shouts. "You men from the bank? . . . Daddy told me I'm to shoot whosoever from the bank!" The trio convinces the boy, who turns out to be Wash Hogwallop's son, that they're not from the bank.

THE TEAM is gathered outside the farmhouse. They've been up since Dawn appeared fresh and rosy-fingered. Ethan is wearing the same shirt as yesterday, or rather, it has the same pattern. Besides that, he has a neat haircut and trimmed beard. Joel's beard and hair are unkempt, but he has changed into a clean, white shirt. Clooney, wearing a brown cap, is extremely tanned, has a five o'clock shadow, a pencil mustache and gray streaks in his hair. Turturro is shaven headed. Nelson, as slim, but a little shorter, has more hair.

They are sitting around talking and laughing with the Coens, waiting for the shot to be set up. They are called for the scene. Scene 12
take 1. The three cons walk toward the shack. Everett is explaining to
the other two about the prophecy of the blind seer who told them:
"You seek a great fortune, though it will not be the fortune you seek."
Everett expounds: "Though the blind are reputed to possess sensitivities compensatin' for their lack of sight, even to the point of develop-
ing para-normal psychic powers. Now clearly, seein' the future would
fall neatly into that ka-taggery . . ." But Clooney misses a line and apol-
ogizes. Joel pats his star on the back reassuringly. Clooney then goes
over his lines again in a huddle with Turturro and Nelson before the
next take, while the make-up girl makes repairs. Ethan tells Clooney
that he must talk like someone who really enjoys talking. "Yeh, yeh—
got you," says Clooney. On take 2, Clooney dries after a few lines.
"Sorry," he says. Turturro and Nelson nod sympathetically. They don't
have such convoluted dialogue. Ethan is pacing up and down.

The three actors gather their chains together in order to advance
on the farmhouse once more. They get through their dialogue without a hitch until the shot rings out and hits a bottle on a branch of a
tree. After the fourth take, which seems to have met with Joel's satisfaction, Turturro asks for another one. Anyway, Deakins wasn't sure
whether the bottle was in shot.

Joel is yawning. "Let's actually do a rehearsal in time. Play the
scene with the boy. See how it feels." He has a word with the little
shaven-haired boy in overalls. The kid's portly parents are sitting on a
log, nervously watching their son. They are keeping cool by holding
up small battery-driven fans to their faces. They're from Little Rock.
The boy grins from ear to ear. He has a broad Arkansas accent. Joel
shows him how to hold the gun to make it seem heavier. "Give it
more weight. Not too much." Joel knows about guns.

After one rehearsal, in which everyone is word perfect, the boy gets
begrimed by the make-up person for the first take. The boy is great.
His parents are relieved.

A GROUP of locals have gathered on a grassy knoll, many of them with
cameras, to watch and ogle the short scene (part of a montage
sequence) where the three cons come out of Templetons General

Merchant and Gas Station, on the corner of a little crossroads town, just as a man in a boater emerges from his car and enters the store. Everett waits for the man to disappear into the store, signals to the others and they pile into the man's car and drive off. There's a man sitting sleeping in a rocking chair on the porch, an archetypal image of the South.

Perhaps there would have been less interest if George Clooney had not been it. Poor George has shaken as many hands as a campaigning politician since he arrived in this neck of the woods. He signs hundreds of autographs and poses with people for photographs. Obviously the star mystique has not diminished since the studio publicity machines stopped creating calculated images in the 1950s.

"I understand the interest," says Clooney. "I grew up in a small town in Kentucky where they shot a series called *Centennial*, and I followed Raymond Burr around everywhere he went. I know what it's like to see someone in person who you've watched on television or seen in the movies, and I don't get upset when people approach me, because I did the same thing."

NOW CLOONEY is at another location for another scene—one set in the boxcar of a freight train. While waiting for the call, Clooney is entertaining the onlookers by throwing a baseball to some members of the crew. "Gee, George Clooney playing ball!" He is wearing a black T-shirt and gray shorts. Now he is retiring to his trailer to escape the glare of the Mississippi sun. The small crowd of onlookers, who don't seem to mind the repetitious process of film-making and the waiting in the sun, stay put. Their patience is rewarded. Clooney emerges smiling from his trailer in his wide-striped prison garb. He is joined by John Turturro and Tim Nelson, who are similarly attired. They are then chained together. Clooney is the first to climb into the boxcar, pulling his two companions after him. He is faced with six silent hobos. Clooney then speaks the first lines of the film, "Say, uh, any a you boys smithies?"

Odysseus's tale was finished. Held in the

spell of his words they all remained still and

silent throughout the shadowy hall, till at last

Alcinous turned to his guest and said:

"Odysseus, now that you have set foot on the

bronze floor of my house I feel assured that

you will reach your home without any further

wanderings from your course, though you

have suffered much."

—**The Odyssey** (Homer)

79 *O Brothers, Where Art Thou?*

THE CIRCUS has left town. Tumbling tumbleweeds are once again rolling down the quiet streets of Jackson, Mississippi. In some of the houses, there are photographs of citizens taken with their arms around George Clooney, the most recognizable person among the film people. The team has moved onto Los Angeles to shoot some interiors. Then Roderick Jaynes and Tricia Cook will be holed up intimately in the dark editing room for days on end. Carter Burwell will compose music while watching the flickering images on the screen. Finally, *O Brother, Where Art Thou?* will be "in the can" and ready to be exploited. After a short break with their families, the Coen brothers will come together again and face the rounds of publicity, answering a range of questions, most of them meaningless and banal.

And they will go through the motions with good humor and courtesy, though they are still not comfortable with the ritualistic exposure to the press. *O Brother* is only their eighth movie in sixteen years. As a result, every new Coen release is an event among thinking filmgoers. Then the critics will descend on it, and the public will have a chance to judge it for themselves. It will be shown around the world, before turning up on the shelves of video stores, on television and on CD-roms. In a few years' time, for youngsters, *O Brother, Where Art Thou?* will be an "old film." Meanwhile, Joel and Ethan will have completed *To the White Sea*, their "silent" movie, and the cycle will begin again.

LAUGHTER IN THE DARK

XII

(In the interests of balance, the author asked

Edward Schulbyte, professor of cinema studies

at the University of Copacabana, to write this

epilogue.)

WHEN ORPHEUS went into the Elysian Fields to look for his beloved wife Eurydice, he was warned that he must not look back at her. Nevertheless, he catches sight of her and she disappears. Lot's wife was turned into a pillar of salt when she looked back. Perhaps these two classic examples of looking back should have been a warning to the Coen brothers not to do the same in terms of the cinema. The Coens have proved that it is futile to try to recapture the golden era of American cinema. The result is that their motion pictures are merely films about films, pastiches of older styles. Therefore, the Coens' films are paradigms of postmodernism.

Modernism tends to present a view of human history (see T.S. Eliot's "The Waste Land") as essentially tragic. Many modernist works also tried to uphold the idea that works of art can provide the unity, coherence and meaning which have been lost in most of modern life. Postmodernism, in contrast, celebrates the meaninglessness of life and art. Modern societies depend on the idea that signifiers always point to signifieds, and that reality resides in signifieds. In postmodernism, however, there are only signifiers. The idea of any stable or permanent reality disappears, and with it the idea of signifieds that signifiers point to. Rather, for postmodern societies, there are only surfaces, without depth; only signifiers, with no signifieds.

François Lyotard argues that totality, stability and order in modern societies are maintained through the means of "grand narratives," which are stories a culture tells itself about its practices and beliefs. A "grand narrative" in American culture might be the story that democracy is the most enlightened form of government, and that democracy can and will lead to universal human happiness. Postmodernism, in rejecting grand narratives, makes no claim to universality, truth, reason or stability.

Like most postmodernists, the Coens lack gravitas. They have not realized, if I might be permitted a joke, the importance of being earnest. This has happened to many an American film director. Woody Allen is perhaps a good example. His best films are undoubtedly *Interiors*, *September*, *Another Woman* and *Shadows and Fog*. But he had to capitulate to the popcorn-crunching crowd. Allen touched on the dilemma in *Stardust Memories*, in which his efforts to be serious about life and death, had people continually saying, "What's the matter with him? Doesn't he realize he has the greatest gift of all—the ability to make people laugh?," "I liked him when he made funny movies, not all this other stuff." This idea that it is more important to make people laugh than think is at the heart of Preston Sturges' philistine *Sullivan's Travels*. The message is that there is no message.

The Coens have never taken an ethical stance on anything. Although the bad are punished in *Blood Simple*, which wallows in the most loathsome murders, the detective, the prime villain, dies laughing. *Raising Arizona* makes the serious crime of kid kidnapping into a farce. The main character, Tom Reagan, in *Miller's Crossing*, gets away with murder, shooting a man in cold blood while making a joke of it. *Barton Fink* makes fun of political playwrights, like Clifford Odets, who wrote with a social purpose. *The Hudsucker Proxy* plays suicide for a laugh, while *Fargo* undermines the solemnity of its subject, by having the leading character speak with a funny accent.

Besides the jokey treatment of death at the end of *The Big Lebowski*, there is a tasteless scene, played for laughs, in which Walter, the Vietnam vet, hoists the wealthy Lebowski out of his wheelchair by the armpits and tries to get him to walk. "Walk—you fucking phony!" he says. When he finds out that the man is not faking, all he says is "Shit. He didn't *look* like a spinal."

Sir Anthony Forte-Bowell, editor of *Cinema/Not Cinema*, agrees with me in his essay, "But Is It Funny?," on *The Big Lebowski*. "Repeated viewings of the movie have failed to clarify for me the genre-relevance of the themes of bowling, physical handicap, castration and the Jewish Sabbath. But perhaps we should not dismiss the possibility that they are simply authorial mistakes. Certainly the script could not be held up as a model of artistic coherence."

The sad pattern has continued with O *Brother, Where Art Thou?*, for which the Coens have taken one of the greatest literary achievements of Western civilization, Homer's *Odyssey*, and reduced it to a Three Stooges comedy.

It is also typical of them that they should have tried shamelessly to hoodwink the public by inventing certain people. For example Roderick Jaynes, whom they credited as editor on most of their films, was a figment of their imagination. I have also investigated the existence of Rabbi Emmanuel Lev-Tov, author of the memoir *You With the Schnozz*, and found that neither the rabbi nor the work exists, and I have tried to trace Professor Dennis Jacobson, a putative colleague of mine in cinema studies at the University of Iowa, as well as Joel Silver, allegedly a Hollywood producer, to no avail.

At the end of *Sullivan's Travels*, the film director says that he doesn't want to make O *Brother, Where Art Thou?* because he is too happy and he hasn't suffered enough. Perhaps the Coen brothers will have to suffer before they can make a significant movie. I hope that day comes soon.

—EDWARD SCHULBYTE, professor of cinema studies
at the University of Copacabana.

IN ANSWER to Professor Schulbyte's damning criticisms of the Coen brothers, I can only offer the pages of my biography as refutation, and a few further reflections. The professor accuses the Coens' movies of being "films about films' or "pastiches of the older styles." I would say that, while having an acute sense of the history of cinema, they have remoulded old material, which reflects their own sharply defined personalities. To possess a sense of the past is to enrich the present as seen through the prism of their own imagination. It is true that all but three of their films are set in an earlier period but, paradoxically, it is this time lag that makes their films seem so dateless.

As for his humorless ideas about comedy, I suggest he read Henri Bergson's famous essay on "Laughter." As James Agee remarked, "All great comedy involves something beyond laughter," and the Coen brothers' films certainly conform to this definition. Besides, to quote the director in *Sullivan's Travels*, "There's a lot to be said for making people laugh. That's all they've got in this cockeyed caravan."

But it is Ethan and Joel who will have the last laugh, an existential laugh at the absurdity of the world.

"Heh, heh, heh!"

RONALD BERGAN
London
May 2000

FILMOGRAPHY

ALL THE films were produced by Ethan Coen, directed by Joel Coen, and written by Ethan and Joel Coen. Only *The Hudsucker Proxy* was co-written with Sam Raimi.

Blood Simple (1984)

Cast: John Getz (Ray), Frances McDormand (Abby), Dan Hedaya (Julian Marty), M. Emmett Walsh (Visser), Samm-Art Williams (Meurice), Deborah Neumann (Debra). *Production*: River Road Productions. *Executive Producer*: Daniel F. Bacaner. *Associate Producer*: Mark Silverman. *Director of Photography*: Barry Sonnenfeld. *Production Designer*: Jane Musky. *Music*: Carter Burwell. *Editor*: Roderick Jaynes, Don Wiegmann. 99 mins.

Plot:

Julian Marty, a jealous bar owner, hires a sleazy private detective to kill his wife, Abby, and her lover, Ray, one of his bartenders. But the detective fakes the killing by doctoring photographs of the lovers in bed to look as though they have been shot. He collects the money for the job and then shoots the bar owner with the wife's gun, which he has stolen. He leaves the gun at the scene of the crime. Unfortunately, the lover comes to the bar that night, finds the body and the gun and assumes that the wife committed the murder. He cleans up the blood and goes to bury the body in a field. However, he discovers that the husband is still alive and is forced to finish the job himself. Abby then believes that Ray has killed Marty, and becomes afraid of him, while he believes she is using him. Ray discovers the doctored photos in Marty's office, and the detective, realizing this, shoots Ray and then tries to kill Abby. He chases her into the bathroom, but she escapes through the window into the next room. He puts his ear to the wall, and reaches out to open the window of the room, but she stabs his hand with a knife, pinning it to the window sill. In order to free his hand, he shoots scores of bullets into the wall. He punches a hole in the wall with his one hand in order to free the other on the other side. In terrible pain, he confronts her cowering in a corner. She shoots him, crying, "I ain't afraid of you, Marty!" As the detective dies, he says, "Well, ma'am . . . If I see him, I'll sure give him the message."

Raising Arizona (1987)

Cast: Nicolas Cage (H.I. McDonnough), Holly Hunter (Ed), Trey Wilson (Nathan Arizona Sr), John Goodman (Gale), William Forsythe (Evelle), Sam McMurray (Glen), Frances McDormand (Dot), Randall "Tex" Cobb (Leonard Smalls), T.J. Kuhn Jr. (Nathan Arizona Jr.). *Production*: Circle Films. *Executive Producer*: James Jacks. *Co-producer*: Mark Silverman. *Associate Producer*: Deborah Reinisch. *Director of Photography*: Barry Sonnenfeld. *Production Designer*: Jane Musky. *Costume Design*: Richard Hornung. *Music*: Carter Burwell. *Editor*: Michael R. Miller. *Storyboards*: J. Todd Anderson. 94 mins.

Plot:

Incompetent robber H.I. (Hi) McDonnough keeps getting caught and returned to the same penitentiary. Every time he gets arrested, he is fingerprinted by the same female cop, Edwina—Ed for short. They fall in love and marry. Ed wants a baby but discovers she is infertile. When they hear that wealthy furniture store owner Nathan Arizona's wife has had quintuplets, they decide to kidnap one of them because five babies must be "more than they can handle." They kidnap Nathan Arizona Jr. and take him to their trailer home. Meanwhile, two of Hi's former cellmates, Gale and Evelle, escape from prison seeking shelter with Hi and Ed. When they discover that the baby is the kidnapped Arizona child, they decide to get the ransom money themselves. On the trail of the reward money is Leonard Smalls, a bounty-hunting biker. After confronting the biker and seeing him being blown up by his own hand-grenade, Hi and Ed decide to return the baby to his parents. They can only dream of having a family.

Miller's Crossing (1990)

Cast: Gabriel Byrne (Tom Reagan), Marcia Gay Harden (Verna Bernbaum), John Turturro (Bernie Bernbaum), Jon Polito (Johnny Caspar), J.E. Freeman (Eddie Dane), Albert Finney (Leo), Steve Buscemi (Mink). *Production*: Circle Films. *Executive Producer*: Ben Barenholtz. *Co-producer*: Mark Silverman. *Director of Photography*: Barry Sonnenfeld. *Production Designer*: Dennis Gassner. *Costume Design*: Richard Hornung. *Music*: Carter Burwell. *Editor*: Michael R. Miller. *Storyboards*: J. Todd Anderson. Released by Twentieth Century Fox. 115 mins.

Plot:

Gangster Johnny Caspar tries to convince his rival mob boss Leo to let him kill Bernie Bernbaum, a bookie whom he suspects of doing the dirty on him. But Leo refuses because he is in love with Bernie's sister Verna. Gambler Tom Reagan, Leo's friend, advises Leo not to get into a gang war. Meanwhile, Tom is sleeping with Verna. Caspar's men try to kill Leo, and a series of killings result. Leo finds out that Tom has betrayed him and their friendship is broken. Tom goes over to Caspar's side, where he is forced to prove his loyalty by killing Bernie. He takes Bernie into the woods at Miller's Crossing, but fakes the murder and lets Bernie escape. However, Bernie returns to blackmail Tom, who has to kill him at the end.

Barton Fink (1991)

Cast: John Turturro (Barton Fink), John Goodman (Charlie Meadows), Judy Davis (Audrey Taylor), Michael Lerner (Jack Lipnick), John Mahoney (W.P. Mayhew), Tony Shalhoub (Ben Geisler), Jon Polito (Lou Breeze), Steve Buscemi (Chet). *Production*: Circle Films. *Executive Producers*: Ben Barenholtz, Ted Pedas, Jim Pedas, Bill Durkin. *Co-producer*: Graham Place. *Director of Photography*: Roger Deakins. *Production Designer*: Dennis Gassner. *Costume Design*: Richard Hornung. *Music*: Carter Burwell. *Editor*: Roderick Jaynes. *Storyboards*: J. Todd Anderson. 116 mins.

Plot:

Barton Fink has just had a hit on Broadway with his social problem play "Bare Ruined Choirs." He accepts an offer to go to Hollywood as a writer for Capitol Pictures. In Los Angeles, he finds himself staying in the eerie, cavernous old Hotel Earle. The head of the studio, Jack Lipnick, asks Barton to write a wrestling picture for Wallace Beery. But Barton does not know what they expect from him and he seeks the assistance of W.P. Mayhew, an alcoholic Southern novelist in Hollywood to make money, and Mayhew's mistress Audrey Taylor, who helps write her lover's scripts. Barton has writer's block, and when he has to deliver a treatment to Lipnick the following day, Audrey comes to his hotel room to help him out. They go to bed together, but when Barton wakes up, he finds Audrey dead beside him with multiple stab wounds. He screams, attracting the attention of his next-door neighbor, the insurance salesman Charlie Meadows, with whom he has become friendly. Meadows disappears for a while, and the police ask Barton for information about his neighbor, informing Barton that Charlie is really a serial killer called Karl Mundt. Meadows returns to the hotel, and shoots one of the cops as the hotel catches fire. Barton manages to complete a script, but Lipnick rejects it. "You ain't no writer, Fink," the mogul tells him. "You're a goddamn write-off." Dejected, Barton goes to the beach holding a box that Charlie had asked him to keep for him.

The Hudsucker Proxy (1993)

Cast: Tim Robbins (Norville Barnes), Jennifer Jason Leigh (Amy Archer), Paul Newman (Sidney J. Mussburger), Charles Durning (Waring Hudsucker), John Mahoney (Chief), Jim True (Buzz), William Cobbs (Moses). *Production*: Silver Pictures/Working Title Films. *Executive Producers*: Tim Bevan, Eric Fellner. *Co-pro-ducer*: Graham Place. *Director of Photography*: Roger Deakins. *Production Designer*: Dennis Gassner. *Costume Design*: Richard Hornung. *Music*: Carter Burwell. *Editor*: Thom Noble. *Storyboards*: J. Todd Anderson. 113 mins.

Plot:

New York 1958. Norville Barnes has arrived in New York from Muncie, Indiana, hoping to become a success with his idea for a hula hoop. On his first day in his job in the mail room of Hudsucker Industries, the founder, Waring Hudsucker, commits suicide by throwing himself out of the window of the 44th floor of the Hudsucker building. The next in line, Sidney J. Mussburger, decides to place a pawn in the chairman's seat so stocks will fall and he can buy them cheaply and take control of the company. When Norville comes to Mussburger's office to deliver a letter, Mussburger discovers that the young simpleton would be ideal as the Hudsucker proxy. Meanwhile, top reporter Amy Archer gets a job as Norville's secretary, in order to expose him as a phoney. But when the hula hoop becomes a great success, the company's shares rocket, and Norville is feted as a hero. Meanwhile, he has fallen in love with Amy. Mussburger tries to get Norville declared insane, and exposes the truth about Amy. On New Year's Eve, a depressed Norville jumps off the top of the building, but is rescued by Moses, the clock-keeper, who stops the clock while Norville is in mid-air. He meets Waring Hudsucker, now an angel, who comes floating down to greet him. Hudsucker tells Norville that his will states that his share of the company is to go to his successor.

Fargo (1996)

Cast: William H. Macy (Jerry Lundegaard), Frances McDormand (Marge Gunderson), Steve Buscemi (Carl Showalter), Peter Stormare (Gaear Grimsrud), Kristin Rudrüd (Jean Lundegaard), Harve Presnell (Wade Gustafson), Tony Denman (Scotty Lundegaard), John Carrol Lynch (Norm Gunderson). *Production:* Polygram/Working Title Films. *Executive Producers:* Tim Bevan, Eric Fellner. *Director of Photography:* Roger Deakins. *Production Designer:* Rick Heinrichs. *Costume Design:* Mary Zophres. *Music:* Carter Burwell. *Editor:* Roderick Jaynes. *Storyboards:* J. Todd Anderson. 98 mins.

Plot:

Minneapolis car-dealer Jerry Lundegaard, in financial difficulties, hires two petty gangsters, Carl Showalter and Gaear Grimsrud, to kidnap his wife so that when his rich father-in-law pays the ransom, he will get the money, less what he owes the kidnappers. After they have kidnapped her, they are stopped by a state trooper on the road. Gaear shoots him dead, as well as a witness to the crime. Police chief Marge Gunderson, seven months pregnant, investigates the murders. Meanwhile, Jerry's father-in-law Wade Gustafson has taken a suitcase with the money to hand over to Carl, but is shot while doing so. Marge's investigations lead her to Jerry, and finally to the isolated cabin where the kidnappers are holed up, and where Jerry's wife has been killed. Marge arrives to find that Gaear has chopped up his partner, and is feeding him into a wood-chipping machine. Marge manages to wound him with her gun and arrest him. Jerry is also arrested. Marge returns to her husband Norm, and domestic bliss.

The Big Lebowski (1997)

Cast: Jeff Bridges (The Dude), John Goodman (Walter Sobchak), Steve Buscemi (Donny), Julianne Moore (Maude Lebowski), David Huddlestone (The Big Lebowski), Philip Seymour Hoffman (Brandt), Tara Reid (Bunny Lebowski), John Turturro (Jesus Quintana), Ben Gazzara (Jackie Treehorn). *Production*: Polygram/Working Title Films. *Executive Producers*: Tim Bevan, Eric Fellner. *Director of Photography*: Roger Deakins. *Production Designer*: Rick Heinrichs. *Costume Design*: Mary Zophres. *Music*: Carter Burwell. *Editor*: Roderick Jaynes. *Storyboards*: J. Todd Anderson. 113 mins

Plot:

Los Angeles 1991. Jeff "Dude" Lebowski returns to his beach cabin to find two heavies waiting for him. They shove his head down the toilet and piss on his carpet. He discovers that they had mistaken him for the wealthy philanthropist Jeff Lebowski. Dude visits the Big Lebowski's mansion to seek compensation for his rug. Lebowski, who is in a wheelchair, refuses. Later, his namesake tells Dude that his young wife Bunny has been kid-napped and wants Dude to hand over the ransom. But Dude is persuaded by his bowling buddy Walter Sobchak to steal the ransom as he doesn't believe Bunny has really been kidnapped. However, the plan goes completely wrong, and the pals decide to track down Bunny themselves. Dude is abducted and taken to the house of Jackie Treehorn, a porn film producer, who wants to know where Bunny, one of his stars, is. Dude is then seduced by Maude Lebowski, the Big Lebowski's artist daugh-ter, who tells him she wants a baby. Three German anarchists, who pretended to have kidnapped Bunny for the ransom, con-front Dude, Walter and their friend Donny outside the bowling alley. They send the anarchists fleeing, but Donny dies of a heart attack.

O Brother, Where Art Thou? (2000)

Cast: George Clooney (Ulysses Everett McGill), John Turturro (Pete), Tim Nelson (Delmar O'Donnel), Michael Badalucco (George "Baby Face" Nelson), Charles Durning (Pappy O'Daniel), John Goodman (Big Dan Teague), Wayne Duvall (Homer Stokes), Holly Hunter (Penny McGill Wharvey), Tommy Johnson (himself). *Production*: Universal. *Executive Producers*: Tim Bevan, Eric Fellner. *Director of Photography*: Roger Deakins. *Production Designer*: Rick Heinnichs. *Costume Design*: Mary Zophres. *Music*: Carter Burwell. *Editor*: Roderick Jaynes. *Storyboards*: J. Todd Anderson.

Plot:

Ulysses Everett McGill has escaped from a Mississippi chain gang with Pete and Delmar. He tells them that he wants to get home to his wife Penny and six daughters, and to find the money from a bank heist that he has buried. The trio arrive at Pete's cousin's farm, where they get rid of their leg irons. However, the cousin, Wash Hogwallop, betrays them to the county police, and they go on the run again. They meet up with Tommy Johnson, a black guitarist, and the four of them make a recording of "Man of Constant Sorrow" as the Soggy Bottom Boys. They then meet up with "Baby Face" Nelson, with whom they rob a few banks. Meanwhile, Pete has been seduced by three women and got himself rearrested. While Everett and Delmar are having a meal in a restaurant, they are approached by Big Dan Teague, who claims to be a Bible salesman. At a picnic, Big Dan beats them up and steals their money. After rescuing Pete from the prison camp, they come across the lynching of a black man, Tommy, by the Ku Klux Klan. They rescue Tommy and make for a political rally where they perform their song, which has now become a hit. Everett comes across his wife, who has divorced him and is about to marry Vernon T. Waldrip. However, as the valley is flooded, Everett convinces her that he has changed.

BIBLIOGRAPHY

Gates of Eden by Ethan Coen (Doubleday, 1998)
Joel & Ethan Coen by Peter Körte and Georg Seessien (Titan
   Books, 1999)
*Two Views Of Wittgenstein's Later Philosophy by Ethan Coen
   (Seeley G. Mudd Manuscript Library, Princeton University
   Library—May 1979).

* Extracts published with permission of the Princeton University Library.

Blood Simple

Blood Simple—screenplay (Faber & Faber, 1996)
Film Comment, April 1985
American Cinematographer, July 1985
Film Directions, v7 1985
Newsweek, January 1985
Village Voice, January 1985
New Republic, February 1985
New York Times, January 1985
Film Journal, March 1985
Film Comment, March/April 1985

Raising Arizona

Raising Arizona—screenplay (Faber & Faber, 1996)
Monthly Film Bulletin, July 1987
Film Comment, March/April 1987
Interview, April 1987
Positif, August 1987
Positif, July/August 1987

Miller's Crossing

Miller's Crossing—screenplay (Faber & Faber, 1991)
Empire, March 1991
Positif, February 1991
Hollywood Reporter, May 1989
Premiere, April 1989
Premiere, March 1990
Films In Review, September/October 1990
New York Times, 1990

Barton Fink

Barton Fink—screenplay (Faber & Faber, 1991)
Empire, February 1992
Film Comment, September/October 1991
Sight & Sound, September 1991
Positif, September 1991
New York Magazine, August 1991
Positif, September 1991
Empire, March 1991

The Hudsucker Proxy

The Hudsucker Proxy—screenplay (Faber & Faber, 1994)
Observer Life Magazine, August 1994
Scene By Scene Projections, 6 p. 33 (Faber & Faber, 1996)
Premiere, July 1994
Premiere, September 1994

■
Fargo

Fargo — screenplay (Faber & Faber, 1996)
Empire, June 1996
American Cinematographer, March 1996
American Cinematographer, June 1997
Sight & Sound, May 1996
Interview, March 1996
Positif, September 1996
Premiere, March 1996
Sight & Sound, May 1996
New York Times, March 1996

■
The Big Lebowski

The Big Lebowski — screenplay (Faber & Faber, 1998)
The Making of *The Big Lebowski* (Faber & Faber, 1998)
Positif, May 1998
Total Film, May 1998
Premiere August, 1997
Screen International, January 1997
Interview, March 1998
Film Review, Summer 1998
Film Scouts interviews, July 1999
Projections, 8 p. 183 (Faber & Faber, 1998)
Cinema/Not Cinema, April 1998

INDEX

Miller, George, 95
Miller's Crossing
  budget, 114
  casting, 115-118
  dream sequence, 196
  ethics, 126-128
  filming, 118-124
  filmography, 230
  influences, 113-114, 120-124
  music, 123
  symbolism, 35
  writing, 2, 114-115
Minneapolis, 38-39, 53-54, 167-168, 206
modernism, 222
Montgomery, Robert, 102
Moore, Julianne, 193
Müller, Robby, 73
Musky, Jane, 119

N

The Naked Man, 135
Neeson, Liam, 112
Nelson, Tim, 208, 212, 215-216
Neter, Ron, 54, 56
Newman, Paul, 7, 74, 150, 158-159, 180
Nicholson, Jack, 53

O

O Brother, Where Art Thou?
  casting, 211-213
  characters, 48
  filming, 211-217
  filmography, 234-235
  influences, 208-211
O'Connor, Flannery, 16, 74
The Old Country, 39, 42
Yanagita, Mike, 39
Orloff, Lee, 124
Oscars, 122, 182-186

P

Passer, Ivan, 190
Patterson, Frank, 123
Peckinpah, Sam, 53
Pedas, Ted and Jim, 92
Peterson, Pete, 50
Pitt, Brad, 205
Place, Graham, 159
Poe, Edgar Allan, 2, 74
Polanski, Roman, 143
political correctness, 124-125
Polito, John, 10, 13, 116-117, 201
postmodernism, 26, 35, 85-86, 222, 223
Powell, Dick, 155
Presnell, Harve, 71, 168, 178

Q

Quinn, Aidan, 206

R

Raimi, Sam, 13, 15, 21, 38, 48, 64-67, 69-70, 87, 93, 112, 113, 158-159, 161,
Raising Arizona
  budget, 24, 113
  camera effects, 101-104
  casting, 95-100
  dream sequence, 109-110
  filming, 99-106
  filmography, 229
  financing, 92-93
  influences, 95, 106-110
  slapstick chase scene, 105
Rappaport, Michael, 205
Red Wing, 126
Reeves, Steve, 52
Reinisch, Deborah, 78
Robbins, Tim, 57, 150, 154-155, 157
Robertson, William Preston, 13-14, 34, 166
Rudrüd, Kristin, 173
Russell, Ken, 196

S

Sanders, George, 5
Savini, Tom, 67
Scafolini, Romano, 67
Schoolcraft, Alan J., 5-6
Schulbyte, Edward, 221-225
Scorsese, Martin, 19, 21, 45, 51
Seattle Film Festival, 189
Seessien, George, 28, 83, 153
Sellers, Peter, 14
Sennett, Mack, 105
Shakicam, 65, 66101, 103
short stories
  The Boys, 71
  Cosa Minapolidan, 126
  Destiny, 75
  Gates of Eden, 48
  Have You Ever Been to Electric
    Ladyland?, 45, 150
  The Old Country, 39, 42
  Red Wing, 126
Silver, Joel, 7, 148-150
Simon's Rock College of Bard, 50
Sonnenfeld, Barry, 138
  13, 15, 13
  66-67, 69, 78-79, 66
  95, 101, 115, 119
Spielberg, Steven, 21, 51, 88
Spies Like Us, 66
Staiger, Janet, 21
Steadycam, 101

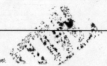